AF682256

Information and Communication Technologies in Rural Society

The field of information and communication technologies has become an increasingly complex subject arena. While there is little doubt about the impact of the immense changes in the use of digital data on urban areas, it can be argued that e-commerce, e-learning, e-government, e-services and all of the diversity of this digital renaissance, are having a proportionally greater impact among rural communities due to their geographical location and the sparse distribution of their population.

This book explores and documents the extent to which the experiential nature of being rural, whether as a business manager in an SME (or micro-enterprise), a non-business person, a retired inhabitant, a housewife, etc., is changing as information and communication technologies (ICTs) become more widely applied and facilitate connection across geographies. The contributors investigate ways in which these ICTs are being variously experienced in rural areas of Europe, in order to provide a commentary on changing ruralities and their implications for European, national and regional Information-Society policies. These changing ruralities are presented here as the lived experiences of individuals, businesses and communities, and the ways in which their experiences are being enhanced, undermined and variously modified through application of ICTs within business, home, leisure and social relations. The book examines the space and place implications of these changes, as reported in a range of rural settings within Scandinavia and Western Europe.

This book will benefit postgraduate students in areas of research such as rural development, regional development and new technology management among others.

Grete Rusten is Associate Professor at Department of Geography, University of Bergen, Norway. **Sarah Skerratt** is Senior Researcher and Team Leader in Rural Development and Society Research at the Scottish Agricultural College in Edinburgh.

Routledge studies in technology, work and organizations
Edited by David Preece
University of Teesside, UK

1 **Information Society and the Workplace**
Edited by Tuula Heiskanen and Jeff Hearn

2 **Technological Change and Organizational Action**
Edited by David Preece and Juha Laurila

3 **Managing Complex Projects**
Networks, knowledge and innovation
Neil Alderman, Chris Ivory, Ian McLouglin, Alfred Thwaites and Roger Vaughan

4 **Information and Communication Technologies in Rural Society**
Being rural in a digital age
Edited by Grete Rusten and Sarah Skerratt

Information and Communication Technologies in Rural Society

Being rural in a digital age

Edited by Grete Rusten and Sarah Skerratt

Routledge
Taylor & Francis Group
LONDON AND NEW YORK

First published 2008
by Routledge
2 Park Square, Milton Park, Abingdon, Oxon OX14 4RN

Simultaneously published in the USA and Canada
by Routledge
270 Madison Ave, New York, NY 10016

Routledge is an imprint of the Taylor & Francis Group, an informa business

© 2008 Selection and editorial matter, Grete Rusten and Sarah Skerratt; individual chapters, the contributors

Typeset in Times by Wearset Ltd, Boldon, Tyne and Wear
Printed and bound in Great Britain by TJI Digital, Padstow, Cornwall

All rights reserved. No part of this book may be reprinted or reproduced or utilised in any form or by any electronic, mechanical, or other means, now known or hereafter invented, including photocopying and recording, or in any information storage or retrieval system, without permission in writing from the publishers.

British Library Cataloguing in Publication Data
A catalogue record for this book is available from the British Library

Library of Congress Cataloging in Publication Data
A catalog record for this book has been requested

ISBN10: 0-415-41116-5 (hbk)
ISBN10: 0-203-93429-6 (ebk)

ISBN13: 978-0-415-41116-5 (hbk)
ISBN13: 978-0-203-93429-6 (ebk)

Contents

Illustrations

Figures

Tables

Boxes

Contributors

John R. Bryson, Professor of Enterprise and Economic Geography, School of Geography, Earth and Environmental Sciences, University of Birmingham, UK. Email: j.r.bryson@bham.ac.uk. Professor Bryson's research focus is on organisational change and specifically knowledge- or expertise-intensive firms and regional economic development. He is Vice-President of RESER, the European Network for research on services and space.

Winfried Ellingsen, Senior Researcher, Agderforskning, Gimlemoen, Postbox 415, N-4604 Kristiansand, Norway. Email: wge@aforsk.no. Dr Ellingsen's main research focus is on regional development, both in city regions and rural areas. More recently, he has also incorporated political issues into his research.

Andrew Gillespie, Professor of Communications Geography at the University of Newcastle, currently Head of the School of Geography, Politics and Sociology, and formerly Executive Director of the Centre for Urban and Regional Development Studies (CURDS). Email: Andy.Gillespie@ncl.ac.uk. His research is concerned with information and communication technologies (ICTs) and the development of cities, regions and rural areas, on which he has published extensively. He has had a particular interest in the development of regional telecommunications and Information-Society strategies in Europe, and has advised the Commission of the European Union on policy developments in these fields since the mid-1980s.

Rosemarie Gannon, UCD School of Information and Library Studies, University College Dublin, Belfield, Dublin 4, Ireland. Email: rosemarie.gilligan@ucd.ie. Rosemarie Gannon completed her PhD in Information Studies in UCD. Her thesis title was 'Exploring the 'spatial' dimension of an 'Information Society': an investigation of the 'friction of distance' in a rural Irish community. Her research interests include the social and cultural impacts of ICTs, adoption and use of ICTs in rural areas, mobile-phone adoption and use and eInclusion issues. She is a current member of the COST 298 Action 'Participation in the Broadband Society' and a past member of the COST 269 Action 'User Aspects of ICTs'.

James Hosea, Managing Director, jhosea consulting, is an independent consultant based at NHH, the Norwegian School of Economics and Business Administration, Helleveien 30, 5045 Bergen, Norway. Email: jhosea@jhosea.com. James Hosea's research and consulting interests are focused on marketing and branding niche food products and the use of the Internet as a marketing and branding channel. He is a Fellow of the Royal Geographical Society in London.

Ingeborg Astrid Kleppe, Associate Professor, Norwegian School of Economics and Business Administration, Department of Strategy and Management, Discipline of Marketing, Bergen, Norway. Email: ingeborg.kleppe@nhh.no. Kleppe's research focus is on consumer behaviour in international markets. She served seven years as the Head of the Board for the National Institute for Consumer Research (in Norway) and has international research experience from the World Bank and from several visits to universities in the US and Australia.

Frode Kristiansen, Researcher, Institute for Research in Economics and Business Administration (SNF) Breiviksveien 40, N-5045 Bergen, Norway. Email: frode.kristiansen@snf.no. Kristiansen's research includes studies of regional development, and internationalisation and ICT. His more recent work is mainly in the field of health economics.

Marsaili MacLeod, Research Student, Department of Geography and the Environment, University of Aberdeen, AB24 3UF, Scotland. Email: marsaili.macleod@abdn.ac.uk. Marsaili MacLeod is conducting doctoral research which explores how minority-language speakers' gain access to, and control over, language choice through formal and informal work structures. Her research interests include the role of e-communication in minority-language networks and the language of technologies in bilingual institutions.

Frank Rennie, Head of Research and Postgraduate Development at Lews Castle College and Course Leader of the MSc in Managing Sustainable Rural Development at the UHI Millennium Institute in the highlands and islands of Scotland. Email: frank.rennie@lews.uhi.ac.uk. His research interests lie in rural and community development, particularly community-based approaches to integrated sustainable development. Recent work focuses on new approaches to online education and distributed learning on and in rural communities. He is an advisor to several government programmes and committees and a fellow of a number of learned societies. Dr Rennie has been involved in developing and delivering various combinations of distributed learning solutions (with a particular emphasis on networked solutions for rural areas) with colleges and university partners in Europe, Amazonia, Bhutan, Nepal and New Zealand. He has published a wide range of materials related to rural issues and is a regular keynote speaker at international conferences. For further details see URL: www.lews.uhi.ac.uk/Research/StafRec1.htm.

Grete Rusten, Senior Researcher, Institute for Research in Economics and Business Administration (SNF) Breiviksveien 40, N-5045 Bergen, Norway. Email: Grete.Rusten@snf.no. From 1 September 2007 Dr Rusten is an Associate Professor at Department of Geography, University of Bergen. Her research focus is on industrial and regional development, service economies, ICT, design and other creative industries. She has also examined entrepreneurship in rural areas. She is an Honorary Research Fellow of the School of Geography, Earth and Environmental Sciences, University of Birmingham, and a Council Member of the European Research Association on Services and Space (RESER).

Sarah Skerratt, Senior Researcher and Team Leader in Rural Society Research, Scottish Agricultural College, King's Buildings, Edinburgh, Scotland, EH9 3JG, UK. Email: sarah.skerratt@sac.ac.uk. Dr Skerratt has been researching processes of rural community development, and particularly the roles of ICT as an enabler or disabler in those processes. She focuses on how people in rural areas experience technology. She is particularly interested in definitions of the digital divide, and implications for policy and practice. She is an Honorary Research Fellow at Glasgow Caledonian University and the University of Helsinki. She is a Member of the International Rural Network, the European Society for Rural Sociologists (ESRS) and the European Federation of IT in Agriculture (EFITA).

Hilary Talbot, PhD Student, Centre for Urban and Regional Development Studies, University of Newcastle, NE1 7RU, UK. Email: Hilary.Talbot@ncl.ac.uk. Her research interests include rural society, the community sector and ICTs, and policy and governance at multiple levels. Prior to completing her PhD, she worked in the Centre for Rural Economy at Newcastle University for ten years, where her specialism was in rural telematics.

Foreword

For many years I have repeatedly stated my opinion that the most significant impacts of the digital revolution will be felt in the rural areas. This is not said simply to challenge the impact of the stunning changes in the use of digital data that are happening in urban areas, but to acknowledge that e-learning, e-commerce, e-government, e-services, and all the diversity of this digital renaissance, are having a proportionally greater impact among rural communities due to their geographical location and the sparse distribution of their population. The digital changes that are documented, analysed and discussed in this book are not only of academic value – they represent innovations of great potential and meaningful influence on the quality of rural life.

This is an increasingly complex subject arena, and much emphasis is frequently given to the frenetic speed of technological changes, but the real significance lies not in speed, nor even in the undoubted increase in convenience, but in the abilities of the users both to create their own contents and to enable hyper-interactivity between other users. These affordances can be utilised to reinforce community identity, minority cultures and authentic interpretations of heritage, customs or landscapes as rural people wish to portray them. They enable small groups of people, far away from centres of high population density, to provide rich and highly valuable contributions to the diverse framework of our society – a countercurrent to the dominant and dominating influence of a commercialised media culture. They also enable real people to communicate authentically with global media, global ideas and global markets. It is true, as authors in this book point out, that there are many variations in the level of uptake of this new digital society by the 'net citizens' of the world, both between countries/regions, and between individuals within the same region/community. This book is a valuable contribution towards understanding what influences and drives these differences. Implicit and explicit in every chapter is a staggering range of further research questions and opportunities to explore the changing *experience* of being rural in the digital age. Staggering and exciting.

Equally important for me is the fact that this book tries to understand issues relating to the access, contents and context of digital resources mediated by the web from the perspective not merely of the technical possibilities, but, much more importantly, from an analysis of the social and human perspectives. Whether a farmer in rural Norway, an individual businessperson in rural Ireland, or a digitally literate Gaelic-speaker in the Scottish highlands and islands, we are all interconnected – the digital media simply allows us to make these connections over large distances more easily and more frequently. It helps to reduce the 'friction of distance', but is that enough? The paradox of focusing on a basket of technologies that claim to be global and 24/7, yet to be looking at this through the lens of a rural community of place, is that it enables us to bring to ground the hype and hyperbole of the dotcom age and confront it with the realities of a genuine sense of place. What are the real options and obstacles to being rural in a digital age? This book is an honest attempt to uncover and understand that reality, and as such it is a welcome addition to the literature on this subject. Let's continue to push the quest a little further.

Frank Rennie
Head of Research and Postgraduate Development
University of Highlands and Islands
Isle of Lewis
Outer Hebrides
February 2007

Acknowledgements

This book project started as part of a dinner conversation in the town of Sligo in the western part of Ireland. The reason for this visit was to participate in the European Society for Rural Sociology Congress (2003), convening a working group examining the roles of ICTs in rural development. Since then, the germ of the idea has developed further among the various researchers who have combined fieldwork and face-to-face interviews, surveys, online and book studies and discussions with colleagues. In spring 2005, the authors came together and discussed the different projects and chapter drafts at a workshop hosted by the Institute for Research in Economics and Business Administration (SNF) in the city of Bergen, western Norway. Since then, this project has developed through numerous emails exchanging ideas, requests, draft comments, reminders and reading and adjusting final chapters. Running the project across geographies and with a range of academics would probably not have been possible without ICT. We hope this book will be an inspiration for further collaborative research on the Information Society in the future. Thanks so much to everyone who has taken part.

Grete Rusten
Associate Professor,
University of Bergen

Sarah Skerratt
Senior Researcher and Team Leader,
Rural Society Research
Scottish Agricultural College, Edinburgh

1 Being rural in a digital age

Grete Rusten and Sarah Skerratt

Setting the scene

The aim of this book is to describe ways in which Information and Communication Technologies (ICTs) are being variously experienced in rural areas of Europe, in order to provide a commentary on changing ruralities and their implications for European, national and regional Information-Society policies. These changing ruralities are presented here as the lived experiences of individuals, businesses and communities, and the ways in which their experiences are being enhanced, undermined and variously modified through the application of ICTs within business, home, leisure and social relations. We examine the space and place implications of these changes, as reported in a range of rural settings within Scandinavia and Western Europe.

Throughout the chapters of this book, it is possible to see the ways in which people's experiences of rurality are dynamic and vary across territories. We consider it important to be informed about these differences and dynamic experiences, because they have implications for how 'rural' continues to be defined, together with implications for the debate over the persistence of place, place-based identity, culture and language. Further, such an understanding informs us of the range of settings, applications, constraints and opportunities for ICTs inherent within rural Europe, illustrated through selected themes and case studies. This variety is important in itself as indicative of the need for ICTs to 'fit' within context. It is also of significance for our commentary on Information Society policies, since aspects and determinants of rural digital divides remain multifaceted and thus require tools and interventions which are sensitive to such a variety of place, which include the range of structural characteristics and social and economic relations.

We propose and discuss these aspects within the context of a Europe where harmonisation, liberalisation, regulation and forming an inclusive Information Society are given high priority. These are addressed by stimulating investments such as broadband infrastructure and the deployment of e-services, such as e-government and e health projects (European Commission, 2006). Linked to these initiatives is the development of comparable statistics to measure progress and identify weaknesses in the adoption of Information and Communication

Technologies (ICTs). Two examples of ICT indicators covering households and enterprises respectively both illustrate how performance levels differ across Europe.

First, Table 1.1 shows the proportions of individuals that use the Internet on a regular basis. The pattern represents a broad picture of an international digital divide between the various countries as a result of differences in access to technology and services, training and culture for uptake and use, with the Nordic countries at the top and the southern and south-eastern parts of Europe at the lower end. However, the table does not reveal any further details regarding the composition of these factors, their relative interaction and importance, and how they may vary across space. The second table (Table 1.2) includes commercial activities by firms often referred to as 'e-business'. These statistics list firms' external communication as well as flow of information within organisations, regardless of whether individuals are located at the same site or geographically separated.

Table 1.1 Share of individuals regularly using the Internet (percentage of individuals who accessed the Internet, on average, at least once a week)

	2004	*2006*
Iceland	77	84
Sweden	75	80
Denmark	70	78
Norway	68	77
Netherlands	–	76
Finland	63	71
Luxembourg	59	65
Germany	50	59
Belgium	–	58
United Kingdom	49	57
Austria	46	55
Estonia	45	56
Slovenia	40	47
Latvia	27	46
Ireland	27	44
Slovakia	33	43
Hungary	21	42
Spain	31	39
France	–	39
Lithuania	26	38
Czech Republic	25	36
Malta	–	36
Poland	22	34
Italy	26	31
Portugal	25	31
Cyprus	28	29
Greece	17	23
Bulgaria	13	22
Romania	10	–

Source: Eurostat, October 2005 (http://europa.eu.int/comm/eurostat/).

Table 1.2 Percentage of enterprises with Internet access and a website having placed purchases or received orders via Internet or other computer networks (2005)

Country	*Internet*	*Website*	*Purchases*	*Sales*
Finland	98	76	19	17
Denmark	97	82	32	32
Sweden	96	85	41	23
Austria	95	70	36	25
Belgium	95	65	18	16
Germany	94	72	41	16
Norway	93	67	36	26
Czech Republic	92	67	21	13
Netherlands	91	72	20	14
UK	90	74	51	25

Notes

1 Including percentage of all enterprises with ten or more employed. The table include the ten EU/EEA countries with highest Internet access score.

2 Data for France is not available (for further details see Eurostat, 2006).

The first column starts with Internet access, followed by use of a website, a sign that the firm has an active set of e-operations rather than simple Internet access. The latter columns of the table specifically focus on e-commerce, which usually refers to external transactions related to goods and services. Adoption of online sales is typically a more sophisticated use since it will often require the establishment of applications for receiving electronic payment. Measuring indicators column by column place the three Nordic countries of Finland, Denmark and Sweden at the top; however, the UK is in the lead when measuring purchasing activity, followed by Sweden and Germany, Austria and Denmark, while Finland comes much lower down on the list. Sales activities rank Denmark, Norway and the UK in the first positions. Comparing rankings across the four indicators does however place Sweden and Denmark together at the top, followed by Finland and the UK, with the second highest score. Within our book therefore, we aim to explore the experiences, barriers and contextual factors which exist behind these statistics, to generate a greater comparative understanding of these observable differences.

Being rural in a digital age

The book's sub-title is thus deliberately chosen to suggest an *experiential orientation* to the analyses and presentations presented here, that is: '*being* rural'. We wish to focus on the complex ways in which people, communities and businesses in rural areas are experiencing rurality and the manner in which these experiences continue to change as ICTs become more prevalent.

Thus we focus upon the ways in which, for instance, 'distance' from services is not only measured in miles or kilometres, but is experienced in terms of time, need, convenience and access to transport, human networks, as well as cost and affordability. Further, the experiences of 'digital divides' among rural populations may not only relate to the amount and type of high-speed telecommunications infrastructure ('broadband')[1] that is in place. Rather, issues of capacity and 'soft infrastructure', as well as cost, all play their part. By looking at this issue *experientially*, from the 'worldviews' of those living in rural areas, we contribute in an essential and complementary manner, to those investigations of rural change, digital divides, e-business, regional governance, and service and government delivery online.

Specifically, we argue that the new e-economic relations within society in general, including access to online (public) services, are about much more than smart technological solutions. Access, equality, efficiency and democratic processes can all be considered as having an overall importance in forming an inclusive society which meets individual needs. In practical terms, individual and corporate use of ICTs is also about motivation, competence, resources and ways of organising among senders and recipients. The society at a national level may wish to deliver services to all inhabitants. Even so, there will always be a divide in such a society which reflects those who for technological, economic and social reasons are not online. In fact it seems reasonable to distinguish between, on the one hand, three spatial concepts of such digital divides as they occur across territories such as nations, regions and communities, and, on the other hand, those digital inequalities (Hargittai, 2003) where non-access has social or demographic (age, gender, ethnic) explanations and therefore does not systematically vary across space. One may likewise want to question purpose and effects of ICT use, for those taking part and thus connected, contrasting their experience with those who are left out. For these reasons therefore, as presented in the various chapters that follow, this book is not merely a discussion about use or non-use; rather, we present the complexities of social, economic and place-based contexts as key components of divides and their bridging.

The perspectives presented within this edited volume contrast with national statistics on ICT usage, which show a very inaccurate picture concerning these different levels just mentioned. In fact, the rather high scores seen for instance for some of the Nordic countries do not tell us if these societies really offer broadband or ICT services in all geographical corners, nor can we divine the difference in the quality of the services on offer. Data on national level are in fact often measures of 'access possibilities' for the municipality as a whole, rather than details about connectedness and specific use in every locality. What kind of economic priority, for instance, offers ICT provision to communities that are so sparsely populated as to be of no commercial interest to providers? For instance, might sufficient access to PCs at public schools compensate those who cannot, for practical or economic reasons, enjoy this technology at home? In other instances, government and private telecommunications sectors work together to provide infrastructure. This still presumes affordability and ease-of-use for home users, however. Educating the population to access online (public) services is a way of diminishing the knowledge gaps or what may be characterised as 'digital illiteracies'. Examples from Norway are tax reporting, online application forms for building activity, kindergarten or music school, as well as the opportunity for citizens to read political documents or follow town-hall meetings online. One of the major challenges for public authorities in a society is to secure digital inclusiveness, meaning access for most user-group categories. It is especially higher-educated inhabitants and younger people that, through studies or jobs, have access to, and take advantage of the Internet. Diminishing the gap has therefore led to a targeting of the older generation, women or ethnic groups that are either outside or not engaged in jobs where they use ICT. It is also important to be able to establish services and programmes that are user-friendly even for individuals with little training or with disabilities. Reducing the digital gap will therefore also be about collating sources for users, easing online searches, as well as offering personalised information portals with flexible and inclusive solutions. However, the need to deliver another access alternative for those who are not online of course persists, particularly as online sources of service delivery and basic transactions have increased in the past five years, and this trend is set to continue.

Therefore, when adopting the term '*digital age*' in our working title, we wanted to propose a discourse that moves beyond one which focuses only on either the 'Information *Society*' or the 'Knowledge *Economy*'. We propose that 'digital age' indicates a time period in which digitised experiences are increasing (*The Economist*, 2005), thus changing how living and working in rural areas are experienced on a day-to-day basis. This hypothesis is explored directly through the following chapters. We do not want to focus only on 'information' and 'knowledge', or indeed only on 'society' or 'economy', as distinct categories. Instead, in the following pages, the authors examine the interrelated experiences and changes taking place in rural areas, many of which do not fall neatly into a particular analytical field. Thus we feel that this term gives us the scope to present 'thick descriptions' of rural experiences, rather than categorise them, *a priori*, as falling within either a 'social' or 'economic' domain (Heiskanen and Hearn, 2003).

It is important to emphasise, at the outset of this book, that we are not suggesting that ICTs are ubiquitous, available everywhere, or being used by everyone. In fact, we set out to challenge this largely metropolitan assumption (*The Economist*, 2005; Cairncross, 2001; Wellman, 2001, 2002). However, we recognise that ICTs *are* increasingly applied in many spheres of life, and that this in turn raises two questions for debate. First, are rural areas being disadvantaged because of poor hard or soft e-infrastructure – that is, compared with more densely populated areas, are they being left behind, excluded or marginalised? Second, how is 'being rural' changing for those living and/or working in rural areas, through their own adaptation of ICTs, for example, reducing distance, increasing market share, developing closer ties between producer and client (Kolarova *et al.*, 2006) allowing niche marketing, overcoming isolation, or increasing their place-based isolation (see the Pew Internet and American Life Project range of reports which address these issues: http://207.21.232.103/reports.asp).

Complex ruralities

It is important to state that we do not aim to focus our discussions on 'Is there a rural?' or 'What is rural?' (there are authors within rural sociology, and geography, who explore these debates thoroughly and coherently, e.g. Cloke, 1997; Ilbery 1998; Phillips, 1998). Rather, for the purposes of this book, we propose that 'rural areas' possess defining characteristics, which raise specific challenges and opportunities, some of which can be addressed through ICT, some of which cannot. We argue that this territorial and spatial focus on rural areas *is* worthy of investigation when evaluating wider trends within the 'digital age'. We therefore propose that the key defining characteristics of rural areas include:

- a physically dispersed population;
- weaker infrastructure (roads, rail, air, telecommunications), particularly compared with urban areas;
- a narrower (than urban) industrial structure and demand for certain qualifications;
- increasingly limited access to a declining set of 'offline' services in many western EU countries, such as the UK and Ireland (including job centres, public libraries, post offices, banks, citizen's advice, and local government offices), contrasting with some Nordic countries, where welfare policy and public services are designed to compensate for lack of local commercial, physical alternatives;
- a parallel decline in public transport, making physical access to such services (increasingly centred in 'hubs'), problematic, thus arguably disadvantaging the rural poor or those without ready access to private transport;
- a 'public' sort of life where declaring a personal need to acquire new skills, and find supportive learning places, comprise two key challenges in themselves, and can also reflect gender dimensions.

Although valuable in helping us to identify those rural characteristics which directly interact with ICTs, we must also use caution in our analyses, and differentiate such broad characteristics according to 'remote rural' and 'accessible rural' contexts. It has been argued that rural areas now rarely exist in isolation but do, in some way or another, relate to (and may be interdependent with) the economic and social activities of urban areas. This means that 'accessible rural' areas are in the fringe or shadow of urban districts and therefore exist primarily as places where people may live while working in the city. Some of these rural regions also serve as recreation areas for city dwellers. The other broad category of rural areas are what may be characterised as 'remote rural'; that is, deep rural, including both 'idylls' and areas facing major problems such as an ageing and declining population, unemployment or a lack of qualified labour to fill vacant jobs. It has been argued that, even in the remote rural, the life and conditions of such places are integrated with urban areas as these form the major markets as well as the location for higher-level public services such as health and higher education. The dependency may also very well go in the opposite direction. In Norway, for instance, every twelfth inhabitant has a cabin as a second home, usually rurally located, which they visit during holidays or at weekends. This living pattern represents important income and job opportunities for rural areas in a whole range of sectors, including trade, transport, maintenance and recreation services. In other words, it represents an increased opportunity for several people to remain and work in rural areas. In fact, being late-movers into the digital age also means that several communities not only offer broadband but fibre optics to their weekend residence and permanent inhabitants within Norway. We can therefore question whether this Nordic example shows the Internet virtually connecting these territories offering what may be characterised as 'closeness-at-a-distance'. One additional example comprises the case of customers interested in organic food being granted the chance to become involved in what is grown on a farm – a kind of virtual vegetable parcel – or to adopt a sheep (Holloway, 2003).

The spread of information technology constitutes a technological breakthrough that has penetrated different corners of our world. This process moves our economies in the direction of increased globalisation alongside political, financial and regulatory integration. It will, however, take some time before ICTs reach everyone in an efficient way, eroding the special problems of rural areas such as geographical isolation, peripherality and specialisation. Infrastructure difficulties still exist for many smaller communities and variable take-up and efficient use of ICT still varies considerably. Performance seems obviously to peak within knowledge-intensive sectors such as business services. These are mostly located in urban areas where active integration (including meetings with clients) is more easily organised than in cases where the firms are based in more isolated rural settings. Models of ICT adoption are in some literature described as a stage-model or ladder, ranging from simple to advanced, describing the spread of the technology to the individual firm or even populations of firms or regions as a whole (Gray, 2006). It may be to some extent that major economies and larger urban areas have already been at the forefront for a long time as earlier adopters supporting an already dominant position. At the same time, can some of the previous lagging areas that have recently entered the scene now pick up more modern versions of the technologies? In fact, are some rural areas in the Nordic countries now able to move directly from non-digital directly into becoming users of the latest developments within fibre and wireless technologies, these are not yet offered to all in urban areas, due partly to inertia, and partly to capacity constraints?

Moving to the firm perspective clearly illustrates how ICT facilitates coordination at a distance, parties do still often need to meet to socialise and create the trust essential to establishing a formal agreement. Further, there is an assumption that ICT will ensure that rural firms will be able to operate in markets elsewhere national and internationally; in some cases, this is possible – if the product or service concept is unique, convincing and in demand. One example comprises well-established designers and engineers who have no difficulties in generating projects regardless of their business address; a decision to employ them is influenced by reputation and product branding (Rusten and Bryson, 2007a). In other cases, however, companies seeking knowledge-intensive services may prefer local expertise since relations are already established and the search costs are low; an additional advantage is that the parties are socially proximate, facilitating mutual trust and an understanding of the tasks. By contrast, businesses may wish to employ expertise more independent from local, social and business networks, or arrange contracts from knowledge-suppliers that only exist in certain centres. The search process may even in some cases be relatively distance-insensitive, meaning that a firm will seek the best supplier irrespective of location (Rusten *et al.*, 2005). The delivery of expertise in itself may be a complicated combination of face-to-face contacts and digital transfers. Many business contracts are still a result of longstanding business relations with much emphasis on meetings (Ramsey *et al.*, 2005).

It is our contention within this edited volume that – even with all their variation – these rural characteristics, and their layering and interlinking, comprise the 'active context' within which ICTs are experienced. This contrasts with the contention that recent developments in ICTs, in particular around the Internet and related digital technologies, lead to the 'death of distance' (Cairncross, 1997), or the end of geography, with the potential to overcome, rather than reflect, spatial disparities. If we simply follow the logic of this argument, rural areas, given their physical sparsity of population and services, stand to benefit most from such a 'digital revolution' (Skerratt, 2003; Skerratt and Warren, 2003). However, research demonstrates the existence of an urban–rural digital divide, and intra-rural digital divides (Skerratt, 2003; Nurmela, 2003; Montagnier *et al.*, 2002; Berkeley *et al.*, 1996; Clark *et al.*, 1995; Grimes, 2000; Hindman, 2000; Parker, 2000) suggesting that, to date, potential technological benefits have not been realised in rural settings. This finding is linked with analyses which suggest that the role of ICTs in economic development is not a 'magic' solution for rural areas in itself (e.g. Richardson and Gillespie, 2000; Malecki, 2003), since technology is 'wrapped up' in human capital and is complicated by processes that go beyond rural and urban (Kitchin, 1998; Rusten *et al.*, 2005). In addition, the theoretical focus in much of the literature has been on death of distance, whereas fewer authors have raised the question as to whether ICT might *undermine* the qualities of geographical proximity that characterise rural areas such as a sense of 'community' or 'civic connectedness' – although there are a number of urban-based commentaries which paint (dystopian) views of 'networked individuals' divorced from place (e.g. Wellman 2002). In addition, research has rarely consistently addressed whether ICTs as tools simply allow users to enjoy the benefits of both worlds – urban and rural, that is, irrespective of physical location. These, therefore, are the complexities, and paradoxes perhaps, which are identified and discussed within the following chapters.

Further, the exploration represented by this book, we believe, adds considerable value to current debate which still seems largely to compartmentalise 'rural' and 'ICTs'. The following examples are illustrative of the extent of analyses to date. First, Ilbery (1998), in *The Geography of Rural Change*, provides an examination of the processes and outcomes of rural change, placing emphasis on relevant principles, concepts, theories and case studies. He mentions briefly how ICTs may open up new opportunities for rural areas, but also points out that considerable barriers exist in rural areas: financial reasoning may mean that ICTs are given a lower priority. A second barrier is perceived as being connected to the lower degree of utilisation due to lack of training and skills. A second discussion of ICTs in rural areas is found in Lievrouw and Livingstone (2002) – *The Handbook of the New Media* – which again addresses the issue about access within communities, institutions and households, referring specifically to the digital divide. Third, *Worlds of E-commerce* (Leinbach and Brunn, 2000) addresses major issues concerning the growth of ICT across different business sectors; the authors discuss the 'tyranny of geography' and how ICTs might be both decentralising and centralising, since face-to-face contact is still important (referred to as 'co-presence' by Urry, 2001). They argue that the agglomeration of demand and skilled labour further bifurcate geography into a core and a periphery. Finally, the role of ICTs in contributing to the decentralisation of activities, and how telecommunications can be an important element within economic development in rural areas are discussed in Wilsdon (2001) *Digital Futures*. These, largely, remain the exceptions, and thus this book aims to develop the debate – connecting ICT experiences *as embedded within* their rural contexts – more deeply and consistently.

The book in relation to wider (non-rural) ICT analyses of 'place-lessness'

In addition to addressing those arguments concerning the end of geography and place in the place-less world of the Internet, our book also complements those texts relating to the Information Society, Knowledge Economy, and processes of global connectivity, which typically focus either on urban, metropolitan or business sectors (e.g. Sassen, 2001, Bryson *et al.*, 2004; Hellawell, 2001), often with the implication that rural areas will experience ICTs in a similar way (Servon, 2002). Further, our analytical focus on 'place' contrasts with, and complements, research into online communities of practice or interest (Kim, 2000; Powazek, 2002; Wilcox, 2005), where the rise of the 'networked individual' is replacing commitment to, and identification with, place (e.g. Smith and Kollock, 1999; Wellman, 2001). In addition, this book also adds to the debates concerning the interdependency of offline and online worlds (Malecki, 2003; Rusten and Bryson, 2007b) and the scope for ICTs to change social relations (Ritchie and Brindley, 2005).

European territorial dimension

Further, in addressing the European context, our book complements those texts which *do* focus on rural ICT, such as Allen and Dillman (1994) and Kline

(2000) which are primarily US-based and US-oriented, or are situated in Australia (e.g. Gurstein, 2000). Although very informative and important texts, their authors do not address the current and future issues facing rural areas in a European context. Where 'rural' *is* addressed within European ICT commentaries (such as by the OECD), it generally comprises one element within regional reviews, rather than being subject to a stand-alone critical analysis, and is often reported at aggregated regional levels (exceptions to this including OECD, 2001, 2004; Cornford *et al.*, 2000).

Thus, by incorporating the territorial dimension from a range of rural settings within Europe, we illustrate how various types of ICT-related experiences are linked with the presence/absence of specific rural cultural and spatial conditions. We develop an empirical and academic contribution regarding ICT and Internet access, performance, economic and socio-economic impact, and social shaping and 'construction of relevance' (McCown, 2002; Brown and Duguid, 2000). The empirical evidence that we present embraces examples across different European and Nordic countries, and reflects how capacity for and interest in adoption, engagement and adaptation are influenced by different economic and geographical settings.

Finally, in presenting contributions from Norway and Gaelic-speaking Scotland, we complement those studies which are based to a large extent on empirical evidence from large complex economies which have enjoyed the benefits of an Internet dominated by Anglo/American language. This issue of online language is seen as increasingly important, particularly given the rise in Internet acess in India, for example (Lund and McGuire, 2005), and thus has added pertinence when looking at the next 10–15 years.

Implications within the wider rural development context

Although the issue of ICT in rural areas could be conceived by some as being an over-specialised area, we situate the issue of 'ICT' within the wider debate of how the experience of rural is changing, and will continue to change. This is of great concern, theoretically, empirically and in the policy arena, and – for example – has been reflected in the International Congress themes of the International Rural Sociology Association (Norway, 2004), the European Society for Rural Sociology (Ireland 2003, Hungary 2005) and the International Rural Network (US, 2005). We are therefore investigating and presenting a key dimension of rural change, which is integral in mediating the range of impacts from those drivers affecting wider Europe's rural areas. Further, we touch on the mew Member States through illustrations in our chapters, and we thus highlight enlargement issues, of key concern to the European Commission, as well as to the academic community. The work presented in this volume therefore, examines how the *experience* of rural is changing in a digital age, through pulling together disparate threads into a coherent academic commentary and analysis.

The chapters: a story

We have aimed to create a book which is much more than simply an edited volume of disparate or weakly connected chapters. Typically, rural ICT research relies on case studies or 'vignettes' which are unique, stand-alone, and often idiosyncratic to the extent that 'generalisability from the specific' remains inherently problematic. Our text, however, enhances the existing literature base by presenting 'patterns' in the experiencing of rurality within a digital age – underpinned by these specific examples; we believe this to be a valuable contribution to the research literature. Thus we are presenting a 'story', with each chapter illustrating an aspect of that story relating to elements of experiencing ICTs in rural settings.

We also build towards an examination of the implications of the presented findings for the broader policy vision of *e*Europe, where digital connectivity and social inclusion are espoused for all citizens, irrespective of location (Europe's Information Society: Thematic Portal). That is, how do rural inhabitants' experiences of being rural, in a digital age, support – or counter – *e*Europe claims and targets? How does the variability of that experience, and its dynamism, challenge future predictions and strategies?

The chapters presented here are not intended as exhaustive, either of instances, themes or geography. Rather they are illustrative of the main contested themes emerging within rural Information-Society debates, policy and practice. That is: first, the embedding of ICTs within practices of small and medium enterprises (SMEs) in rural areas, and the importance of capacity; second, the persistence of place, both as an active modifying context, and as a marketable commodity; third, the significance of 'fitting' ICTs within details of social and cultural context, such as within place-based communities and among those with a shared minority language. Therefore, the underlying thread which unites all chapters is this: *that context remains all-important in analyses of the appropriation, adaptation, and 'fit' of ICTs, and that rural remains a key component of that context.* The experience of 'being rural' is, by association, changing, and the effects of rurality on those change processes is itself being modified by people's engagement with ICTs in business, home, leisure and within social networks. These interacting elements, in turn, modify and filter the implementation of a European Information-Society 'vision'.

Chapters 2 (Rusten *et al.*) and 3 (Bryson) illustrate the first of these three themes – that of the *embedding of ICTs within practices of small and medium enterprises (SMEs) in rural areas*, and the organising of work. Rusten *et al.* explore rural firms' e-business performance through five different case studies. Their analysis shows how niche producers may create distinctiveness related to which product they sell, their promotion activity and not least by communicating effectively with their customers as part of the trade process. All these components represent elements of the ways in which niche producers can create distinctiveness, trust and a large enough market to produce a profit. The ICT tool in fact makes these firms a viable alternative to more inward-looking firms producing and selling traditional goods predominantly locally. Bryson in chapter 3, meanwhile, clearly shows how urban and rural settings can be integrated by individuals utilising the benefit from both geographical settings. It also illustrates how rural areas – due to lower costs of living and quality lifestyles – may represent interesting locations both for living and recreation. Further, it also shows how the Internet makes it easier to work from home. Bryson sets this analysis within a compelling historical context, critiquing those approaches which privilege an exclusive focus on the Internet's impacts while bypassing the historical trajectory of technological adaptation through which many firms have already passed, for example, thanks to the telephone.

The second theme – *persistence of place, both as an active modifying context, and as a marketable commodity* – is illustrated in chapters 4 (Kleppe and Hosea) and 5 (Skerratt). In their chapter, Kleppe and Hosea explore the way in which ICT can become a virtual tool in promotional activities and place-based branding by firms located in rural areas. Meanwhile, Skerratt examines the significance for e-inclusion of 'participation environments' in the provision of shared, informal ICT facilities in rural areas of the UK.

The third theme, which addresses *the significance of 'fitting' ICTs within detailed experiences of social and cultural context*, is illustrated through Chapters 6 (Gannon) and 7 (MacLeod). In her chapter, Gannon describes variations in rural household usage of ICTs, and analyses implications for the 'frictions of distance' and Information-Society models. MacLeod tackles the persistent, and increasingly debated, issue of minority languages on the Internet, and the implications for sustained rural usage.

In arguing that European Information-Society policy needs to be sensitised to these elements of context, and particularly to these three themes, the final chapter (Talbot and Gillespie) comprises a critical review of such policies, particularly in the light of a persisting digital divide.

The book concludes with a postscript, which both synthesises these four main themes and the elements of the 'being rural in a digital age' story, and indicates potential research, policy and practice areas of focus, in working towards a digitally inclusive range of rural experiences.

Note

1 Within the following chapters, the issue of differential speeds of broadband is naturally referred to. We do not set out to explore this specifically. However, we do highlight it as an area requiring further research and consistent policy attention, since new divides are emerging related to varying 'broadband speeds' from *up to* 512KB per second in rural areas to between eight and 16MB per second in urban centres.

References

Allen, J.C. and Dillman, D.A. (1994) *Against All Odds: Rural Community in the Information Age*, Rural Studies Series, Oxford: Westview Press.

Berkeley, N., Clark, D. and Ilbery, B. (1996) 'Regional Variations in Business Use of

Information and Communication Technologies and Their Implications for Policy: Case Study Evidence from Rural England', *Geoforum* 27 (1): 75–8.

Brown, J.S. and Duguid, P. (2000) *The Social Life of Information*, Harvard, MA: Harvard Business School Press.

Bryson, J.R., Daniels, P.W. and Warf, B. (2004) *Service Worlds. People: Organisations, Technologies*, London: Routledge.

Cairncross, F. (1997) *The Death of Distance*, Boston, MA: Harvard Business School Press.

Cairncross, F. (2001) 'The Death of Distance 2.0', in *How the Communications Revolution Will Change Our Lives*, London: Texere Publishing.

Clark, D., Ilbery, B. and Berkely, N. (1995). 'Telematics and Rural Businesses: An Evaluation of Uses, Potentials and Policy Implications', *Regional Studies* 29 (2): 171–80.

Cloke, P. (1997) *Rural Studies: A Reader*, Abingdon: Hodder & Stoughton.

Countryside Agency (2000) *Rural Services in 2000*, Cheltenham: Countryside Agency.

Cornford, J.R., Gillespie, A. and Richardson, R. (2000) 'Regional Development in the Information Society', in K. Ducatel, J. Webster and W. Herrmann (2000) *The Information Society in Europe: Work and Life in an Age of Globalization*, Boulder, CO: Rowman and Littlefield, pp. 21–44.

Economist, The (2005) 'Totally Digital' by Fiorina, in *The World in 2005*, p. 128.

European Commission (2006) *Bridging the Broadband Gap (SEC (2006) 354 and SEC (2006) 355)*, Brussels: European Commission.

Eurostat (2006) 'The Internet and Other Computer Networks and Their Use by European Enterprises to do eBusiness', Statistics in Focus 28/2006.

Gray, C. (2006) 'Stage Models of ICT Adoption in Small Firms', in S. Zappalà and C. Gray (eds) *Impact of e-Commerce on Consumers and Small Firms*, Aldershot: Ashgate, pp. 3–20.

Grimes, S. (2000) 'Rural Areas in the Information Society: Diminishing Distance or Increasing Learning Capacity?', *Journal of Rural Studies* 16: 13–21.

Gurstein, M. (2000) *Community Informatics: Enabling Communities with Information and Communications Technologies*, London: Idea Group Publishing.

Hargittai, E. (2003) 'The Digital Divide and What to Do about It', in D.C. Jones (ed.) *New Economy Handbook*, San Diego, CA: Academic Press.

Heiskanen, T. and Hearn, J. (2003) *Information Society and the Workplace: Spaces, Boundaries and Agency*, London: Routledge.

Hellawell, S. (2001) *Beyond Access: ICT and Social Inclusion*, London: Fabian Society.

Hindman, B. (2000) 'The Rural–Urban Digital Divide', *Journalism and Mass Communication Quarterly* 77 (3): 549–60.

Holloway, L. (2003) 'Virtual Vegetables and Adopted Sheep: Ethical Relations, Authenticity and Internet-mediated Food Production Technologies', *Area* 34: 70–81.

Ilbery, B. (1998) *The Geography of Rural Change*, London: Prentice Hall.

Kim, A.J. (2000) *Community Building on the Web: Secret Strategies for Successful Online Communities*, Berkeley, CA: Peachpit Press. (See also: www.naima.com/community.)

Kitchin, R.M. (1998) 'Towards Geographies of Cyberspace', *Progress in Human Geography* 22 (3): 385–406.

Kline, R.R. (2000) *Consumers in the Country: Technology and Social Change in Rural America*, Baltimore, MD: Johns Hopkins University Press.

Kolarova, D., Samaganova, A., Samson, I. and Ternaux, P. (2006) 'Spatial Aspects of ICT Development in Russia', *The Service Industries Journal* 26 (8): 873–88.

Leinbach, T.R. and Brunn, S.D. (2000) *Worlds of E-commerce: Economic, Geographical and Social Dimensions*, Chichester: John Wiley.

Lievrouw, L. and Livingstone, S. (2002) *The Handbook of New Media*, London: Sage Publications.

Lund, M.J.F. and McGuire, S. (2005) 'Institutions and Development: Electronic Commerce and Economic Growth', *Organization Studies* 26 (23): 1743–63.

McCown, R.L. (2002) 'Probing the Enigma of the Decision Support System for Farmers: Learning from Experience and from Theory', *Agricultural Systems* 74: 1–10.

Malecki, E.J. (2003) 'Digital Development in Rural Areas: Potentials and Pitfalls', *Journal of Rural Studies* 19: 201–14.

Montagnier, P., Muller, E. and Vickery, G. (2002) *The Digital Divide: Diffusion and Use of ICTs*, Paris: Information, Computer and Communications Policy Division, Directorate for Science, Technology and Industry.

Nurmela, J. (2003) *A 'Great Migration' to the Information Society? Patterns of ICT Diffusion in Finland in 1996–2002*, Helsinki: Statistics Finland.

OECD (2001) *Information and Communication Technologies and Rural Development*, Territorial Economy Series, Paris: OECD.

OECD (2004) *The Development of Broadband Access in Remote and Rural Areas*, Working Party on Telecommunications and Information Services Policies, available online at: www.oecd.org/dataoecd/38/40/31718094.pdf.

Parker, E. (2000) 'Closing the Rural Digital Divide', *Telecommunications Policy* 24 (4): 281–90.

Phillips, M. (1998), 'The Restructuring of Social Imaginations in Rural Geography' *Journal of Rural Studies* 14: 121–53.

Powazek, D.M. (2002) *Design for Community: The Art of Connecting People in Virtual Places*, Indianapolis: New Riders Publications. (See also: www.designforcommunity.com.)

Ramsey, E., Ibbotson, P., Bell, J. and McCole, P. (2005) 'Internet-based Business among Knowledge Intensive Business Services: Some Irish Regional Evidence', *The Service Industries Journal* 25 (4): 525–45.

Richardson, R. and Gillespie, A. (2000) 'The Economic Development of Peripheral Rural Areas in the Information Age', in M.I. Wilson and K.E. Corey (eds) *Information Tectonics*, New York: Wiley, pp. 199–217.

Ritchie, B. and Brindley, C. (2005) 'ICT Adoption by SMEs: Implications for Relationships and Management', *New Technology, Work and Employment* 20: 3.

Rusten, G. and Bryson, J.R. (2007a) 'The Production and Consumption of Industrial Design Expertise by Small and Medium-sized Firms: Some Evidence from Norway', *Geografiska Annaler, SerieB, Human Geography* 89 (51) forthcoming.

Rusten, G. and Bryson, J.R. (2007b) Understanding the Relationship between Information Communication Technology and the Behaviour of Firms Located in Regional Clusters', in J.R. Bryson and P.W. Daniels (eds) *The Handbook of Service Industries in the Global Economy*, Cheltenham: Edward Elgar, pp. 311–30.

Rusten, G., Bryson, J.R. and Gammelsæter, H. (2005) Dislocated versus Local Business Service Expertise and Knowledge: The Acquisition of External Management Consultancy Expertise by Small- and Medium-sized Enterprises in Norway, *GEOFORUM* 36: 525–39.

Sassen, S. (2001) *The Global City: New York, London, Tokyo*, Princeton, NJ: Princeton University Press.

Servon, L.J. (2002) *Bridging the Digital Divide: Technology, Community and Public Policy*, Oxford: Blackwell Publishing.

Skerratt, S. (2003) *The Implications for Rural and Regional Populations of the Irish Government's Provision of Broadband Communications Infrastructure*, National Institute of Regional and Spatial Analysis, National University of Ireland.

Skerratt, S. and Warren, M. (2003) 'Rural Communities and Broadband: Local Appropriation of a Global Technology?', in P. Cunningham, M. Cunningham and P. Fatelnig (2003) *Building the Knowledge Economy: Issues, Applications, Case Studies*, Oxford: IOS Press, pp. 150–7.

Smith, M.A. and Kollock, P. (1999) *Communities in Cyberspace*, London: Routledge.

Urry, J. (2001) 'Mobility and Proximity', Web-paper, www.ville-en-mouvement.com/interventions/John_Urry.pdf, last accessed December 2006.

Wellman, B. (2001) 'Physical Place and Cyberspace: The Rise of Networked Individualism', in B. Keeble and B. Loader (eds) (2001) *Community Informatics: Shaping Computer-Mediated Social Relations*, London: Routledge, pp. 17–42.

Wellman, B. (2002) 'Little Boxes, Glocalization, and Networked Individualism', Web-paper, www.chass.utoronto.ca/~wellman/publications/littleboxes/littlebox.PDF, last accessed January 2007.

Wilcox, M. (2005) 'Describing Networks: Joining Us, Joining in, or Joining up', Paper for Partnerships Online Blog, 9 March 2005. Accessed online at: www.partnershipsonline.org.uk/index.cfm?fuseaction=main.viewBlogEntry&intMTEntryID=2401.

Wilsdon, J. (2001) *Digital Futures: Living in a Dot-com World*, London: Earthscan Publications Ltd.

Zappalà, S. and Gray, C. (2006) *Impact of e-Commerce on Consumers and Small Firms*, Aldershot: Ashgate.

Websites

Europe's Information Society Thematic Portal: http://europa.eu.int/information_society.

Pew Internet and American Life Project reports: http://207.21.232.103/reports.asp.

Part I

Understanding ICTs in rural SMEs

2 Lost in cyberspace? Website performance among firms located in rural areas of Norway

The niche food sector

Grete Rusten, Winfried Ellingsen and Frode Kristiansen

Introduction

The reduction of subsidies for conventional agriculture, among other changes in the food industry, has moved some food producers in the direction of alternative products and distribution channels. Online business offers opportunities for marketing and trade of regional products and creates direct links with customers as an alternative to wholesale distribution. The strategic employment of Information and Communication Technology (ICT) depends on the level of a firm's awareness of its value and potential applications. Moreover, performance also depends on internal resources such as knowledge and administrative capacity, and earlier experiences with ICT.

This chapter assesses how rural niche producers in the Norwegian food industry have exploited the Internet to develop their businesses. Although demand and consumption issues are considered, this chapter's primary focus is on the production side of website marketing and trading. Motivations and conditions for setting up the website are also discussed. Five cases based on web analysis and telephone interviews among small niche food producers make up the empirical evidence that illustrates the way the content and role of websites vary across product categories, frequency and volume of orders, market range, and when combined with other distribution channels.

There are in principle three ways in which ICT adds value to the activities of firms. First, technology may enhance organizational efficiency in all parts of the value chain including those that reach beyond the boundaries of the firm. This tool makes it easier to exchange information, to cooperate and to coordinate the production between individuals, units and organizations. ICT can help in collecting information about innovations, markets and regulations. The whole process of searching for suitable suppliers, comparing prices and quality, is far simpler when facilitated by ICT, and suppliers can become more aware of clients' requirements through the development of customer profiles. Software programmes may serve to control resource flows, stocks, production and distribution processes. Online communication also makes it easier for rural SMEs to interact with experts who may be located elsewhere. In practical terms, a firm's supply chain will contain a mixture of firms located in different places; every firm will rely on a distinctive combination of local, regional, national and even international relationships. In fact, ICT is strengthening existing ties in many business relations. For others it may be an efficient tool stimulating cooperation with new partners. ICT can for instance be of service when cooperating on activities such as finance, training, technological developments and marketing to gain the economies of scale, scope and strength generally associated with large companies. Farmers, growers and producers in the UK have for instance formed a joint organization, the *National Farmers' Retail and Markets Association (FARMA)*, which aims to promote and support members and grants certificates to farmers' markets meeting certain agreed criteria. Advertisements about farmer-market events are published on its website (www.farmersmarkets.net).

Second, ICT alters the relationship between customers and firms; the relationship can be more interactive even to the extent of permitting the development of customized products and services. ICT is strengthening existing ties, but can also brings the firm and the product to the attention of new customers. It can also actively promote the local connection and cultural history of a product. Clients and suppliers are able to invest in shared integrated ICT systems that enable real-time exchanges of information about stock levels, logistics, design detailing, and alterations to the technological detailing or function of a product. The latter is especially important where firms are part of a complex production system in which they are contributing elements of a much more complex product. Through the application of ICT, service and sales processes can be coordinated so that the various participants resemble a single integrated supplier, something which might be crucial when matching the requirements of large and complex contracts. In such cases, it is essential that all parties to the supply chain are integrated by the adoption of a shared ICT platform. The incorporation of ICT into a supply chain enhances information flows and contributes to the development of long-term relationships. It also locks firms into a supply chain as well as excluding firms as it may reduce the number of additional firms able to join the supply chain. Lock-in may be beneficial initially, but could also result in pressure to reduce the cost of parts supplied by any one member of the supply chain. One of the major challenges for rural firms is to reach enough customers to be able to make a surplus. Being able to combine different market channels including performance marketing and even Internet selling seems to be useful to firms even when most buyers are located relatively nearby, in many cases in the same community or region. Internet business can be either complementary to traditional market channels or represent a whole new line of trading. ICT gives a wider reach, but may at the same time require more careful credit management. The trust needed for trade can be created by personal relations or via formalized credit-check systems. Another alternative can be to move the responsibility over to the logistic service providers, with the goods delivered to the customer only once payment is received.

Operating in cyberspace does also afford scope to create new linkages and virtual communities between producers and consumers. Network forms of organization or virtual firms constitute an alternative way to grow a business. Small firms and even individuals are able to overcome the constraints of location and capacity by becoming part of a virtual firm. Clients benefit from drawing upon a breadth and depth of expertise that is available from the continually evolving flexible network of members of the virtual firm. The network also permits the rapid creation of a flexible web-based corporate identity. 'Members' of the network benefit from resources (expertise, reputation, services) developed and managed by other firms as well as retain flexibility. The development of virtual organizational forms is part of an ongoing process in which the boundaries between firms are rendered invisible or become increasingly blurred and complex. Sometimes it is important for a firm to show the outside world that it is part of a cluster. To have a 'good address' and present this cluster on the web is a way of signalling this resource position to the rest of the world. At the same time, marketing and shared infrastructure can bind these parties together (Rusten and Bryson, 2007).

Third, ICT is part of the toolkit that a firm can deploy to project itself as an attractive company. Websites may become part of a firm's branding and marketing strategy. This way of presenting the business may also help to project a firm's power in the marketplace in a way that can be read by potential business partners as well as private or public investors. The firm may, for instance, highlight the nature of its activities by supplying information about production conditions, product details, certificates and prizes, sales outlets and key customers. The firm may also display photographs of their traditional farm, or production buildings that symbolize solidity, size, modernity and success in business. This type of marketing activity concentrates on highlighting the positive aspects of a firm's image. A firm's relation to spatial symbols/labels is expressed by its marketing strategies including the way it presents itself on the web. Spatial elements of firms' websites include physical address, accessibility, map, site and spatial references on web addresses. The levels ranges from local to global and are sometimes clearly articulated, in other cases more abstract or tacit. For some rural firms the content of the websites could also serve to promote the local culture. Place-based products capture an individual's attention, encouraging them to relate products to their established maps of place-based meanings, associations and references. In this way, place-based or place-positioned products attempt to capitalise upon consumers' existing knowledge and assumptions. Promoting the geographical origin can add that little extra to a product or service, as some consumers know that certain addresses represent certain qualities.

Some firms do for instance project local connections through pictures of the production process and in some instances references from local suppliers. Other firms wish to avoid community links due to worries about content not being updated or language quality being poor. On the other end of the scale are firms that, instead of fostering an association with a particular place, have developed an identity as global players or networked organizations. Information about export volumes, international markets and the location of production or sales offices are displayed to emphasize the companies' international orientation.

This can be done by publishing images of foreign locations, maps, pictures and place names on the web. Presenting the major customers on the website might be the correct strategy for some firms in order to signal their power and reputation, whereas others might consider this type of information a trade secret. The geographical label can be an important element in the way a firm markets itself and its brand. This may also be a help to customers in their navigation on the net. The promotion of geographical origin is also a clear response to increased globalization, and represents new market opportunities for niche food producers in several rural communities in Norway and elsewhere.

There is in fact a growing interest in food that Ilbery and Kneafsey (2000) refer to as 'authentic', 'traditional', 'wholesome' and 'traceable'. For Norway, as in many other places in Europe, these changes in the market represent an interesting possibility for product development within the food industries in rural regions (Nygård and Storstad, 1998). The agricultural sector in Norway is declining and comprises only about 4 per cent of the total employment at national level. It remains, however, the main employer in many rural communities. The sales of high-quality niche products to certain market segments may yield important additional income to some farmers, allowing them to continue to live off their farms.

Foods that are traceable to a place of origin and that can be incorporated into individual lifestyle projects are becoming more fashionable (Giddens, 1991). Rural lifestyles and commodities, which claim to be authentic, traditional and of high quality stimulate a growing consumer demand for commodities of a distinct rural origin. Food produced in a particular geographical area is often labelled specifically as local or rural. As our cases will illustrate, the geographical market range for these products may differ. Customers may be either urban or rural, living close or more distant from the producers. They may also differ in their use of market channels and buying habits.

The connection between geography and product also differs in other ways. The use of spatial symbols can be part of a branding strategy for certain products and can enhance website performance. These particular place images can be either created or exploited (Pawson, 1997). In other cases, certain products are part of the identity of a community region or nation. Consumers may in some cases wish to buy a product from a particular area. The origin of the receipt or production site or sales outlet is associated with a certain image or quality, and, in that way, geography is linked to the product. Conversely, products may also contribute to a particular image of a region

Then there is the issue about the marketplace. Weatherell *et al.*'s 2003 study from the UK indicates that most customers prefer to buy regional food products in supermarkets. This option should, however, be a supplementary rather than an alternative way of selling, since some customers appreciate the combination of being able to order on the Internet direct from the producer with the products delivered to their doorsteps. Purchases can also be made by post since postal services now include door-to-door deliveries to households in the evenings when most people are home from work. Large-volume deliveries do not, however suit all consumers.

An alternative means of classifying market channels is to take the customers as the starting point, and divide them according to whether they prefer home shopping, retail shopping or production-site shopping. All of these channels may involve the use of Information and Communication Technology (ICT) for promotion, as a communication channel prior to a visit, or for online ordering and/or payment. Whether product delivery is discrete or continuous will also vary.

Limited resources for marketing can be a considerable hindrance when selling products outside the local community and managing a sales volume that will give a decent income (Døving *et al.*, 2002). Information and communication technology can be a way to reach more customers. E-business[1] can also improve trade by leading to more efficient administration and information flows, and reducing distribution costs. Information technology may be a means of reaching new and existing customers. Business over the Internet can either be complementary to traditional market channels or represent a whole new line of business. This chapter assesses how niche producers in the Norwegian food industry have taken advantage of the Internet to develop their businesses.

This chapter discusses some cases of how businesses present and/or sell their products via the Internet. Not only do we find large variations according to type of product, but also in the way the firms are organized. This will eventually have an influence on both the content and the resources firms can employ on their web presentations. In some cases, synergy effects are created by linking different categories of producers together. Food producers, tourism businesses and handcraft producers represent one of several possible combinations, and such websites contain images as well as practical information about how the places can be visited.

This chapter continues with a brief overview of the status of e-commerce in Norway and some existing research analysing website strategies and actual website performance. We address the role of trust in e-commerce, actual website performance and some problems with these forms of product presentation. By referring to some practical examples, we aim to raise awareness of the value of the website as a marketing tool and a communication channel. Case studies afford a flexible design for research, both for research questions and for the choice of cases. All the firms studied were based in Norway, and each website was examined in detail and the various functions performed on the site recorded.[2] Obviously, given the restrictions of the sample, the results presented cannot be taken as representative of the population or as representative of the full range of existing web strategies. Nevertheless, the cases illustrate various ways of organizing businesses and a variety of different products, strategies and actual website performances. The conclusion reflects on the way the content and roles of websites vary due to differences across a number of dimensions.

ICT performance in Norway

Telecommunication systems in the Nordic countries are fairly advanced, with a high coverage of broadband, even in rural areas. Moreover, the user cost is quite low relative to average income (Rusten, 2003). The use of e-commerce in Norway has improved significantly since the late 1990s. In 2006, up to 71 per cent of all firms (10+ employees) had their own homepages. Still, only 23 per cent of firms sell their products and services over the Internet. This figure, however, only refers to those with direct ordering and payment systems. For many firms, their websites are very much awareness tools, and it is therefore difficult to measure the Internet's full role as a marketing and sales channel. Behind the measures shown in Table 2.1 are other important characteristics that influence performance, such as sector, type of product, market orientation and many other aspects that are found in numerous combinations on an individual level. Further, ICT as a communication and sales channel should not be studied independently of other ways of reaching customers. In fact, as the cases presented in this chapter illustrate, communication and sales channels are often combined. Exactly how this is done varies from business to business and even differs within the same organization over time depending on the type of product, the location of customers and a range of other factors. In fact, a case approach to this issue captures a variety of factors in different combinations that would be lost in traditional statistical analysis.

The strategy

The existing literature on website presentation focuses mainly on technical, managerial and marketing issues. One relevant issue in the literature is the analysis of website content, purpose and functionality (e.g. Chang *et al.*, 1997; Cooper and Burgess, 2000). This perspective examines the layers of complexity for the purposes of benchmarking. Similar website studies look at indexing in search engines (Thelwall, 2000). Some of the existing website studies can be criticized for not distinguishing between websites set up for general marketing purposes and websites predominantly established for regular customers, suppliers and/or other collaboration partners. Neither do these studies address the fact that, for many firms, the website complements rather than replaces traditional marketing and distribution channels. In order to evaluate website performance, it is necessary to know the motivations and conditions for setting up the website and how this part of the ICT strategy fits in with the rest of the business.

Table 2.1 The use of ICT by enterprises, measured in relation to Internet access, homepage and sales via Internet. The numbers are expressed as percentages

	1998	*2000*	*2004*	*2006*
Proportion of all enterprises with Internet access	40	74	84	93
Proportion of all enterprises with a homepage	22	48	61	71
Proportion of all enterprises with turnover from sales via Internet	4	8	18	23

Source: Statistics Norway, 2006. www.ssb.no.

We can identify four phases in e-business performance.

1. Firms generally start with some experimental e-business activity, often the establishment of what is sometimes dismissively referred to as 'brochure-ware', or a simple static homepage containing little more than what can be found in standard brochures.
2. The business starts to publish a wider range of information on the web, both to market its products and services, and, occasionally, in other areas such as after-sales support.
3. The website shifts from being a one-way publishing channel to a two-way communication channel so that visitors to the site can send messages back to the company, either by email or through forms (i.e. to order goods and services, even though these may be paid for by more traditional means).
4. The site becomes transactional and capable of supporting the whole purchasing decision, including accepting payment for ordered goods and services. By the use of extranet applications, communication may be limited to existing business contacts.

Outlining different stages of e-business performance does not, however, mean that all firms develop this way. Indeed, many will only ever use their website as a marketing tool.

Website advertising may be one of many ways of convincing customers to enter into a trade relationship. It may be even more important as a tool for serving existing customers more efficiently through announcements in newsletters or email responses. Customers buying a product need to feel sure that they will get what they are paying for. The transaction will, in other words, require trust.

Trust and motivation

A business transaction in its most basic form represents three distinct phases: the information phase, in which the customer searches for a suitable business partner; the negotiation phase, in which details about an agreement are settled; and finally the execution phase, in which delivery and payment take place. Trust is important in every part of this process, and necessitates a measure of predictability.

Notions of trust in relation to food products are inherent in perceptions of quality. Kneafsey and Ilbery (2001) identified four indicators of quality: (1) certification (a quality mark from a professional organization or government);[3] (2) specification (i.e. production methods); (3) association (geographical or historical); and (4) attraction (appealing design, flavour, appearance, taste, etc.). Information on production methods (e.g. 'no additives') and an appeal to rural settlements are factors popularly associated with Norway. Attraction can be easily combined with and attributed to products, particularly in the case of niche food producers operating on the Internet. Trust finds expression in different ways. One way is to supply details of the physical address of the firm. Consumers will generally have more confidence in a business operating on the web if it can be associated not only with a postbox, but also with real physical buildings, facilities and personnel (Doney and Cannon, 1997). In some cases, the existence of an actual store gives customers the chance to inspect the goods before purchasing. Websites can contain information that convinces the parties that they should initiate (or maintain) contact, and can also give further instructions that eventually lead to orders. Examples are authorized certificates that guarantee production conditions and product quality. However, e-commerce does not seem to overcome distance decay. Closeness has value as it strengthens the feeling of security. Most trade relations involving farm products and other small-scale food producers are based on a tacit understanding between the parties, and only a minority are regulated through formal contracts.

A critical quality element for a website is its ability to respond to enquiries immediately. An email not answered within a given timeframe (say, for example, within a day) could result in the loss of a customer. This is no doubt a challenge for small firms with limited administrative capacity.

One of the main points of corporate resistance to e-commerce has to do with culture, i.e. whether the Internet should be part of the core competencies of the firm or just a complementary communication channel. Several key elements make the website an important supplement to traditional market channels – may be suitable for marketing and branding, not only for the product, but also to 'dress up' the firm in order to attract interest from investors as well as customers. For niche food producers it is also important to get media coverage. A website may also be easily assessed for control purposes by the authorities, the financial community or project managers (e.g. through annual-report presentations). For niche food producers it can be effective to join forces in other portals as well as advertising like market activities such as farmers' markets, food shops, book projects, etc. Joining forces will both lower the individual costs and make each firm more visible in the market. A new trend in marketing is to develop horizontal connections between different products and present them together. Electronic mediated contacts can be employed among cooperating firms. One example is that some hotel chains cultivating an environmentally friendly image are actively seeking niche food suppliers. These combinations of products may also be presented together on the web. Our discussion of the niche food industry and website performance using five different case studies (Status, 2005) addresses customers' motives when making purchases via the Internet.

The case studies

Among our cases there seems to be a clear division between those firms that use the web as a tool to communicate with their regular network and defined customer base, and those that exploit it as an advertising tool. This partly explains why some websites are deliberately designed to be search-engine-friendly and others are not. This chapter presents five different case studies to illustrate various ways of performing on the web. Obviously, given the restrictions of the sample, these results cannot be taken as representative of the population of niche food producers and the full range of practices of operating on the Internet that may exist. Nevertheless, the cases illustrate various types of performance affected by the firms, their identities, products and location. To protect confidentiality, firm names have been altered.

Jam on the net

Jam is a food item in the examples that can be considered a standard supermarket product. The company *Jam on the net* has traded directly with customers since it started in 1939, in its early years mostly within the county of Rogaland, where it originated. In 1999, the firm set up webpages with electronic order forms to attract a wider range of customers and their market now covers the whole country. According to the manager (personal communication), the company is not targeting particular groups, but is aware of some structural characteristics of its customers. It concluded from the results of a questionnaire that its customers have above-average incomes and education and also larger families than average.

The company's website focuses on three aspects: tradition, quality and product range. A traditional image can be interpreted as an attempt to build trust. The company has been doing business since 1939, which in itself can be perceived as a guarantee of product quality. Quality is explicitly supported by a guarantee and generated through attractive images that appeal to the subliminal desires of consumers in terms of texture, flavour, taste and appearance. Products are presented on the web with colourful pictures. The main product lines are various types of jam and a range of juices (to be mixed with water). Juice concentrates are not available in shops. Recently, the company began selling jam in a supermarket chain. This is more in the form of an experiment, as there is no particular adaptation to this chain (it receives the same discount as web orders), and direct sales are still predominant. Although jam sold by *Jam on the net* is mass-produced and is nowadays found in some department stores, certain *distinctive* features, such as no adding preservatives, are advertised in order to promote its higher value. This also suggests that the difference between primary and secondary commodities may be fluid, as food is a necessity, but may become a luxury with the addition of certain features (of production) or by associating the product with a certain image. By appealing to the customer's environmental conscience with the cleanliness of the product, or with direct references to the consumer's state of being (as in most *Green* or *Godt Norsk* food), or to novelty, the exchange value of these products can be raised.

The webpages disclose hardly any company information apart from the tradition mentioned above. The region and locality are downplayed in descriptions and pictures in catalogues and on the website. The website gives no information about the origin of the raw material. Most of the fruit comes from national producers (according to national law, a certain percentage of the raw material has to be of Norwegian origin). The marketable quality of the product is that no preservatives except for sugar are added, and the jams are quite tasty since the sugar content is low. We also observe that place promotion, defined as the conscious application of publicity and marketing to communicate selective images of specific geographical localities or areas to a target audience (Gold and Ward, 1994), remains unexplored for this firm.

The company does not support creditcard transactions, but the website includes HTML forms, email and surface mail addresses, as well as fax and telephone numbers. There are no links to other local sites or attractions. The website offers order forms, with customers receiving a small discount for online ordering. The webpages have recently been upgraded and Jam on the net has added other products in collaboration with other suppliers to their online catalogues. *Jam on the net* is the only one of the cases that started out as a traditional mail-order firm before evolving into an e-commerce business.

Meat from land to table

The *Meat from land to table* concerns a farm, which forms part of a larger consortium of six local meat producers located in the counties of Akershus, Østfold, and Hedmark, in eastern Norway. Proximity to the capital city Oslo as well as other urban concentrations seems to play a major role in the business, and many potential customers boast above-average education and income. The producers deliver orders directly to customers' doorsteps. The market range for the product is regional. The home webpage lists the six producers of the consortium, and customers can select any of the members. Although a single external operator designed all the webpages, a great deal of variation exists between the member pages, as each farm producer arranged the design and content of their webpages according to their own needs and wishes.

The idea of selling meat to individual customers directly from the producer builds on the traditional way of distributing farm products. It ensures the traceability of the product, with further details about the farm, its location, ownership and production conditions. The focus is on the ethical aspects of keeping animals, providing them with space to roam and conditions that are as natural as possible. The image produced is one of health, adding to the *green* image of clean food without additives. This appeals to the customer groups implicitly targeted by the webpages. The overall impression is that the target group comprises 'those who are concerned with what they eat and where the food comes from'. For that purpose, content information relates how long the farm has been operating, its physical conditions (soil, etc.), the number of cows and pigs, along with further details about the family that owns the farm. The references to history and family details are meant to ensure *familiarity*, *accountability* or *trustworthiness*. This intention is underlined by images of a well-kept farmhouse in beautiful surroundings (also the logo of the company) and *healthy* animals in the fields rather than pictures of the meat. The photos make exact location impossible and place is referred to only in the context of physical parameters, such as proximity to the longest river in Norway and the farm's distance to the nearest town.

The second issue important to these producers concerns transactions with the customers. The expression 'from land to table' implies that there are no middlemen and no additional retailing, and the producers propose that the product is thus competitive in price and quality with the same food available in stores. Contact between producer and consumer can be established through the Internet, by telephone or mail. Customers can order directly over the web, with the producer informing customers when goods will be delivered to their homes. Email and direct contact form the user feedback systems. Payment is on delivery and creditcards are not accepted. This form of doing business is consistent with the general *green* image of the products. It is clearly the intention of the producers to establish lasting relationships with a limited number of customers. This facilitates transactions as a whole and gives both parties a sense of security. The producers of this consortium still have not reached their full potential for direct sales, and sell their remaining livestock to one of the slaughterhouses owned by an agricultural cooperative (Gilde) which operates across the country. The only links on the farm's webpages are to other farms in the consortium, and, in cases of delivery constraints due to the volume of incoming orders, customers may be transferred to one of the other producers.

Meat from land to table is a good example of the belief of the consumers (the appeal to people living in the city) in the link between product quality and the place of production. The perceived authenticity of rural food is underlined by the delivery to customers' doorsteps, establishing a face-to-face relationship to support the initial web contact. This case also suggests that the Internet can function to sell goods and services outside the normal retail system, thus achieving more than creating and sustaining awareness (Gold and Ward, 1994). This case also shows how the Internet can act to reintroduce the traditional direct sale based on longlasting customer relations.

Herb

Herb started trading in 1992 as an organization comprising more than 250 small-scale farmers all over Norway. The concept was to prepare and distribute dried herbs produced by its members, the products are mainly consisting of various herbal spices and teas. The farmers send their products to regional units that check the quality, before rinsing and packing the products ready for sales in stores or online.

Information about the products, pictures of the flora, labels with product details, together with an online ordering system, make up the central part of the website. It was designed by a third party and in the process of being revised during our inspection. The exact geographical origins of the products, other than that they come from different locations in Norway, are not detailed. Advertising in magazines, including information about the website and stores stocking the products, seems to be an additional important tool for reaching customers. The market is national.

The manager reported that the main challenges for the website operation are visibility and capacity to cope with online orders despite internal constraints. The website does not offer an online payment system.

One could perhaps expect that herbs, being non-perishable, would be an almost perfect product for home purchasing. However, it is questionable whether there is sufficient volume in an individual order to justify the transport costs. Infrequent orders, especially for spices, make a large customer base necessary. Advertising on the web is one of several marketing channels, with most customers buying the products in pharmacies and health-food shops. The manager seemed doubtful about the benefits of marketing the products on the web, believing the consumers were not quite ready for this. The firm had, however, found the Internet effective in developing and maintaining relationships with retailers, restaurants, etc.

Turkey

This fourth case concerns a farmer who combines organic breeding of turkeys, growing apples and practising his skills as a figurative artist. The turkey breeding is based on a 30-year tradition at the farm, with the animals kept grazing outside most of the time. The whole process from breeding to slaughtering and packing the finished cut meat takes place on the farm. All meat is checked by the Norwegian Food Safety Authority before it reaches the customers.

The farmer practises a combination of direct-contact advertising methods, sending newsletters through email and regular post, mostly targeting existing customers. About 40 per cent of the products are sold by this direct method. He previously had a website through the Norsk Gardsmat, a portal featuring information about products and services relating to rural tourism and traditional food in Norway. However, this link to the Norsk Gardsmat website resulted in very few orders, so he eventually decided to withdraw from this network. Products are still presented on the web, and customers may email for further details of the products, conditions for delivery, and place orders. The website also includes information about the farm and visiting possibilities. One method of delivering products to customers living in Bergen, about two hours' away, is using a drop-off point at a farm shop near the city. This shop specializes in locally produced meat products, and therefore has the freezer capacity to keep the goods for *Turkey* until the customers collect them. Appointments can be made by contacting the farmer by email or telephone and the products can be collected from the farm, delivered to the customer's home or elsewhere. Place promotion is a central part of being on the web, but here it is merely a way of informing new customers that they can visit the farm, where the food products or sculptures can be purchased. The farmer prefers payment by cash rather than creditcards.

However, online communication and a sort of direct marketing to dedicated customers is not the most important marketing channel. The farm is also known for its quality and mans a stand at the farmers' market that takes place four to five times a year, and, finally, some of the stock is sold through gourmet shops across the country.

Salmonogram

A farm in western Norway runs a profitable sideline in online salmon sales, with delivery to the customers or as gifts to other addresses. Several marinades for the salmon are available and the volume of orders is about 8,000 yearly. The salmon are delivered by a local fish farmer and smoked and packed in a town nearby. This proximity between the different suppliers is crucial to ensure that the whole value chain runs smoothly and also that quality is good. The firm has tried to increase its sales volume, but logistics present a challenge due to inefficient postal services. The website has an online ordering form. An email order will be dealt with the same day or, if received at the weekend, on the nearest working day, the products being sent by mail. Door-to-door delivery is an important part of the concept which is of high quality and represents the higher-price segment for this type of product.

Private consumers comprise the largest share of the salmon market, in addition to several firms that have employed *Salmonogram* to furnish gifts for business partners and customers. A small quantity of salmon has also been delivered to a couple of high-class restaurants. The fam's Internet presence, combined with guest packages for visitors, as well as stands at food fairs and other exhibitions demonstrate that a mix of different advertising media can serve to increase the number of customers. Payments are based on invoices delivered with the products. Salmon products make up a smaller share of the firm's income than its other activities, which include tourism and deer breeding.

Discussion

In this chapter, we have reviewed the opportunities that websites offer small food producers, and discussed their impact as a marketing and distribution tool. The extent to which the organizations have adopted Internet trading varies among the five cases, both in terms of e-commerce applications on their websites, and how the business is adapted to the web. Of the cases serving as illustrations in this article *Herb*, *Jam on the net* and *Salmonogram* are true e-based mail-order firms in that the customers do not normally have the option of buying the products at a shop at the production site or meeting the producers on delivery as in the case with *Turkey* and *Meat from land to table*. Therefore, the cases vary considerably not only in the content and product characteristics, but also in the extent to which the Internet is employed compared with other communication forms and sales outlets. Obviously some experimentation, through trial and error, is taking place. This study has also shown how website performance should be assessed in the context of the organizations behind these initiatives, and their motivations and strategies.

Although many producers advertise on the web, potential consumers are unlikely to discover them in this way. Nor does the electronic marketplace usually make the physical marketplace obsolete, but the proportion of business handled on the web is likely to change. Websites in general may offer an online ordering system, at least for some products (as with *Jam on the net* and *Herb*). However, the degree to which the web can replace traditional distribution channels may vary considerably. In some cases (such as *Turkey*) the website provides information on the products, ordering and delivery to existing customers or new ones perhaps encountered, at the farmers' market. Buying small portions of meat in the supermarket, rather than a whole animal, as in the case of *Meat from land to table*, means that different customer segments can be targeted. In both cases, the web can be valuable in locating a market, as well as as building a brand and supplying information. In fact, all the cases analysed show the importance of targeting dedicated customers. *Salmonogram*, *Herb* and *Jam on the net* have customers across the country, whereas most of *Turkey* and *Meat from land to table* customers are local or at least within the same region (in most cases within two to three hours' drive).

There are obviously first-mover advantages and capacity constraints for businesses trading online. Duplicating each other's websites can be a threat, but a way to minimize this type of damage is to make use of individual advice instruments or to spread a large set of best-practice options across sectors. Exaggeration, understatement, stereotyping, cliché, repetition, banality, overcrowding, fragmentary assembly of place elements, inability to establish a distinct selling proposition, and failing to specify accurately the target audience are also relevant factors when measuring website performance. There is of course also a real risk of being lost in the enormous mass of information on the web. The ability to use the Norwegian language, if Norwegians are the major customer group, (and we believe this is the fact due to export regulations for food), may be helpful in limiting the marketplace. Data from Statistics Norway based on a representative sample from firms with five or more employees across all sectors showed that 42 per cent only presented webpage information in Norwegian (Statistics Norway 2004, unpublished data).

Being listed in portals with related businesses or in portals sorted by geography may also be a solution. Another challenge for smaller companies is attending to the sometimes high number of enquiries that may be generated by their websites. Staff at one company studied (*Herb*) said that they struggled to deal with all the emails, and remained unsure as to whether it would be profitable to employ more people to cope with the increased activity. Focusing on dedicated customer service, as several of the case firms did, is in fact a way to avoid the number of enquiries getting out of control.

ICT enables the formation of subtly defined niches according to lifestyle and previous buying behaviour. Both customers and suppliers share some common interests and form something like virtual communities where trade may take place. Virtual clusters, created through websites, by parties geographically close (such as *Meat from land to table*) or distant from each other (such as *Herb*), can also be an efficient way of sharing resources. Clusters also represent strong symbols that attract attention, signify market power and may attract government support or private capital. Some newschapter campaigns for small niche food producers organized by Innovation Norway have been proven to increase the interest in this type of food. Important details such as visiting addresses, weblinks or general information needed to get hold of the products are, however, often missing in these articles.

A webpage with unlimited access will present the producer, its product and perhaps details about retailers to a countless number of recipients. It still does not mean that these pages are meant for everyone absolutely everywhere, but that they have instead content that may appeal to some while being of almost no interest to others. This means that the firm will always have to decide how it will present itself to attract interest and be relevant for its prioritised targets. The recipients they wish to reach may be suppliers or dealers, business or private customers. Sometimes the pages are aimed at all of these groups; in other cases, they are only designed for selected recipients. In yet other cases, a firm may have a combined strategy, meaning that some parts are meant for dealers or suppliers while other sections are meant for the customer or the public in general. One problem we have identified through our studies of firm websites is that pages produced for a firm's dealer, featuring mostly technical and practical information, are in the open and read by others. Potential customers seeking product information can be disappointed by these dull pages. Splitting up the website by targeting different categories of readers can help to avoid this. The more dedicated parts of the webpages may adopt effective access restrictions via passwords. These sections called, Extranets, will also prevent competitors or others accessing strategically important business information and other types of confidential content.

Our cases have shown how web communication can strengthen local distribution ties to new or existing customers or in some cases be a way of reaching market niches beyond the nearest neighbourhood. Our research also shows that website performance should not be isolated from discussion about other communication channels, and of the organizations behind these initiatives, their motives and strategies. The introduction of the Internet to already existing businesses is no doubt forcing these firms to transform themselves, to rethink their strategies, their organizational structure and their business models.

The website may also be intended to reach more than just potential markets. For instance, financial information such as an annual report may be of interest to banks or potential investors. It may also serve as an important information source to designers wishing to get a grasp of the history, identity and ambitions of a firm. Others finding the information relevant could include public authorities, politicians, journalists, educational institutions, consultants and researchers or simply members of the general public seeking information about the business community. An interesting issue related to Internet presence is whether this reduces pressure on staff responding to inquiries, or in fact increases their workload in this regard. Of capacity-constraint reasons, we even know of small production firms that have decided against setting up their own website, preferring to deal with customers and others directly either face-to-face or via phone, post or fax or indirectly through retailers.

For policy-making in this area, there is a strong need to launch projects and initiatives offering individual advice on website performance to small and medium enterprises (SMEs) in all sectors. Unfortunately, public support for these measures has so far been scarce at the national level. This policy must be grounded in the experiences of small firms in Norway, rather than being based on international management literature. It is clear from our research on SMEs across various sectors that some owners/managers are better able to adapt technology and competence to their businesses, and that the success of this is determined by a wide range of factors within and external to the firm (Rusten, 2003). Motivation, knowledge and capacity are critical elements in the firm's e-performance.

To demonstrate the Internet's potential, programmes that target small-scale food producers should raise awareness of technology, content and design and provide advice, information and training. In some cases, where these firms have reached a certain size, the upgrading of existing businesses could include the recruitment of ICT experts.

Part of an awareness strategy would be to downplay the notion that operating on the Internet means global markets. Many SMEs, particularly the niche food producers, should be focusing on using this tool for local, regional, and national customers. Advice initiatives should operate across sectors in order to transfer ideas from one business area to another and thereby avoid duplication of strategy or product within the same sector. E-commerce performance should also be combined with projects to stimulate the development of joint e-business platforms as well as other market arenas, eventually leading to new business opportunities in rural areas. As producers seem to have only a vague image of their customer base, analysis of customer trends and behaviours could help improve business. Our different cases have also illustrated the interplay between online and offline communication sources and various sales channels.

In this chapter we have not been able to do justice to all aspects of website performance relevant to the niche food industry. Further research may look beyond the limits of the individual firm, and investigate how business performance related to web strategies is tied to the presence or absence of appropriate cultural and spatial conditions in general, and to rural locations in particular. Niche products within the food industry may be associated with particular places and vice versa. It is important that the images of these places are employed when operating on the web.

Our main results relate to the way the content and role of websites varies across product categories, frequency and volume of orders, market range, and other distribution channels. In future studies, it will be important to further differentiate between these dimensions to fully understand niche food producers in general. The range of products, different categories of customers and the size of the market need to be taken into account when one tries to understand the role of the web.

Notes

1 Business activities that involve the use of ICT for promotion, communication, financial transactions and/or distribution.
2 Investigations of the websites and additional telephone calls took place in spring 2003. To protect their confidentiality, the actual names of the firms have been changed in the text.
3 Certification can be construed as a lack of trust. Farmers are obliged to hold certificates of cleanliness, slaughter procedures, etc. and produce them on demand to demonstrate their trustworthiness.

References

Chang, L., Arnett, R.P., Capella, L.M. and Beatty, R.C. (1997) 'Websites of Fortune 500 Companies: Facing Customers through Home Pages, *Information and Management* 31: 334–45.

Cooper, J. and Burgess, L. (2000) 'A Model of Internet Commerce Adoption (MICA)', in S.M. Rhaman and M.S. Raisinghani (eds) *Electronic Commerce: Opportunity and Challenges*, Hersey: IDEA Group Publishing, pp. 189–201.

Doney, P.M. and Cannon, J.P. (1997) 'An Examination of the Nature of Trust in Buyer–Seller Relationships', *Journal of Marketing* 61: 35–51.

Døving, G., Sand, R., Jakobsen, S.-E., Haugum, M., Rusten G. and Sand, A.G. (2002) *Følgeevaluering av Verdiskapingsprogrammet for matproduksjon*, Report 50, Bergen: Institute for Research in Economics and Business Administration.

Giddens, A. (1991) *Modernity and Self-identity: Self and Society in the Late Modern Age*, Stanford, CA: Stanford University Press.

Gold, J. and Ward, S. (eds) (1994) *Place Promotion: The Use of Publicity and Marketing to Sell Towns and Regions*, Chichester: John Wiley & Sons.

Ilbery, B. and Kneafsey, M. (2000) 'Registering Regional Speciality Food and Drink Products in the United Kingdom: The Case of PDOs and PGIs', *Area* 32: 317–25.

Kneafsey, M. and Ilbery, B. (2001) 'Regional Images and the Promotion of Speciality Food and Drink in the West Country', *Journal of the Geographical Association* 86: 131–40.

Nygård, B. and Storstad, O. (1998) 'De-globalisation of Food Markets? Consumer Perceptions of Safe Food: The Case of Norway', *Sociologia Ruralis* 38 (1): 35–53.

Pawson, E. (1997) 'Branding Strategies and Languages of Consumption', *New Zealand Geographer* 53 (2): 16–21.

Rusten, G. (2003) *IKT og regional utvikling*, Working Paper 40.03, Bergen: Institute for Research in Economics and Business Administration.

Rusten, G. and Bryson, J.R. (2007) 'Understanding the Relationship between Information Communication Technology and the Behaviour of Firms Located in Regional Clusters', in J.R. Bryson and P.W. Daniels (eds) *The Handbook of Service Industries in the Global Economy*, Cheltenham: Edward Elgar, pp. 311–30.

Thelwall, M. (2000) 'Commercial Web Sites:Lost in Cyberspace?', Internet Research, *Electronic Applications and Policy* 10 (2): 150–9.

Weatherell, C., Tregear, A. and Allinson, J. (2003) 'In Search of the Concerned Consumer: UK Public Perceptions of Food, Farming and Buying Local', *Journal of Rural Studies* 19: 233–44.

3 Lone Eagles and High Fliers

Rural-based business and professional service firms and information communication technology

John R. Bryson

> Economists, most of whom have long ignored or despised economic geography, are now taking a fresh interest in it.
>
> (Cairncross, 2001: 203)

> If he chooses, [a country solicitor] can save hours of dull letter-writing by walking up and down streets, where he is certain to meet his clients, or he can transact business with them at the club or at a tavern. For my own part, though I have taken instructions on golf courses, and in cricket pavilions, I prefer in half-idle moments to consort with my clients, after the eighteenth-century fashion in coffee houses.
>
> (Hine, 1945: 69)

Introduction

In 1945 Reginald Hine, a British solicitor, published an autobiography in which he described his experiences of working in one of the oldest firms in England (established 1591), Hawkins & Co., of Hitchen in Hertfordshire. Hine was a prolific author and is known for 17 books he wrote on the local history and people of Hitchen. He had an interesting and in some ways leisurely working life as 'the best of my days were spent half doing my duty … devoting the other half to the discovery of manuscripts for the history of a royal and ancient manor' (Hine, 1945: 5). His autobiography is an account of a small-town legal practice that had to alter as new technologies were introduced. Hine notes that, over the 35 years he spent as a 'half-practiced' lawyer, new technology had disturbed his working routine:

> Gone too, is that ruminating, spider-like existence that a lawyer used to lead in his be-cobwebbed chambers. Nowadays, what with telephones, and callers hurrying in by train or omnibus or car, life in the law is one long interruption …
>
> (Hine, 1945: 4)

It is very easy to forget that businesses have always had to respond to developments in communication technologies. These include the development of the railway, tram, road and shipping networks as well as the semaphore, the development of the postal service, the introduction of the telephone, fax machines and, more recently, the the Internet and teleconferencing. The first major communication breakthrough came with the establishment of the postal system. In England this can be traced back to 1635 when Charles I allowed the general public to send letters via the Royal Posts; the first Post-house was established in London in 1635. The postal system came into its own in the UK in 1840 with the introduction of a national minimum price for letters (the penny postage). Railroads also played an important communication role in the nineteenth century as they enabled rural communities to be established across the United States (Hudson, 1985). The railroad opened new territories as agricultural produce could now be transported to the major urban settlements (Bryson and Henry, 2005) and goods and services could now be produced and consumed in previously inaccessible places. The decline of rural communities in the American mid west is associated with the difficulties of attracting and retaining people to what are relatively isolated rural communities. Nevertheless, new forms of Internet-based communication and related working practices enable individuals to live and work in remote rural areas.

Communication over distances in real time only became possible during the later part of the nineteenth century. Casson, in his early history of the telephone, noted that:

> The telephone business did not really begin to grow big and overspread the earth until 1896, but the keynote of expansion was first sounded by Theodore Vail [General Manager of the Bell Telephone Company] in the earliest days, when as yet the telephone was a babe in arms. In 1879 Vail said, in a letter written to one of his captains:
>
> 'Tell our agents that we have a proposition on foot to connect the different cities for the purpose of personal communication, and in other ways to organize a *grand telephonic system*.'
>
> (Casson, 1910: 170)

The development of the postal systems, telephony and, most recently, the Internet led to radical alterations in business behaviour. It is far too easy to overemphasis the importance of the most recent technological developments while forgetting the difficulties companies and customers had in adjusting to earlier rounds of technological innovation.

The development of the telephone and the Internet can be viewed part of the same technological development. Both involved substantial infrastructural investments by service providers and consumers and both enabled people to communicate together in real time. The telephone permitted people to talk over great distances, but the technology was synchronous in that both parties to the conversation had to be available at the same time. The rapid adoption of the Internet by businesses enhanced the real-time interactions associated with the telephone, but with two major differences. First, digitally encoded documents could be transferred to people in real time. This increased the turnaround time of some business transactions as well as enabled the introduction of a spatial division of labour to paper-based business transactions. Deindustrialisation is associated with the transfer of manufacturing units to low-cost economies. The application of a spatial division of labour to manufacturing was facilitated by telex, fax and telephone. These technologies enabled the relocation of some office activities to low-cost locations, but synchronised work in real time was difficult. Second, the Internet is asynchronous as an individual or company can be contacted when they are unavailable (when they are not logged on, during the night, etc.). It is also extremely flexible as text, pictures and sound can be attached to an email while the recipient can respond instantly and engage in a form of rapid conversation or consider a response and draft a formal reply; the Internet blends the features associated with speech with those of writing.

The development of the telephone and various forms of electronic communication allowed companies to alter existing practices as well as the establishment of companies based on new technologically enabled business models. This means that new technology has the potential to encourage the formation of new economic geographies. In some accounts the new communications revolution is associated with the end of geography (O'Brien, 1992, Cairncross, 2001; Graham, 1998) or a flat world (Friedman, 2005). Cairncross considers the death of distance to be associated with the merger of communications with computers and the introduction of high-capacity fibre-optic networks that carry data, voice and images around the world. The efficiency of these networks means that the cost of sending data an additional 1,000 miles is effectively zero (2001: 2). There is a curious conflict between those that associate information communication technologies (ICTs) with the end of geography as we know it and the vast and ever expanding literature on various forms of clustering and local agglomeration. On the one hand, ICT makes it possible for businesses to be established in unconventional locations while, on the other hand, the clusters literature continues to emphasise the importance of proximity, co-presence, and co-location as an important source of or stimulus to creativity. The difficulty lies in reconciling these conflicting accounts of business organisation.

It is possible to argue that economic geographers as well as the policy-making community have been fixated with a theoretical approach that seeks to explain economic growth as the consequence of a process of clustering. Taylor has argued that the cluster concept has become a brand that is in the ascendancy and, more importantly, that 'it is a model that became a message that is now a mantra', a mesmerising mantra (Taylor, 2005: 1). Similarly, Kotkin argues that the logic underpinning clusters is increasingly tenuous as advanced telecommunications means that it is not difficult to coordinate geographically dispersed individuals and companies (2001). The cluster mantra has had an important influence on the types of questions and related research designs developed by economic geographers. It is not an overstatement to argue that the literature of economic geography has an urban as well as cluster bias. This means that research on the rise of the knowledge economy as well as the creative class has focused on the dynamics of highly visible clusters of urban-based firms. This explains the dominance of global cities in much of this literature as well as the comparative neglect of firms located in rural areas. This is an interesting omission given the importance of rural areas as places to live and work. It means, for example, that there is a literature that explores the activities of major law and accountancy firms (Hanlon, 1999), but the smaller legal and accountancy practices located in market towns and rural areas have been overlooked. The omission in the literature is not just about firms, but also one of lifestyles and the relationship that exists between metropolitan and nonmetropolitan areas. Professional workers require stimulating and high-quality residential and working environments. Many professionals are choosing to live outside metropolitan areas in adjacent rural areas (villages and market towns). They can benefit from the lifestyle and well-being advantages of rural and small-town living, while still able to access urban economies, cultures and societies (business and friendship networks).

This chapter begins to unpack some dimensions of the economic geography of business and professional service (BPS) firms located in rural areas. It is based upon surveys (telephone and in-depth) undertaken in 2002 and 2005 (for accounts of the methodologies, see Daniels and Bryson, 2002, 2006) and an analysis of the functioning economic geography of the regional economy of the West Midlands (Bryson and Taylor, 2006). The argument is organised into three sections. This brief introduction is followed by a discussion of recent empirical studies dealing with BPS firms in nonmetropolitan areas. This section highlights the role of sole practitioners and home-based firms in the knowledge economy that is developing in rural areas. The third section explores the factors that have enabled BPS firms to trade their services from a distance. This is especially important for the development of BPS firms in remote rural areas. The fourth section presents an analysis of some empirical evidence from the West Midlands. This takes two forms; first, an analysis using national statistics and second, three case studies to illustrate the argument.

Lone Eagles and High Fliers

BPS firms provide services that are sold primarily to other businesses as well as governments (Bryson, 1997). It is worth noting that some BPS firms supply services to both businesses and final consumers (for example, solicitors, accountants, architects). Included under the BPS heading is a complex array of business activities including management consultancy, accountancy, architectural services, legal services, design, public relations and marketing. This sector of the economy has been expanding rapidly in urban areas as well as in less traditional rural locations (Bryson *et al.*, 1997). Much of the academic literature on BPS concentrates on urban-based firms and ignores those in small towns and rural areas. The long-held view is that services are non-basic; they function in the local or regional economy as support for the basic goods-related activities that are engaged in interregional trade and which generate the revenues (taxes, employees' incomes) that create the demand for services. The implication is that the majority of BPS firms will be located in urban areas as they must be close to client concentrations. Take away the basic goods-producing activities and the demand for services will decline and they will contract accordingly. Prior to developments in ICT as well as business travel, the majority of BPS firms served local businesses. This is no longer the case as a growing proportion sell services interregionally and internationally.

The competitive advantage of BPS firms is embodied in fee-earning or professional employees. There is an important relationship between company success and the ability to attract and retain highly skilled employees who possess expertise, a known reputation and the ability to commercialise their skills. The latter is an important point as professional expertise does not produce added value by itself. The importance of embodied expertise combined with developments in ICT (computers, the Internet and mobile phones) and airlines implies that the growth of BPS firms in rural areas should be expected. This is especially the case when highly educated individuals are sensitive to the environment in which they live; the implication being that rural areas might yield attractive alternative lifestyles.

Research into rural-based BPS is dominated by American studies. The most important was predicated on a telephone survey of 240 rural-based BPS firms conducted in 1994 (Beyers and Lindahl, 1996). The analysis explored the economic contribution of rural BPS firms and especially those that exported their services outside the area. Exporting firms were identified as those that obtained at least 40 per cent of their revenues from outside their local market. Exporters were further categorised as 'Lone Eagles' (one-person proprietorships) or 'High Fliers' (firms with one or more employees). Thirteen Lone Eagles and 89 High Fliers were identified, with the remaining 136 comprising locally orientated firms. The presence of a significant proportion of exporting BPS firms in this sample should come as no surprise. By the very nature of the kinds of services offered by Lone Eagles and High Fliers, it is unlikely that they will be producing output primarily for consumption in local markets. There will, for example, be very limited demand for high-level management consultancy or advice on the installation and maintenance of corporate ICT systems in the small and dispersed communities typical of rural areas in the US, Canada, Australia or Europe. Much of the output of these advanced services, and indeed those located in the much larger and longer-established urban centres, are of necessity traded between localities and regions.

Respondents were asked to volunteer factors that they considered to have been highly important in determining their locational decision. A high quality of life was the most important factor identified by both High Fliers (66 per cent) and Lone Eagles (73 per cent). Proximity to their home was an important factor and many of the Lone Eagles had home-based businesses. A whole series of 'quality-of-life'-related factors were also identified, for example, 'weather', 'communication links', 'born there' and 'purchased an existing firm'. High Fliers and Lone Eagles appeared to be more footloose than locally orientated firms. Many of them furnished a detailed quality-of-life justification for their current location related to 'environmental conditions', and 'desire to get away from urban setting'. In contrast, locally orientated firms made 'frequent reference to family ties in the region, growing up in the area and returning to run a business, or being pulled there by family conditions' (Beyers and Lindahl, 1996: 6).

In a subsequent paper, Beyers and Nelson (2000) present an analysis of four community case studies of rapidly growing rural communities. The analysis is based on interviews with 30 businesses and government officials in each community and the authors also spoke to a similar number of citizens on the street, in coffee shops, or bars, at airports and even while out hiking. The analysis suggests that the American traditional Old West is still very much alive with rural economies containing significant proportions of resource-dependent sectors (farming, ranching, forestry and mining), but 'the case study evidence suggests that we are witnessing the development of a *newer* West, as new economic activities are emerging alongside more traditional resource based industries' (Beyers and Nelson, 2000: 465). Part of the analysis concerns Lone Eagles and High Fliers. However, they identified very few Lone Eagles and they note that this might be attributable to differences in the research design between the 1996 and 2000 studies. The 1996 paper was based upon purchased name-lists of specified BPS SIC codes while the latter community case study used a random sample of all businesses in the case-study sites. People in each community were aware of Lone Eagles among them as they 'felt their presence, [but] also agreed they were "hard to spot"' (Beyers and Nelson, 2000: 470). Beyers and Nelson supply brief overviews of two ICT-enabled BPS firms:

> An example of a Lone Eagle was a person in the graphic art business, who generated his copy by computer, and shipped almost all his files out of state to his clients. We also interviewed a stock broker who was flying off early on a Monday morning from the local airport to meet with his clients, which he does on a periodic basis. When not meeting with clients, he conducts most of his trades electronically.
>
> (Beyers and Nelson, 2000: 470)

Beyers and Nelson report mixed perspectives regarding the perceived value of Lone Eagles to rural communities. Some people considered that these knowledge-based individuals were an asset to the community, but others argued that they were not a source of capital for local development and that they did not employ local labour. Thus, Lone Eagles were perceived to have limited multiplier impacts for the local economy apart from contributing to the local tax base.

Beyers's work on Lone Eagles has been developed in two subsequent studies. Salant *et al.* (1997) undertook a postal survey of people who had recently relocated to Washington State. The analysis is based on people who had replaced an out-of-state driver's licence with a Washington licence. A typology of firms with different degrees of locational freedom was produced that included:

> **Lone eagles**, who (a) are not constrained by the requirements of their work, can either be self-employed (footloose proprietors) or work for someone else (footloose employees), and (b) use information technologies to sell products or services in a non-local market.

> **Moonlighters**, who own businesses or have jobs that tie them to a particular location, but at the same time, have additional work that would make them lone eagles if it were their primary employment.
>
> **Telecommuters**, who have jobs tied to a particular location but still enjoy enough latitude to work at home some of the time, using telecommunications to stay in touch with a central workplace'.
>
> (Salant *et al.*, 1997: 6)

They identified 58 Lone Eagles or 2.4 per cent of their sample; about two-thirds (33) were footloose proprietors and one-third (12) footloose employees. Just over 6 per cent (83) of employed in-migrants were telecommuters and 14 were classified as moonlighters. Telecommuters and both kinds of Lone Eagle were more likely to use various kinds of ICT than other employed in-migrants. Lone Eagles and telecommuters were also more likely to have a higher income than other employed people and this difference existed prior to and after the move to Washington. Salant *et al.* also explored the push-and-pull factors that led to the relocation. Households containing a Lone Eagle cited quality of the natural environment (92 per cent), outdoor recreational opportunities (83 per cent) and a desirable climate (71 per cent) as the most important pull factors compared with 70 per cent, 66 per cent and 57 per cent respectively for 'other employed people' (Salant *et al.*, 1997: 10). The most important push factor identified was the high cost of operating their business at their previous residence; a factor that is related to the absence of a state income tax in Washington. By extrapolating their findings, Salant *et al.* (1997: 7) estimated that 2,100 Lone Eagles had moved to Washington State during the 12 months covered by the study. Most of these people are engineers, writers, accountants, researchers and small manufacturers (for example, a publisher of medical books, a maker of model trains), who are attracted to rural areas for quality-of-life reasons. Parallel to American rural immigration, Northern Europe is experiencing flows of people from other countries seeking rural lifestyles. For example, Dutch immigrants have settled in several declining rural communities. These modern rural settlers retain their existing social ties and work-based relations through ICT and travel. Some are Lone Eagles who deploy ICT to deliver services from relatively isolated rural locations (Sunnmørsposten 27.3.2004).

In 2004, Wallowa County in northeast Oregon, published the final report of a detailed analysis of Lone Eagles (Northeast Oregon Economic Development District, 2004). Rural Wallowa County has experienced a severe economic downturn that began in the 1980s and was associated with the decline in the region's timber industry. A committee of concerned citizens decided to focus their attention on attracting Lone Eagles on the understanding that the county's quality of life represented a valuable resource that could serve to attract footloose, knowledge-intensive and ICT-enabled professionals to the area. Some 30 Lone Eagles participated in the research. Of these, 63 per cent of the Lone Eagles had moved into the county since 1998; 24 were self-employed and some of the employed worked for a company with employees that telecommute from locations throughout the US. Most Lone Eagles travel outside the county on business with one-third spending a month away on business every year, another third are out of the county for one to six months a year and a quarter spend over six months on business travel.

The analysis confirms the findings of Beyers and Lindahl as well as Salant *et al.* as Lone Eagles 'are moving to the area primarily because of the quality of the natural environment and family life, outdoor recreation, safety and affordability' (Northeast Oregon Economic Development District, 2004: 1). Nevertheless, there is a problem with this account as 'most Lone Eagles either grew up here, had family here or had visited the area. Limited telecommunications services present the biggest business challenge' (Northeast Oregon Economic Development District, 2004: 1). A total of 43 per cent of the Lone Eagles had family living in the area or had relocated because they or their spouse had grown up in the county while another 43 per cent had previously holidayed there; only 14 per cent had identified the location through a process of active research. The importance of family relationships in this study conflicts with that of Beyers and Lindahl, who found that locally orientated firms rather than Lone Eagles were more likely to have kinship ties to their rural locality (1996: 6).

It is noteworthy that the Wallowa county Lone Eagles were not completely footloose as kinship associations were a major influence on the relocation decision. The implication is that kinship ties are an important part of a local and even national economy's asset base; well-educated migrants might be encouraged to return home to enjoy rural lifestyles while still being able to capitalise on their skills. Holiday experiences of an area are also important and policy-makers should focus on attracting frequent visitors who may consider relocating to the area. The Wallowa report proposes a relationship-based strategy to recruit Lone Eagles to the county. The focus of the strategy is to target the county's existing contacts, such as those with family ties and frequent visitors. It involves identifying kinship- and holiday-based relationships by:

- connecting with high-school alumni with market-specific written information and contacts, featuring Lone Eagles from their class, etc.;
- advertising in alumni newsletters and to alumni at annual/summer reunions;
- holding an open forum supplying information to anyone wishing to encourage a family member/friend etc., to move into the area;
- tapping into the 'grandma network' to get information out to Lone-Eagle grandchildren;[1]
- supplying written materials about Lone-Eagle lifestyles and Lone Eagles in Wallowa county to tourism contacts, information booths, chambers of commerce, chamber websites, outfitter guides, county websites and Realtors, etc.

(Northeast Oregon Economic Development District, 2004: 30)

The Wallowa study highlights the importance of the relationship between people and place-based attachments. This issue is frequently overlooked in much of the academic literature on knowledge-intensive employment and globalisation. Perhaps too much emphasis has been placed on the mobility of people in an ICT-enabled world. There are at least two types of mobility – mobility related to work and that related to place of residence. For Lone Eagles and footloose businesses, ICT offers individuals the chance to continue to earn a living but in a location of their choice. The only limitations appear to be access to ICT (broadband) and an airport combined with the influence of a variety of place-based associations that include kinship networks as well as the experience of place through holidays. These relationships, however, need to be explored by further in-depth research as the existing studies have just begun to identify some of the factors behind the development of rural-based BPS firms.

Trading services or consuming services locally

The growth of BPS in rural areas and the rise of Lone Eagles and High Fliers depend on firms being able to provide services from a distance. Many BPS require a professional, in some cases a team of professionals, to be located at the client's premises. In many instances, the client may never visit the offices of the service provider, for example, a consultancy company may obtain a contract by attending a beauty parade held at a client's premises and, if successful, all subsequent work may occur at the client's premises or even in hotels, cars and airports.

The term BPS describes a complex heterogeneous collection of firms; complexity and diversity exists between and within BPS activities. The heterogeneity means that some BPS firms concentrate on supplying services to local businesses as well as to end-consumers while others may be totally disengaged from the local economy (Bryson and Daniels, 2006). The latter may only be located in the area and have no local clients. Firm size, the incidence of co-production, and the geographical distribution of clients all exert some influence on the degree to which BPS firms are largely embedded within a local economy or have a more 'open' relationship incorporating markets elsewhere in a country or in other parts of the world. The balance between local and global links can be expected to evolve over time, shaped by factors such as firm growth or client demands. This can be summarised as a matrix (Table 3.1) that, in the interests of simplicity, relates size/type of BPS firms to the location of their clients. In the ideal case, as BPS firms develop and grow, they will shift their market configuration from left to right across the matrix. This shift may not always be advantageous as it increases the complexity and cost of doing business with clients. Ultimately, there is no correct or normative way of running a firm; thinking locally and acting locally for many of these firms may be as competitive a business strategy as thinking globally and acting locally. Although the diversification of market structures to incorporate a wider geographical spread of clients will intuitively be seen as desirable, servicing local clients does have the effect of reducing imports into a city region (inter and intra) as well as sustaining its local business base.

Table 3.1 BPS firms and their clients: a simple model

	Local clients	*National clients*	*International clients*
Lone Eagle	Services local market	May work with national clients	May work with international clients, may only work with international clients
Small local firm (not growing)	Services local market	May have some local clients that develop national networks of branch plants	
Growing small firm	Local clients	May have some local clients that develop national networks of branch plants	May operate internationally, but usually for local firms
Large local firm	May begin as a local firm	Follows local firms as they develop national markets	Begins to search for 'foreign clients' by developing strategic alliances and opening a London front office and maybe offices in Europe
Branch office	Established to service local market	Works for local clients that operate nationally	Work for local clients internationally, but international clients usually handled by theLondon office

BPS firms that begin the process of disengaging from a local economy can trade their services in four ways (UN, 2002: 1):

> Mode 1, *cross-border supply* occurs when suppliers of services in one country supply services to consumers in another country without either supplier or consumer moving into the territory of the other.
>
> Mode 2, *consumption abroad* refers to the process by which a consumer resident in one country moves to another country to obtain a service.
>
> Mode 3, *commercial presence* occurs when enterprises in an economy may supply services internationally through the activities of their foreign affiliates.
>
> Mode 4, *presence of natural persons* describes the process by which an individual moves to the country of the consumer in order to provide a service, whether on his or her own behalf or on behalf of his or her employer.

Three of the modes of service trade are concerned primarily with service transactions between residents and non-residents. Recently, there has been a particular interest in mode 3 trade, whereby enterprises supply services internationally through the activities of foreign affiliates abroad (Bryson *et al.*, 2004). For services, this 'method of serving foreign markets is particularly important because it is often the only method that permits the close and continuing contact between service providers and their customers necessary to compete effectively with indigenous firms' (UN, 2002: 54). Modes 1 and 4 enable BPS firms located in rural areas to export their services to other regions and countries. The study of Wallowa county Lone Eagles (Northeast Oregon Economic Development District, 2004) seems to suggest that a significant proportion of Lone Eagles export their services by travelling to the client's premises. Some people have labelled this process 'body shipping'; the process by which a company buys the services of an individual for an agreed and relatively short period of time (Pearson, 1995: 279).

BPS professionals acquire their training and reputations while working for large BPS firms or for client companies (Bryson *et al.*, 1993). Their competitive strength is constructed around the personality, reputation and brand of the individual as well as the network of contacts both with clients and other BPS professionals (Bryson, 1996). These characteristics mean that an established BPS professional is able to relocate to a rural area and continue to work with clients as long as they can maintain their reputation and contact networks. The implication is that relocation from an urban to rural area and the subsequent establishment of a new firm will automatically result in the export of services from the new location. This means that trade in services for micro (Lone Eagles) and small BPS firms is dependent not on the ability to establish export relationships from a rural location, but the ability to maintain existing non-local relationships; export behaviour may be one consequence of a relocation rather than the primary driver.

Rural-based business and professional service firms in the West Midlands

No major British study exists that concentrates solely on exploring the dynamics of rural-based BPS firms. Such a study would fill a major gap in our understanding of the development of the knowledge economy. The UK's Labour Force Survey has shown that since 2001 there has been a gradual increase in self-employment. Since 2002 the growth rate has been faster than at any time since the 1980s. In the year ending September 2003, the number of self-employed people in the UK increased by 282,000 or by 8.9 per cent while it rose by a further 108,000 to June 2004. This shift towards self-employment affects men and women as well as full-time and part-time workers and it was spread throughout the UK. During 2003, increases in self-employment were experienced across all industries, but the largest growth was in banking, finance and insurance (120,000) and construction (53,000) (Lindsay and Macaulay, 2004). Lindsay and Macaulay (2004: 402) explore a number of likely drivers of the shift towards self-employment and conclude that, for banking, finance and insurance (BPS firms), there has been a rise in freelancing and a subsequent shift from employment to self-employment. They cite media stories of people being made redundant in the city and moving into self-employment. They conclude that there has been a real rise in the numbers of self-employed people and that this rise is not attributed to any survey effects or taxation influences.

Since 1997, there has been an upward trend in teleworking in the UK. The greatest increase has been among self-employed people; in the spring of 2005 more than two-thirds of self-employed people were teleworkers compared with only 4 per cent of employees (Ruiz and Walling, 2005: 421). By September 2005, around 3.1 million people worked mainly in their own home, or in different places, with their home acting as a base. Of these, 2.1 million were unable to work at home without access to a telephone or a computer. Most teleworkers, however, work in different places and use their home as a base. The shift towards self-employment, the rise of teleworking and the growth of BPS firms in rural rather than urban locations are all related: the Lone Eagles identified by Beyers and Lindahl (1996) in the US are the same as self-employed teleworkers who work at home all the time, or exhibit a 'nomadic' working lifestyle as they move between the premises of their clients. It is worth noting that Lone Eagles and High Fliers may be based in urban as well as rural areas; urban-based micro BPS firms (Urban Lone Eagles) have been largely ignored by academics and require further investigation. The diversity of BPS locations is one of the justifications for exploring rural-based BPS firms in the West Midlands (UK).

The West Midlands is an extremely complex region characterised by immense variety. The region includes large cities, sparsely populated rural areas, affluent small market towns and villages as well as communities which experience extreme disadvantage and deprivation. The West Midlands workforce of almost 2.6 million is employed across a very wide range of activities. Traditionally, the region's economy is associated with metal-based industries as well as high-profile food-manufacturing. The main sectors are automotive; plastics and rubber, software, food and drink, electronics and telecommunications; and business services. The region's economic structure is still dominated by manufacturing, but this is under threat as the competitiveness of low-value-added or labour-intensive manufacturing is undermined or value-added creation in other economic sectors outstrips that of manufacturing. As a consequence, over the last 30 years the region has been experiencing considerable economic restructuring. This restructuring has caused considerable turbulence related to the rise of unemployment linked to the closure, relocation or downsizing of manufacturing facilities. Manufacturing still has an important role to play in the regional economy, but it must increasingly be based around the production of high-value-added products rather than price-based competitiveness. Alternative employment opportunities have arisen as the service-side of the economy has grown, for example in retail distribution, education, business and professional services and the public sector. After manufacturing, the most important sector in employment terms is financial and business services; the region boasts the largest financial and business services centre outside London and this is driving service output growth in the region. By 2002, this sector accounted for 16.7 per cent of all employees compared with a British average of 19.6 per cent.

The West Midlands has a major concentration of BPS firms in central Birmingham, complemented by a secondary concentration located to the south and east of the city (Figure 3.1). There is significant dispersal that also incorporates

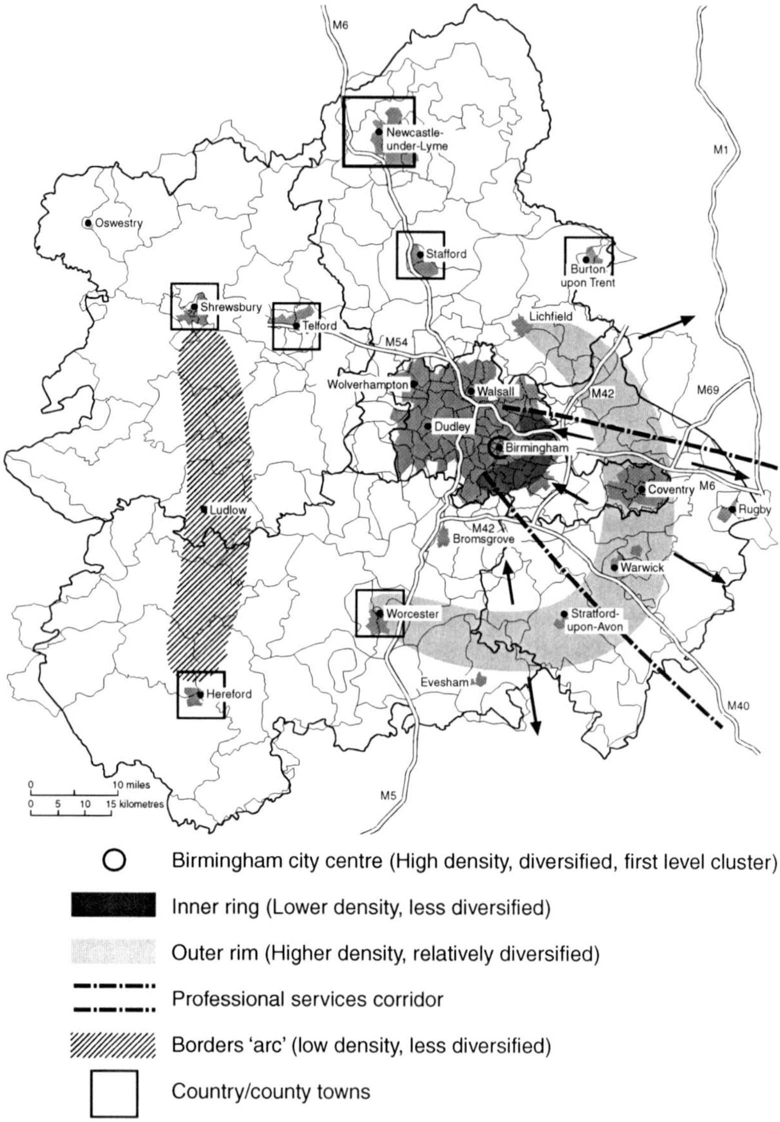

Figure 3.1 Schematic map of professional services in Birmingham and the West Midlands (source: Daniels and Bryson, 2002).

an east-west distinction between a well-served east and a less diverse and probably under-provided (rural) western half of the region. A detailed postcode analysis of BPS firms (Daniels and Bryson, 2002, 2005) in the West Midlands identified the geography of BPS firms in the region (Figure 3.1). Six elements were identified:

Urban elements

1 A *high-density concentration* of professional services in Birmingham city centre.
2 A lower-density *inner ring* of professional services, especially to the south, west and north of the city centre (not including Wolverhampton and Walsall).
3 A *professional services 'corridor'* linking central Birmingham with parts of the outer arc extending southeast from Birmingham city centre, via Solihull and the Coventry–Warwick area to Rugby. It also extends but as a weaker feature northwest of the city-centre cluster towards Wolverhampton.

Rural elements and smaller market towns

4 A higher-density *outer arc* of professional services to the east and south of Birmingham incorporating key market towns including Lichfield, Coventry, Leamington Spa, Warwick, Stratford-upon-Avon, Evesham, Worcester and Bromsgrove.
5 Local clusters of professional service firms in the region's *county/country towns* with mainly rural market areas. Activities in this category include insurance and pension services, telecommunications, multimedia consultants, consultancy services and design-related services
6 Weakly developed local clusters of BPS firms to the west of the region extending from Bridgnorth via Hereford to Ross-on-Wye. The firms in this area tend to be highly localised and are interspersed with small numbers of firms spread across largely rural areas.

An analysis of data from the Annual Business Inquiry (ABI) survey for 2004 reveals a slightly different pattern (Bryson and Taylor, 2006). Mapping location quotient scores of over 1.5 hides the 'Borders' arc (Figure 3.2); this is not surprising as this predominantly supports local demand and could not be expected to be highlighted by location quotients. More importantly, the arc surrounding the Birmingham conurbation is much more extensive and has a horse-shoe or u-shaped profile (Figure 3.2). This does not necessarily reflect the development of a 'rural' arc of BPS firms between the 2002 and 2006 study, but rather the application of a different research design. The 2002 analysis was based on very detailed postcode data while the 2006 one is based on location quotients and the ABI dataset. The 'arc' or 'belt' of BPS firms surrounding the conurbation is involved in a number of functions: some of this activity is closely integrated into the economy of the conurbation, some supports the developing economy surrounding the conurbation and some firms are disengaged as the

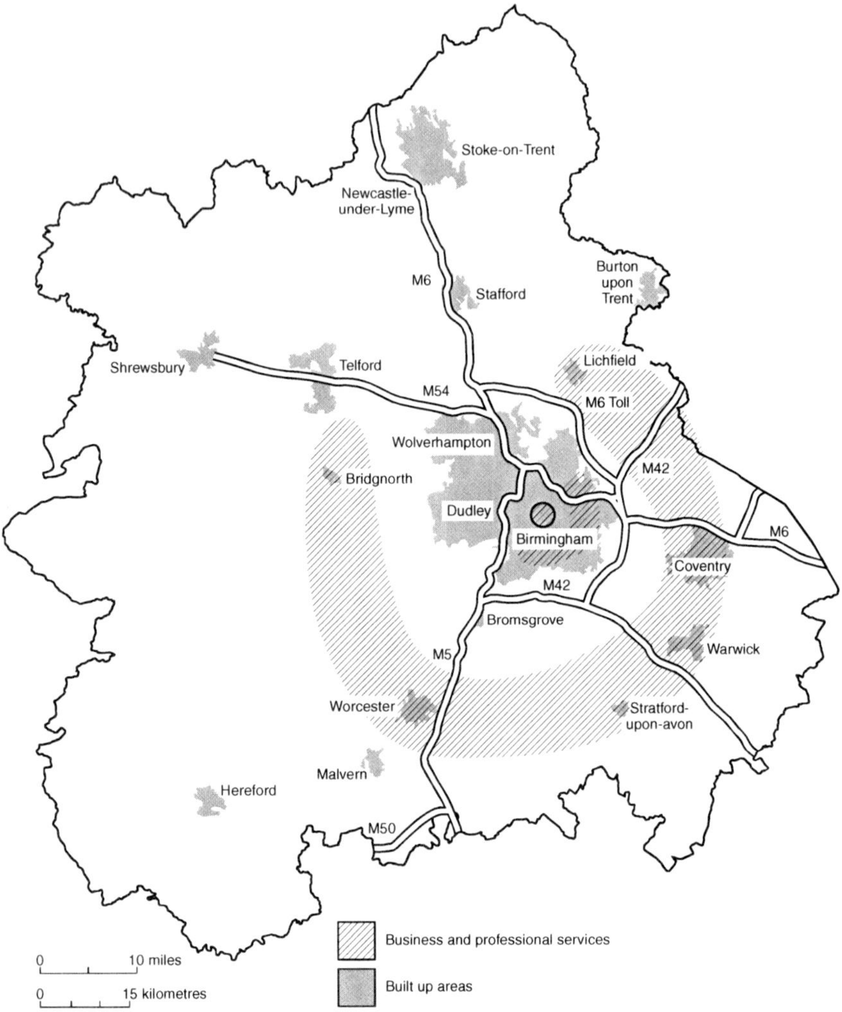

Figure 3.2 The arc or belt of business and professional service firms surrounding the Birmingham conurbation (source: modified from Bryson and Taylor, 2006).

majority of their clients are not located in the region. The belt is partially formed by the relocation of Birmingham professionals to the rural areas and market towns surrounding the conurbation. Initially, the majority of professionals will continue to commute to the city, but over time a proportion will establish their own firms. Research has concentrated on the visible urban concentrations of BPS firms to the expense of exploring rural firms and the relationship between rural- and urban-based firms. Further research is urgently required to explore the relocation of professionals to rural areas contiguous to cities.

The existence in the West Midlands of a complex rural economy of BPS firms reflects many of the findings of the American Lone-Eagle studies. People are leaving urban areas seeking rural lifestyles in an attempt to avoid traffic congestion, pollution and urban crime. Many of these moves may be occurring as a result of a process of step firm formation. This means that professionals are moving from the city to live in rural areas but still continuing in employment and commuting to work. Over time, some of these professionals may begin to telework for part of the week and finally become self-employed. The 2001 UK Census enables the identification of BPS workers who work mainly from home. There were 44,328 home workers in the West Midlands engaged in real estate, renting and business services (SIC K), or 17.36 per cent of all workers in this sector (Table 3.2). These home workers are distributed throughout the West Midlands regions, but appear to be more important in predominantly rural areas (for example, south Shropshire, (41.2 per cent), Bridgnorth (36.3 per cent), Herefordshire (33.4 per cent) compared to urban environments (Birmingham (9.89 per cent, Coventry (11.90 per cent), Telford (12.3 per cent)).

A focus group composed of representatives of six businesses and professional service firms was held in the northern part of the West Midlands in February 2002. These professionals were asked to highlight the most important issues impacting on their business activities. All six stressed the importance of people and expertise and, perhaps more importantly, the difficulty of attracting and retaining professional people in a rural area or small market town:

- It is a people-based industry – training and environment and quality of life are important for this and should be at the heart of any regional policy.
- The quality of the environment in which people live, work and travel. This is important as it will attract and retain people because services are people-orientated activities.
- If people are coming to the region, then the physical location has to have the attractions. This part of the region is rural and the office does not have to be in the town centre as long as people have access to the resources.

Environment and quality of life are key elements in the growth of BPS in rural areas. Perhaps ironically, newer forms of ICT may be less important than the telephone and the postal system with email and attachments escalating the speed at which digitally encoded documents can be delivered to clients. However, the growth of BPS firms in the countryside predates the commercialising of email and the Internet.

Along with many other regional authorities, the West Midlands has developed a regional ICT strategy to ensure that

> By 2010 the West Midlands will be an exemplar region, exploiting and coordinating its Information Communications Technologies to help drive the UK economy beyond the knowledge divide through enhanced productivity, competitiveness and efficiency.
>
> (Advantage West Midlands, 2006: 2)

Table 3.2 Travel to work distances in the West Midlands (UK), real estate, renting and business activities (SIC K), 2001

Local authority district	*Total*	*<2 km*	*2 km < 10 km*	*10 km < 30 km*	*30 km < 60 km*	*>60+*	*Works mainly at or from home*	*% working at home*
Birmingham	62,104	5,430	27,206	16,960	3,997	2,367	6,144	9.89
Bridgnorth	1,718	356	280	380	40	39	623	36.26
Bromsgrove	4,184	581	1,015	1,058	182	186	1,162	27.77
Cannock Chase	3,355	754	1,213	555	110	62	661	19.70
Coventry	15,193	2,175	6,329	3,261	1,065	555	1,808	11.90
Dudley	11,309	2,052	4,614	1,907	382	306	2,048	18.11
East Staffordshire	5,058	975	1,656	940	347	204	936	18.51
Herefordshire	6,623	1,347	1,424	1,210	286	145	2,211	33.38
Lichfield	3,992	638	974	893	206	124	1,157	28.98
Malvern Hills	4,771	959	1,287	1,021	198	126	1,180	24.73
Newcastle-under-Lyme	4,705	808	1,925	751	198	120	903	19.19
North Shropshire	2,095	418	395	464	93	56	669	31.93
North Warwickshire	2,542	319	669	721	147	85	601	23.64
Nuneaton and Bedworth	3,235	684	1,208	390	106	41	806	24.91
Oswestry	1,386	409	387	232	48	31	279	20.13
Redditch	3,793	699	1,173	875	161	131	754	19.88
Rugby	4,324	800	1,440	813	227	143	901	20.84

Sandwell	9,898	1,542	4,562	2,012	362	207	1,213	12.26
Shrewsbury and Atcham	4,225	993	1,096	935	196	85	920	21.78
Solihull	14,857	1,330	4,958	4,431	1,077	660	2,401	16.16
South Shropshire	1,488	304	189	248	76	58	613	41.20
South Staffordshire	2,641	430	608	419	56	35	1,093	41.39
Stafford	6,056	1,175	1,580	1,545	301	228	1,227	20.26
Staffordshire Moorlands	1,964	498	333	289	52	21	771	39.26
Stoke-on-Trent UA	8,369	1,345	4,221	1,349	241	131	1,082	12.93
Stratford-on-Avon	8,450	1,214	1,523	2,484	792	327	2,110	24.97
Tamworth	2,949	590	856	611	162	119	611	20.72
Telford and Wrekin UA	9,343	1,323	3,767	2,083	680	339	1,151	12.32
Walsall	8,270	1,500	3,641	1,362	231	139	1,397	16.89
Warwick	13,090	2,072	3,490	3,661	1,189	716	1,962	14.99
Wolverhampton	9,147	1,366	4,358	1,673	270	165	1,315	14.38
Worcester	5,346	1,234	1,735	1,065	286	117	909	17.00
Wychavon	5,419	921	1,219	1,188	271	136	1,684	31.08
Wyre Forest	3,461	794	1,014	494	98	35	1,026	29.64
Total	255,360	38,035	92,345	58,280	14,133	8,239	44,328	17.36*

Source: Census, 2001, accessed Nomis, 16 May 2006.

Note
* Average rather than total.

The policy debate on ICT suffers from naive generalisations regarding the role ICT plays and can play in improving business performance. It is assumed that ICT is a 'one-size-fits-all' technological fix that is suitable for all types and sizes of business without any significant attempt to address the diversity of practices that make up economic life. This is a major problem as some business models do not require extensive use of ICT while others may be ICT-dependent. The analysis of BPS in the West Midlands as well as the American research on Lone Eagles (Beyers and Lindahl, 1996; Salant *et al.*, 1997) found that the majority of firms predominantly serve local clients. A rural-based consultancy company (15 employees), specialising in business transfers, housecleaning companies for future sale and general consultancy, was encouraged by a publicly funded agency to establish a website. The company's business was focused on the West Midlands in the area between Manchester and Oxford and it did not engage in proactive marketing to foreign firms. The new webpage caused a major problem in producing a series of enquiries from companies in Scotland, Spain and Italy. The company did not seek or desire these enquiries and it had to decide whether or not to respond to them. It decided that it would lose face if it ignored the requests and so eventually provided services to three Scottish, one Spanish and one Italian company. However, this involved extensive travel and was seen as a distraction from the company's core business. One consequence was the removal of the website and the return to more conventional client acquisition strategies.

The relationship between a rural location and the use of ICT is best illustrated through the following three case studies. First, a design company, established in the 1970s, located in the 'belt' to the southeast of the Birmingham conurbation. The owner, henceforth known as Rachel, was trained in London and initially began working for a London design company that managed an account for a major theatrical client. Rachel was asked to handle this account and this enabled her to marry a passion for theatre with her working life; more importantly, it afforded her the opportunity to establish her own business. She developed a reputation for the design of posters and graphics for theatrical companies. She was recruited by a Birmingham-based theatre company and given a brief to win the company prizes for its print art (posters, graphics, etc.). After four years, this relationship ended and Rachel 'did the rather obvious thing' of approaching another large theatrical company in the West Midlands. She obtained a freelance contract with this firm, but continued to do a lot of work for London clients and was always 'going backwards and forward to London by train'.

The company employs four people and, according to Rachel,

> Geography does not matter apart from the first meeting [with a client]. We … kick off a job by meeting the client. There is so much you can glean with our amount of experience from what people tell you and how they tell it to you and listening and understanding what is being said. For running the jobs it is not important to see people anymore – we can Pdf jobs to them – it is all

> electronic and this has really changed our lives. Thirty years ago you would say I have just finished this rough and I am popping it into the post to you and they might look at it the following day and you might get some good feedback the day after that, now it is instant and the pressure is absolutely beyond words to keep it coming, to be fast – it has really speeded up.
>
> (Interview, Managing Partner)

ICT facilitates the company's location in rural Worcestershire, but the company could also operate using the postal service. The key difference is the speed and client expectations regarding the speed at which the company can deliver a project. The company is able to win contracts on the basis of its website, referrals and repeat business. The partnership tries to keep up-to-date with computers and ICT developments, with one partner responsible for reading the computer magazines and ensuring that the right decisions are made. The company's clients are distributed throughout the UK, but its suppliers are based in the local area as well as in London. They employ a London display company to manufacture signage for museum displays and this company also subcontracts more specialist work to Rachel. Local firms are favoured as a relationship based upon loyalty can be established that can be beneficial during times of need:

> We feel sure that if you are loyal to them that they are loyal to you – if a client suddenly needs something printed by Friday we can say to a printer can you do this and they are likely to say 'ok' as we are a regular user
>
> (Interview, Managing Partner)

The company has very few competitors as it occupies a specialist niche it has created for specialist print and digital designs. It does not compete on price, but rather reputation and the quality of its designs. Design innovation is important, but very elusive as:

> We take magazines, but it is in the air – to be a designer is to kind of walk around the world with your eyes open, almost your pores open – we are very different designers in 2002 than when we left College in 1971, but I can't say how that happens – it is because we are alive – it is not conscious – there is fashion to it and your eye becomes accustomed to it.

Recently, the partnership has begun to work with other companies to provide services to clients. This joint production enables the firm to offer expertise that they are unable to development and retain inhouse.

The second case is very different as it involves two businesses (property developer and compensation specialist) run from the same office and by the same people. The company is a husband-and-wife team that employs one personal assistant (PA). According to the partner interviewed,

> This is a rural business, very rural. Basically it is in the middle of a load of fields and we've just had a load of baling done, it is a home office, and our PA has got the hay fever to prove it.
>
> (Interview, Partner)

The businesses are based on reputation and word-of-mouth but also targeted direct mailing or mailshots. There is a major problem in that the PA and husband-and-wife team do not completely understand some of the standard software packages. Their rural location means that it is too far to travel to obtain training as this would involve an 80-mile journey. The two sole proprietorships, while sharing the same office, are radically different businesses:

> On a professional basis, my husband's business and the one that I am also a partner of, the compensation specialist, we are one of probably a very small handful throughout the country that specialise in that particular field. Up until recently we were one of two that did court work, the only one of two that did court work in the country, so our area or work is basically borders of Scotland right the way throughout the country. We even go over to the Isle of Man. So it is a very specialist field if you like. My business is more local, I'm based in the Midlands and I am basically a property developer for want of a better word. So really I am using contract staff all the time.... So you've got two very different businesses.
>
> (Interview, Partner)

The compensation specialist works by travelling to work with clients and acts in a similar way to an American Lone Eagle while the property developer is closely connected to the local regional economy and is not engaged in regional trade.

The final case concerns a small company specialising in the design and testing of specialist circuit boards. The company is located on the edges of the Malvern Hills, an area of outstanding natural beauty. The company produces specialist customised printed circuit boards and the managing director noted that it was neither a manufacturing nor a service company, but a combination of the two. The company was founded in one of the owners' bedrooms and traded from this location for the first three years, before moving to a trading estate. Eventually, it purchased a site and developed a building that is also partly let to another company. The company is located in Malvern, enjoying the beauty of the countryside, the hills and the lifestyle associated with rural living. It has no difficulty in recruiting staff as professionals want to live and work in this rural area. Designing complex customised printed circuit boards that are produced specially to meet the needs of a client is a complex business. The designer of the more complex circuit boards:

> does all the more complicated hardware and he lives near the Lake District – so he can work from home. He does the schematics on the computer and

> sends them down and we ship out the electronic files and parts to the manufacturer and [the designer] will come down for a day or two to test the board when we have assembled the first one.
>
> (Interview, Partner)

The company has no constraints on its location as its customer base is distributed throughout the UK. They are able to access all clients via ICT and the motorway network and in most cases only need one face-to-face meeting with a client. During this meeting, the designer learns the client's expectations and determines what it is possible to achieve with the current technology. The benefits of the location are:

> that it is close to home and it happens to be nice here. You may be interested to know that the company next door has a number of divisions located around the country, and each division specialises in different things, but they are having trouble recruiting. It is all software based. It is easier to get people to live here. So they are having people working from different divisions in the offices next door and doing electronic transfers because it is easier to get people to come and work here.
>
> (Interview, Partner)

For these two design companies, location is important in attracting and retaining expert employees and has no influence on client interaction.

Conclusion

This chapter presents an overview of some of the issues surrounding the relationship between the growth of BPS in rural areas and developments in ICT. New technologies have always altered existing business practices and also offered the scope to develop new business models. The growth of BPS firms is related to enhanced competition, increasing complexity and client demand (Bryson, 1996; Bryson *et al.*, 2004). These pressures have stimulated a rapid growth in BPS firm formation that has also yielded opportunities for the establishment of firms in rural locations. BPS firms can be relatively footloose; they often work at clients' premises and in many cases clients never visit the offices of a BPS provider. Once a reputation and a contact network have been established, a BPS firm or professional does not have to be located close to clients. ICT facilitates the growth of BPS in rural locations, but the ultimate driver behind the growth of rural BPS firms is not ICT, but the ability to maintain friendship networks and a reputation over distances (Rusten *et al.*, 2004, 2005).

The relationship between BPS and ICT is complex. ICT is becoming an ubiquitous resource that is equally available to all firms. In the West Midlands in 2002 many rural locations did not have access to broadband, but this has altered and the majority of places now enjoy access either via satellite or cable (Daniels and Bryson, 2002). Not all BPS firms compete using ICT, but some firms have developed business models based on ICT while others have had their working practices facilitated by new technologies. The relationship between BPS and ICT appears to be ambiguous and requires further detailed research. ICT enables some firms to 'offshore' or global-source service inputs, but it can also expose local firms to the attentions of unwanted foreign clients as well as competitors.

The activities and geographies of Lone Eagles and High Fliers have been partially identified by previous studies, but some of this work is based on anecdotal evidence that needs to be supported by detailed research. The relationship between kinship networks and holiday place-based experiences needs further elaboration. Are the locational decisions of Lone Eagles determined by kinship networks or are they truly footloose firms? Perhaps these are just different but complementary locational determinants. The Lone-Eagle phenomenon is important, but its comparative significance still needs to be elaborated. Beyers and Nelson's anecdotal evidence suggests that some communities treat Lone Eagles with suspicion because they are not integrated into the local community and do not employ local people. Their 'ambiguous conclusion' regarding Lone Eagles (Beyers and Nelson, 2000: 471) needs to be explored by further in-depth analysis, for example, into the indirect local multipliers generated by the activities of Lone Eagles.

It is not surprising that 'quality-of-life migrants' play an important role in the establishment of rural-based BPS firms. Quality of life and environment are nebulous concepts that are difficult to define and research. On the one hand, urban push factors related to noise, overcrowding and crime might be forcing BPS professionals to search for alternative rural lifestyles. On the other hand, rural environments and perceived quality of life might be acting as major rural pull factors and, of course, ultimately house-price differentials, affordability and availability might lie behind many of the relocation decisions. The importance of perceived quality of life and environment should not be underestimated, but these factors merit detailed study using sophisticated research designs as well as further theorisation.

It is perhaps worth concluding this chapter by reiterating the fact that this topic warrants substantial further research. Throughout this chapter, reference has been made to the following research lacunae:

- the relative neglect of rural-based BPS firms in the academic literature;
- the identification of the factors and processes behind the development of rural-based BPS firms;
- research into the relocation of professionals and their families to rural areas contiguous to cities;
- the interactions that occur between rural- and urban-based BPS firms;
- detailed research into the working practices and lifestyles of Lone Eagles and High Fliers in the European context.

References

Advantage West Midlands (2006) *Digital West Midlands: The Regional Strategy*, Birmingham: Advantage West Midlands.

Beyers, W.B. and Lindahl, D.P. (1996) 'Lone Eagles and High Fliers in Rural Producer Services', *Rural Development Perspectives* 12: 2–10.

Beyers, W.B. and Nelson, P.B. (1999) 'Service Industries and Employment Growth in the Nonmetropolitan South: A Geographical Perspective', *Southern Rural Sociology* 15: 139–69.

Beyers, W.B. and Nelson, P.B. (2000) 'Contemporary Development Forces in the Nonmetropolitan West: New Insights from Rapidly Growing Communities', *Journal of Rural Studies* 16: 459–74.

Bryson, J.R. (1996) 'Small Business Service Firms and the 1990s Recession in the United Kingdom: Implications for Local Economic Development', *Local Economy Journal* 11: 221–36.

Bryson, J.R. (1997) 'Business Service Firms, Service Space and the Management of Change', *Entrepreneurship and Regional Development* 9: 93–111.

Bryson J.R. and Daniels, P.W. (2006) 'A Segmentation Approach to Understanding Business and Professional Services in City-Regions: Shifting the Horizon beyond Global Cities', in L. Rubalcaba, H. Kok and P. Baker (eds) *Business Services in European Economic Gowth*, London: Palgrave Macmillan.

Bryson, J.R. and Henry, N.D. (2005) 'The Global Production System: From Fordism to Post Fordism', in P.W. Daniels *et al.*, *Human Geography: Issues for the 21st Century*, London: Prentice Hall, pp. 313–36.

Bryson, J.R. and Taylor, M. (2006) *The Functioning Economic Geography of the West Midlands*, Birmingham: West Midlands Regional Observatory.

Bryson, J.R., Daniels, P.W. and Warf, B. (2004) *Service Worlds: People, Organizations, Technologies*, London: Routledge.

Bryson, J.R., Keeble, D. and Wood, P. (1993) 'Business Networks, Small Firm Flexibility and Regional Development in UK Business Services', *Entrepreneurship and Regional Development* 5 (3): 265–77.

Bryson, J.R., Keeble, D. and Wood, P. (1997) 'The Creation and Growth of Small Business Service Firms in Post-industrial Britain', *Small Business Economics* 9 (4): 345–60.

Cairncross, F. (2001) *The Death of Distance 2.0: How the Communications Revolution Will Change Our Lives*, London: Texere.

Casson, H.N. (1910) *The History of the Telephone*, Chicago, IL: A.C. McClurg, available online at http://etext.lib.virginia.edu.

Daniels, P.W. and Bryson, J.R. (2002) *Professional Services in Birmingham and the West Midlands: Strengths, Opportunities and Threats*, A Report Prepared for Birmingham Forward and Advantage West Midlands.

Daniels, P.W. and Bryson, J.R. (2005) 'Sustaining Business and Professional Services in a Second City Region: The Case of Birmingham, UK, *Service Industries Journal* 25 (4): 505–24.

Daniels, P.W. and Bryson, J.R. (2006) *Skills Needs of Business and Professional Services in Objective 2 Areas of the West Midlands*, Learning and Skills Council and European Social Fund.

Friedman, T. (2005) *The World Is Flat: A Brief History of the Twenty-first Century*, London: Allen Lane.

Graham, S. (1998) 'The End of Geography or the Explosion of Place? Conceptualizing Space, Place and Information Technology', *Progress in Human Geography* 22 (2):165–85.

Hanlon, G. (1999) *Lawyers, the State and the Market: Professionalism Revisited*, London: Macmillan.

Hine, R. (1945) *Confessions of an Un-Common Attorney*, London: Dent.

Hudson, J.C. (1985) *Plains Country Towns*, Minneapolis: University of Minnesota Press.

Kotkin, J. (2000) *The New Geography: How the Digital Revolution is Reshaping the American Landscape*, New York: Random House.

Lindsay, C. and Macaulay, C. (2004) 'Growth in Self-Employment in the UK', *Labour Market Trends* October: 399–404.

Malecki, E. (2003) 'Digital Development in Rural Areas: Potentials and Pitfalls', *Journal of Rural Studies*: 201–14.

Northeast Oregon Economic Development District (2004) *'It's Time to Come Home, Even if You've Never Lived Here Before': Wallowa County Lone Eagle Research Final Report*, Enterprise: Northeast Oregon Economic Development District.

O'Brien, R. (1992) *Global Financial Integration: The End of Geography*, London: Pinter Publishers.

Pearson, R. (1995) 'Gender Perspectives on Health and Safety in Information Processing', in S. Mitter and S. Rowbotham (ed.) *Women Encounter Technology: Changing Patterns of Employment in the Third World*, pp. 278–302.

Ruiz, Y. and Walling, A. (2005) 'Home-based Working Using Communication Technologies', *Labour Market Trends* October: 417–26.

Rusten, G., Bryson, J.R. and Gammelsæter, H. (2005) 'Dislocated versus Local Business Service Expertise and Knowledge and the Acquisition of External Management Consultancy Expertise by Small and Medium-Sized Enterprises in Norway', *Geoforum* 36 (4): 525–39.

Rusten, G., Gammelsæter, H. and Bryson, J.R. (2004) 'Combinational and Dislocated Knowledges and the Norwegian Client Consultant Relationship', *Service Industries Journal* 24 (1): 155–70.

Salant, P., Carley, L.R. and Dillman, D.A. (1997) 'Lone Eagles among Washington's In-migrants: Who Are They and Are They Moving to Rural Places?', *Northwest Journal of Business and Economics*: 1–16.

Sunnmørsposten 27.3. (2004) 'Stordal lokkar travel byfolk'.

Taylor, M. (2005) Clusters: The Mesmerising Mantra', paper presented to the Regional Studies Association Conference, Aalborg, Denmark, May.

United Nations (2002) *Manual on Statistics on International Trade in Services*, New York: United Nations.

Part II

The persistence of place

4 Connecting local food to global consumers via the Internet

Ingeborg Astrid Kleppe and James Hosea

Introduction

This chapter focuses on how local food products can help to market rural places on the Internet. It deals with two seemingly unconnected contemporary consumer trends: the increasing consumer demand for authentic qualities in food products (Amilien, 2005), and the escalation of consumer activities on the Internet (Castells, 2001; Kozinets, 1999; Anon, 2005). It will be argued here that, from a marketing perspective, these trends should be considered together and that, if strategically interlinked, they offer interesting opportunities for the promotion of rural areas, products and communities.

In developed markets there is a growing interest in authentic, traditional, wholesome and traceable food, and a growing demand for cultural identification, culinary heritage and value-added food products that can be strongly linked to a particular geographic place or region (Homefjord, 2000; Loureiro and McCluskey, 2000). At the international political level, formal trademarks or branding labels have been introduced to protect local heritage foods, for example the Protected Geographical Indication (PGI) and Protected Designation of Origin (PDO) trademarks established by the EU (EU council reg. No. 510/2006). In addition consumer and producer communities organise globally to protect heritage food through their own brand labels (e.g. www.slowfood.com). Moreover, local communities collaborate to create gastro-tourism concepts where the idea is to enjoy heritage food in its local environment (e.g. www.theseafoodtrail.com). These projects are working to increase the variety, amount and quality of locally produced food on offer, and one of their tools is the Internet.

The other trend is the escalation of consumer activities on the Internet. The Internet is now a major arena for information search and social interaction (Castells, 2001; Kozinets, 1999; Anon, 2005). The 16 million users of computer communication in the first years of the Internet (1995) are estimated to grow to 2 billion in 2010 (Castells, 2001). Moreover, networked computers empower consumers around the world to find one another and to gather in groups based on a wide range of cultural and subcultural interests and social affiliations (Castells, 2001; Kozinets, 1999; Anon, 2005). The ability to get information about whatever you want whenever you want, from wherever you are, has given consumers unprecedented strength. They demand quality and can compare their experiences worldwide. Consumers can initiate word-of-mouth campaigns – on the Internet called 'word of mouse' – to boycott or buycott specific goods or services (Castells, 2001).

This chapter explores how local foods are communicated on well-established websites that address consumers locally and globally, such as the Slow Food movement, local food brands and national tourism portals. First, the two main concepts introduced above are reviewed: the increasing demand for authentic qualities in food products, and the escalation of consumer activities on the Internet. Second, a conceptual framework is introduced and explained, followed by a content analysis of specific websites. The chapter then concludes with a discussion of the marketing implications for promoting rural identities through local food on the Internet.

Does it matter where our food comes from?

Food products would appear to embody strong associations with rural places as they have a geographic origin by nature. There are often strong historical and symbolic links between places and foods due to the interactions between natural resources and people's lifestyles (Tregear *et al.*, 1998). Geographic associations may be considered quality cues by making reference to socially constructed concepts such as: authentic, healthy and traditional (Dimara and Skuras, 2003), and the use of geographic names to identify products from a particular, normally rural, region is a very ancient custom (Loureiro and McCluskey, 2000). The renown and perceived value of products such as certain French wines demonstrate that geographic indication can be important to consumers (Tregear *et al.*, 1998). The consumption of denominated food and drink may be a statement of taste, fashion, sophistication, lifestyle, status, beliefs, opinions, ethnocentrism, etc. (Dimara and Skuras, 2003; Loureiro and McCluskey, 2000; Bjørkum 1999). It may also be a response to public health and food safety concerns by emphasising the source of production and so providing a greater degree of traceability for these products (Dimara and Skuras, 2003; Tregear *et al.*, 1998). Emphasis on the origin of rural food products can differentiate them from generic competitive offerings, enhancing their commercial appeal and competitiveness (Tregear *et al.*, 1998). Online information can serve to attract and hold on to the hearts and minds of consumers.

Local food as terroir brands

The French concept of 'terroir' conveys a better understanding of how the source of origin of local, rural food products may affect consumers' perceptions of these products (Amilien, 2005). A place/territory may have unique social, environmental, cultural and institutional capitals that distinguish it from another place as a result of its spatial limitation. The terroir concept captures the combination of these different types of capital, which constitute the symbolic capital of the terroir (Amilien, 2005). Aurier *et al.* (2005) explored the meanings that consumers associate with terroir food products, and they found three common characteristics:

1 a product made of local raw materials;
2 a localised traditional recipe or know-how, and
3 location of the firm in the terroir region for a long time.

Perceived sources of terroir were categorised in a geographical and cultural dimension. The geographic dimension embodies the link between products and land and serves as an identification function – an origin cue that allows consumers to identify products. The cultural and historical dimension implies that consumers perceive that a terroir product must *not* be produced elsewhere because it is linked to the history and culture of a specific region. Consumers appreciate that local know-how is developed over time, and is embedded in unique rituals and traditions that cannot be exported or copied elsewhere.

Moreover, perceptions of proximity in local food production, distribution and consumption come forward as crucial in consumers' representations and evocations associated with terroir (ibid.). Proximity between producer and consumer, with region, with product, and with the producer are all strong associations. Proximity implies an intimate relationship with local products, meaning that knowing the region includes knowing its most typical food products rather than just its monuments or tourist areas. Ability to see, feel and interact are important in terroir production and distribution.

The image of a terroir product is generally associated with a production style such as 'craft', 'small-scale producer', 'traditional', or 'from a farm' (ibid.). Each terroir producer is different and distribution channels must be kept as short as possible. The look of terroir products should be authentic and easily distinguished from perfectly or professionally styled consumer goods. The link with the geographic origin is also important, as illustrated by a quote from the study by Aurier *et al.* (2005) – 'when purchasing a terroir product, it is just as if you buy the image of the place, not only the product quality' (ibid.: 8). Terroir products have a strong affective dimension and consumers link nostalgic and idealised associations of past times and indigenous cultures and regions to terroir products.

Labelling foods with their source of origin offers a method of differentiation through branding in response to consumer needs, and a change in labelling or information can change consumers' perceptions and behaviour (Loureiro and McCluskey, 2000). The concept of terroir fits well with the hypothesis that place can be viewed as a type of brand. Indeed terroir could be viewed as a specialist type of place brand for food and drink products. In marketing terms, terroir would translate into unique, complex and authentic brand association, coupled with a level of awareness among consumers. Terroir as a brand is unique because a source of origin cannot be copied. The nature of terroir associations is anchored in the unique interaction between nature and people evolved over a long period of time and embodied in institutions and culture. Information published on the Internet can support these food traditions.

The Internet as a social arena

Over the last 15 years the information available to ordinary users of the Internet and the web has taken on immense proportions (Castells, 2001). The development is so rapid that even the concepts employed to describe the activities on the Internet are still in the making – at least how the concepts are used by the layman.[1]

The Internet has radically changed the nature of and motivation for social interactions. Communities are networks of interpersonal ties that provide sociability, support, information and a sense of belonging and social identity, with the family playing an important role in the construction of these ties (Wellman, 1999; Wellman and Giulia, 1995). Place-based interaction has traditionally been an important source of support, information and social interaction, with this interaction based not just on neighbourhoods but also on workplaces (Castells, 2001). These traditional, family and place-based interactions are what can be termed 'real-life' communities. One of the drawbacks with real-life communities is that they are not so easy to maintain once people move away, and these people end up joining communities in their new home neighbourhood and workplace.

Initially seen as a sophisticated method of information exchange, the Internet has led to the establishment of a new type of community: the virtual community (Kozinets, 1998; Castells, 2001). This new type of community brings people together online around shared values and interests, and creates ties of support and friendship that can also extend into face-to-face or real-life interaction. Kozinets (1999) goes further and defines virtual communities as affiliate groups whose online interactions are based upon shared enthusiasm for, and knowledge of, a specific consumption activity or related group activities. Two of the greatest benefits of the Internet are the ease with which people with similar values or interests can find each other (for example, via search engines), and the ease with which weak ties can be maintained that may otherwise be lost in the trade-off between the effort to keep in contact and the value of doing so (Castells, 2001).

Using the Internet as a social space is to a large extent a grassroots-driven process (Anon, 2005). Democratic ideology gives the Internet credibility and integrity as a social arena (Anon, 2005; Kozinets, 1999). For the first time in history, the Internet both allows 'many-to-many' and 'one-to-one' communication on a global scale (Castells, 2001). Hence the marketing value of the Internet as a social space is unprecedented (Briscoe *et al.*, 2006; Reiss, 2006; Reed, 2001). Core economic, social, political and cultural activities throughout the planet are being structured by and around the Internet, and other computer networks. Exclusion from these networks is one of the most damaging forms of exclusion in our economy and in our culture (Castells, 2001; Kelley, 1997). Therefore everybody wants to be on the Internet; nation-states, geographical regions, places, companies and private individuals.

Since the social content of the Internet has grown from grassroots and user activity, the enormous amount of information lacks governance, structure and hierarchy (Castells, 2001; Leiner *et al.*, 2003; Reiss, 2006). The impact of information search engines, such as Google and Yahoo!, are therefore formidable, both as retrievers and gatekeepers of information on the Internet. One of the most recent business concepts is to assist companies and other agents who want to be on the Internet to design their websites in such a way that they can climb higher in the search hierarchy. Presence on the Internet alone is not enough – accessibility of information to relevant users is also necessary.

What this chapter seeks to explore is how the Internet can influence the development of brand knowledge for terroir products. Based on the above discussion we propose that:

1 rural places can be promoted on the Internet through terroir food products;
2 active Internet consumer communities and information portals designed for consumers can enhance the impact of such promotion.

Framework

If we assume that terroir is a special type of brand, the knowledge held by consumers about a terroir can be broken down into two key elements: brand image, a combination of the strength, uniqueness and favourability of brand associations; and brand awareness, a measure of the consumers' ability to recall and recognise a brand (Keller, 1993). It is the development and spread of this knowledge that is of interest to this chapter.

According to Nonaka and Takeuchi (1995), the creation and development of knowledge is a dynamic process requiring the presence of three environmental factors. The first of these is the interaction of individuals. This deals with the dynamic interaction of different kinds of knowledge. The second factor is the location or context where knowledge creation takes place. This means the real cultural, social and historic context which is of importance to each individual involved, and which enables them to understand and appreciate the information that they receive. The final factor concerns the assets or resources required to enable knowledge creation, such as trust that stimulates knowledge sharing, roles and routines, so that people in different roles handle time and place and frequencies for knowledge creation equally. One of the key issues for the development and dissemination of knowledge is the dynamic interaction of individuals with different types of knowledge. As more interaction occurs, the knowledge becomes more widespread. Social networks and communities play a major role in this process, and the rapid growth of information and communication technology has had a major impact on the nature of this interaction.

The power of technology to scale up the size of networks or communities has been hypothesised in the formulation of Metcalfe's Law and later Reed's Law, although it has been suggested more recently that these overstate the additional value gained by scaling up a virtual network (Briscoe *et al.*, 2006). Metcalfe's Law states that the value of a communications network grows with the square of the number of devices or people connected to it, while Reed's Law asserts that the utility of large networks can scale exponentially with the size of the network (Briscoe *et al.*, 2006; Reed, 2001). It is the extra reach that online networks and virtual communities can provide that is the key to online marketing. In the virtual world, websites and portals provided by companies, public bodies and other organisations act to disseminate information to consumers and the world at large, while virtual communities are actively gathering and sharing information on a whole variety of topics and interests. The amount of information exchanged, the number of people involved and the value of these interactions far outweigh the traditional, real-life means of exchanging information. The power of the Internet can be summed up in the term 'word of mouse', as opposed to the more traditional 'word of mouth'.

Spatial and technological dimensions

Two dimensions have been considered in exploring the development of terroir brand knowledge: a spatial dimension and a technological dimension. The spatial dimension refers to how widespread knowledge of a terroir product is, that is to say if the product is only known to a select few locally or if the product has become known on a larger scale. The technological dimension refers to the nature of the interaction between producers and consumers, with real-life face-to-face contact on one side and Internet or virtual communities on the other. By combining these two dimensions, four theoretical spaces are created along the axes, localised versus globalised, and real life versus virtual.

A short description of each of the categories presented in the above framework (see Table 4.1.) illustrates their relevance to terroir products:

Parochial. When a terroir product has localised brand knowledge that is only present or accessible in the real world, it is generally restricted to a small area or a dedicated group of followers. Brand knowledge only develops outside this area/group slowly through word-of-mouth interactions. An example of a parochial product would be the local fisherman who sells fresh prawns from his boat at the quayside in a small fishing village.

Ubiquitous. When awareness of the terroir product has been significantly raised through traditional channels such as word of mouth and the more traditional forms of media, and brand knowledge has become widespread on a large scale, it can be considered to be ubiquitous. Scotch whisky provides an example

Table 4.1 Framework: conceptual typology of real life, virtual and global, local spaces

	Real life	*Virtual*
Global	Ubiquitous	Networked
Local	Parochial	Connected

of such a product. Although strongly linked to Scotland in the minds of consumers, the product can be found almost anywhere in the world.

Connected. The term connected implies that the terroir product has a presence on the Internet. This is likely to be a quite simple presence involving a stand-alone website. The site may well provide a good presentation of the terroir product and the producer, but is only known about by a select few or by those who have received a recommendation or have discovered the website by chance, for example, via a search engine.

Networked. When a terroir product has a web presence, and this is linked in with consumer-interest websites, tourist-board portals, producer portals and other sites, it becomes networked. By being connected to relevant sites that consumers are actively looking at and interacting with, a producer may greatly increase the brand knowledge of his/her products.

Methods: sample and analytical approach

The geographical frame of reference is Scotland and Norway, which have well known generic rural images (e.g. Scottish highlands, Norwegian fjords) but relatively few famous terroir product places. In comparison, countries like France, Greece, Italy and Spain have long traditions for promoting terroir food products through wine, olive oil, cheeses, ham and other agricultural produce. Evidence suggests that terroir products are mainly associated with agricultural produce. Of the 740 EU-approved PGIs and PDOs, only nine were terroir fish or seafood products.[2] Hence there is great potential in developing terroir seafood brands. In Norway and Scotland seafood is a very important food export, which is another motivation to select seafood producers as exploratory cases for this study.

Another requirement for selection of cases was substantive content on the terroir products on the website. The terroir consumer associations identified in the Aurier *et al.* (2005) study served as a guide. Hence the consumer websites should contain information on place with name and geographical location; information on production methods and presentation of producers should be included; information on the link between product and the history, culture and climatic conditions at the place; and images or pictures of the product, place and producers. This type of information signals proximity between product and place, producers and consumers, which are all strong consumer association for terroir produce.

Finally, the framework guides the sample based on the interaction of the two dimensions: localised and globalised space and real life versus virtual technology. Two broad categories of Internet sites served the research needs: 1) *networked* consumer communities run by consumers and 2) information websites and portals run by producers and public bodies that *connect* to broad groups of consumers. After extensive exploration on the Internet and application of the sampling criteria, a convenience sample of three cases was selected, shown in Table 4.2.

Table 4.2 Presentation of sample of websites

	Virtual
Global	Networked *Global consumer food community:* Case I: The Slow Food Foundation for Biodiversity websites presenting three Norwegian Fish Presidia *Consumer information and sales portals* Case II: The www.VisitScotland.com Sea Food Trail website
Local	Connected *Terroir food brand:* Case III: The Scottish seafood company Loch Fyne Oysters Ltd. website

The analytical approach is inspired by techniques from semiotic and narrative methodology (Silverman, 2005). By identifying narrative themes, frequently used concepts and signs, we will get some insight into how terroir food products are communicated on the Internet, which will subsequently serve as input for the discussion of marketing implications. The web-texts on terroir produce are typically short (from 100–500 words; Slow Food Presidia) and informative in nature. The depth of the analysis is therefore limited by this.

Presentation and analysis of cases

Case I: Consumer community: The Slow Food case

Presentation of Slow Food. Slow Food is both real life and virtual, and local and global. Slow Food members are organised into local groups – Condotte in Italy and Convivia elsewhere in the world. More than 800 Convivia are active in 50 countries (including 400 Condotte in Italy). Apart from being a real-life social group whose aim is to enjoy slow food, the Convivia also promote local food to the whole Slow Food organisation internationally by proposing local food producers for the Ark of Taste. The Ark of Taste is designed to discover, catalogue and safeguard small, quality food products and defend biodiversity around the world. To assist artisan producers, Slow Food has established Presidia, which are small projects approved by Slow Food, designed to save artisan foods. Similar to the EU's PDO and PGI trademarks, seafood products are in the minority of Presidia products – nine of the 81 international Presidia and three of the 195 Italian Presidia represent fish or some other seafood. Each Presidia has its webpage on the Slow Food website with detailed information on the terroir details embedded in the product. The product is visually presented with high quality artistic pictures (www.slowfood.com).

The Slow Food website has many functions: information, edited feature articles, bulletin boards (including information about local events), food and wine shops, web logs (or blogs), etc. Sloweb – a round-the-clock food news and review website draws on the resources of Slow Food's vast global network of collaborators. Distinguished journalists, food and wine writers, technical experts and members of Slow Food staff supply updates on the many facets of biodiversity and food in all its shapes and forms.

Norwegian fish Presidia. There are three Fish Presidia from costal Norway on the Slow Food website: Kristiansund Baccala (western Norway), Stockfish from the Isle of Sørøya (northern Norway), Cured and Smoked Herring from Sunnmøre (western Norway). The content of these webpages promotes the complex environmental, cultural and social qualities that constitute the uniqueness of the rural production place (www.slowfood.com). In the following we will use quotes from these pages to illustrate terroir content.

There are four constants that seem to guide the narratives of all Slow Food Presidia:

1 the name of the terroir place in the Presidia label;
2 a description of the unique environmental resources and characteristics of the place;
3 the products identified as anchoring in long cultural traditions; and
4 a detailed description of production methods.

The narratives capture the unique interplay between people, culture, history and the environment in the local areas covered.

Environmental resources. Geographical source of origin is already established in the name of the Presidia, which signals geographical identity and uniqueness. Kristiansund Baccala can only be made in Kristiansund; Stockfish from the Isle of Sørøya can only originate there; and Cured and Smoked Herring from Sunnmøre is unique. Kristiansand, Sørøya and Sunnmøre are all known for their rich fishing grounds, and their environmental conditions are communicated to establish their unique qualities. For example, the Kristiansund area is particularly suitable for production of baccala ('klippfisk') because of the rich cod fisheries, rocks for drying the fish and a climate with long periods of good, stable weather. Moreover, information on seasonal fluctuations and constraints underline dependency and closeness to nature.

Product anchoring in local history and long traditions. The Slow Food Presidia cleverly present the products to promote terroir qualities. For example the following text appears in the online presentation of Cured and Smoked Herring from Sunnmøre:

> What generations of Norwegians born after the 1920s remember most clearly from their childhoods is the tradition of smoked herring. Those who spent their youth in villages along the coast can still picture the fat silver fish their mothers would roast on burning coals and leave hanging over the fireplace. They would serve the herring with mashed potatoes. For hundreds of years, herring have been an essential part of the Norwegian diet: the remains of this fish have been found all over Norway in archaeological sites dating as far back as 600 BC.
>
> (www.slowfood.com)

This quote assigns historically long ties and cultural, as well as nutritional, values to smoked herring. Many would agree that the herring was instrumental in bringing coastal Norway out of poverty. The herring therefore has come to symbolise the silver fish that saved people from starvation and nourished new generations of healthy Norwegians. Its high fat content makes the herring suitable for different conservation methods and the picture of lines of smoked herring hanging from barns and boathouses along the coast of Norway is a classic coastal Norwegian image. The Slow Food website photographs of the smoked herring and stockfish perfectly capture and support the images constructed in the text.

Production methods. The production methods are embedded both in environmental, cultural and social capital at the place. This interdependence of the multiple capital sources is communicated on the webpage through an explanation of how baccala is made. The importance of the fishermen's skills, the freshness before processing and the short-travelled distance between fisherman and processor is documented. For example, the producer of baccala buys fresh fish from the fisherman, alreayd salted with sea salt.

> The salted fish is washed and placed to mature at about 10–13 °C for 23 days. The fish is then moved to cold storage, at a temperature of about 2–5 °C. Then it will be washed and salted once more. It is being stacked and thereafter laid out to dry. The fish must be stacked every evening and covered with a fle, a circular wooden cover, to protect it from moisture. The fish shall dry for 14–21 days, depending on the size. After being dried, the fish will be moved to storage for a few days in a cool room, so that the salting process can continue. Then the actual klippfisk production starts. First, the fish is sorted in three sizes. Then it is cured with salt at above 10 °C. It will be stored and restacked every seven day for at least 23 days. The fish is sorted in three sizes. Then the fish will be washed and the black membrane removed. The fish is then stored under pressure at 2–5 °C. The drying is started once more, and the fish are then sorted by quality. There are 8 degrees of dryness. If the fish was exported dry it was at 8/8. Then there is a new round with storing and pressing at 2–5 °C. The fish can now be placed in storage to mature for 1–3 years. The klippfisk is then sorted and graded for export in the categories: Superior extra, Superior and Imperial.
>
> (www.slowfood.com)

This detailed description on the website illuminates the strong interplay between man and nature. The production process – very dependent on nature – is complex and time-consuming and demands sophisticated skills. Every day, for the three weeks it is laid out to dry on the cliffs, the fish has to be carefully attended in order to protect it from moisture and environmental hazards. The very fine-tuned sorting in quality categories is an indication of sophisticated craftsmanship and pride in supplying the customers with the best product.

Case II: Information portal – the www.eatscotland.com case

Presentation of EatScotland. EatScotland is an initiative launched by VisitScotland (formerly the Scottish Tourist Board) in January 2005 to promote excellence wherever food is served in Scotland. The scheme was initially conceived as a simple pass-or-fail quality assurance scheme for all eating places in Scotland, replacing the one-to-five medal system of its predecessor, Taste of Scotland. EatScotland has since expanded to include a series of annual awards and an eating and drinking guide (both printed and online) that promotes traditional, natural cuisine as well as local eating places and local specialities. The guide also features information on food and drink trails that tourists can follow to indulge themselves in particular types of food.

VisitScotland estimates that the eating and drinking market is worth £719 million to UK's tourism each year. A recent survey of tourist perceptions found that two-thirds of Britons said that food and drink influenced their holiday choice, with the West Country, Wales and Scotland being the top three destinations. EatScotland aims to capitalise on this.

As well as promoting quality in the Scottish food and drink and hospitality sectors, EatScotland also acts as a bridge between local businesses and people (mostly tourists) interested in finding more authentic, original food-and-drink experiences. The initial pilot involved a cross-section of 100 volunteer businesses from across Scotland, and the scheme is now actively recruiting firms to continue building and developing the content of the eating-and-drinking guide. Companies pay a fee of between £125 and £195 to take part in the scheme, and they must pass the required quality standards before they are allowed to join.

The online guide has a searchable database of quality-assured places to eat, special offers from members, suggestions for activities (such as food trails, festivals, culinary breaks and specific visitor attractions), a database of accommodation quality-assured by VisitScotland, guides to traditional and natural food-and-drink products and producers, profiles of chefs and individual businesses, a guide to regional specialities, and the ability to register for an e-newsletter.

Narrative themes. The EatScotland online guide represents an efficient and relatively easy way for people, both familiar and unfamiliar with Scottish food and drink, to find out more about authentic, natural and traditional cuisine, while enjoying the beautiful nature of Scotland. People and their background and local culture are also important in the context of food and drink, and much space is given to talk about individuals and their links to food and drink. These themes are all key elements of the terroir, and they are made clear in the language employed on the website. A feature webpage about the seafood trail illustrates how the themes of authentic, natural and traditional cuisine, the beautiful nature of Scotland, and the people involved in producing and preparing Scottish food and drink are woven into the texts presenting the food places. The scene is set early on: 'The idea is to lap up the beauty of this magical area from Tighnabruaich and the Mull of Kintyre to Loch Fyne and Oban, while relishing a sensory feast of some of the world's best seafood' (www.eatscotland.com).

The link between freshness, natural produce, local producers and the nature itself is reinforced through the webpage. Much is made of the 'breathtaking views, unique waterfront locations, access to the freshest local produce and an understanding of the environmental issues that concern the Scottish fishing industry'. In addition, the webpage emphasises that 'Seafood Trail members are determined to showcase Argyll's natural larder from the deep and have built strong relationships with local producers' (www.eatscotland.com).

The link between the local people and the produce is established with phrases such as 'the real heroes are the fishermen themselves who deliver the lobsters, halibut, crabs and scallops all the way to our shores' (www.eatscotland.com). Each establishment along the seafood trail is described with an introduction to the people who run it and the surrounding nature. The webpage contains maps and more detailed information, as well as links to a stand-alone website for the seafood trail (www.theseafoodtrail.com), and websites for each individual restaurant. In this way, potential visitors glean a lot of information and at the same time are put in contact with the local restaurants themselves, instead of just being left with some vague generalisations about seafood along the west coast of Scotland.

Authenticity reinforced through language. Scottish words are also adopted in the text to reinforce the feeling of authenticity and originality, while lending an extra helping of local flavour. This is illustrated on the webpage by a reference to the owner of the Cairnbaan Hotel, who is described as being 'a lover of wine and seafood, (who) also likes a good blether and enjoys telling the tale of the hotel's more seedy reputation in the past, dating back as it does to 1801' (www.eatscotland.com). Blether is an old Scottish word meaning to talk, and can be used to describe someone who talks a lot.

Stereotypes. Stereotypes are another tool employed in the text, as in the case of the description of the owner of the Hunting Lodge at Bellochantuy, who is introduced to readers as being 'the bearded, kilted, exuberant owner' with 'a penchant for malt whisky, which he loves to bestow on his unsuspecting guests' (www.eatscotland.com). To connect to a more outward, cosmopolitan focus, this stereotype is challenged when mentioned later that he and his wife brought up their family in 'diverse destinations such as Yemen, Poland and the extremely remote island of Tristan da Cunha before coming back to roost on the dramatic coast of the Kintyre peninsula.

Case III: Being Connected – Loch Fyne Oysters

Introduction to the company. Loch Fyne Oysters was originally set up in 1977 by two oyster enthusiasts John Noble and Andrew Lane. Both Noble and Lane thought the pure water of Loch Fyne would add distinction to the flavour of their product and, after some experimenting, they started farming oysters and selling them to restaurants and hotels all over the UK. In the following decade the company took over a local smokehouse, broadened its product range, opened a seafood shop and a restaurant in an old cattleshed at the head of Loch Fyne. It also started exporting, and in 1994 it won the Queen's Award for Exports. During the 1990s a chain of restaurants was developed in the UK under the Loch Fyne Restaurants brand, and by 2005 the company owned 25 restaurants. In 2002 John Noble died and in 2003, ownership of Loch Fyne Oysters was transferred to a trust on behalf of the employees. The Loch Fyne Restaurants chain (excluding the original Loch Fyne Oyster Bar) was sold to a management buy-out, backed by private equity, for £33 million (Bolger, 2005).

Terroir is a key element in the Loch Fyne success story. From early on, the company focused on the quality of their produce, their natural production methods, sustainability, the clean, pure environment their products come from, and the close bonds they enjoy with the local area. The company further branched out to sell local meat products under the Glen Fyne brand, as well as a selection of other authentic and artisan products.

Total sustainability. This is a key concept on the Loch Fyne website, and the following analysis concentrates on this topic. Loch Fyne's mission statement has a direct link with an elaborate text documenting how they live up to the ideal. The presentation of a key supplier of fresh farmed salmon on the website, Loch Duart, emphasises Loch Fyne's commitment to total sustainability. Although Loch Fyne does not farm salmon itself, it operates a smokehouse and sells its own smoked salmon. The close relationship with Loch Duart illustrates how important it is for Loch Fyne that their suppliers share their principles. It may be helpful to have in mind the common perception of farmed seafood as modern, high-tech and in conflict with nature, notions quite at odds with core terroir associations such as natural, sustainable and in harmony with nature. Loch Fyne is therefore a particularly interesting case since the company has managed to build a famous terroir food brand for farmed seafood, while working closely with other companies and organisations that share the same ethos.

Narrative themes. The themes in the mission statement of the company are to:

1 respect the animal and its habitat by actively working to understand the environment and the needs and welfare of the animals grown;
2 actively work to enhance biodiversity;
3 underpin the economy of the community by the provision of skilled work, fairly rewarded and in line with the tradition of the locality (www.lochfyne.com).

Respect for the animal and its habitat. This is documented on the webpages by reference to several accreditations awarded to the company. Its production methods have been endorsed as 'operated in a sustainable and conservation friendly manner' by the Scottish Executive Rural Affairs Department, Scottish Natural Heritage; and the Marine Conservation Society's Good Fish Guide. The website also notes that Loch Fyne's salmon supplier, Loch Duart, became the first fish-farming company in the world to gain approval under the Royal Society for the Prevention of Cruelty to Animals' (RSPCA) Freedom Foods animal welfare scheme (www.rspca.org.uk). The RSPCA is a UK charity, founded in

1824, dedicated to improving animal welfare. The Freedom Food certification mark assures consumers that the producers concerned are endorsed by the RSPCA, one of the most respected animal charities in the world. Moreover, Freedom Food is recognised by the UK government as a 'higher-level' assurance scheme. A web link to the RSPCA enables consumers to find out more about the Freedom Foods scheme.

Documenting these awards and approvals on the website lends external validity to the company's mission statements. It has proven not only through words but also through action that its production and processing routines are sustainable and animal-friendly. This can make the company stand out among the many fish-farming companies who would like to project a similar image often without such solid approval from certifying bodies.

Food safety and quality control linked to terroir capital. The Loch Fyne website indicates how the company anchors its entire value chain in terroir capital. First, it specifies its own feeds, relying on a small local feed supplier whom it knows and can survey. It opposes GM feed, using only 'sustainable' diets low in dioxins/PCBs. The low level of these substances in their final produce is shown to be way below the EU and UN standards. Since fish farming cannot evidence quality in accordance with long traditions, Loch Fyne emphasises Loch Duart's pioneering spirit in securing animal welfare and food safety. External endorsements, accreditations and awards support the firm's claims.

Active work to enhance biodiversity. One of the most controversial issues in salmon farming is the conflict between wild and farmed salmon. The website also highlights this discourse and informs the reader that the decline in wild salmon is a result of several factors – farming being only one. Instead of defending farmed salmon, the website explains how Loch Fyne's supplier, Loch Duart, have been active in the establishment of West Sutherland Fisheries Trusts, which aims to restore the stocks of wild salmon and sea trout (www.lochfyne.com).

The website communicates the fact that the company wants its farmed salmon to be as similar to wild salmon as possible. The text disassociates Loch Fyne's product from farmed salmon that are considered to be round (instead of torpedo-shaped) and 'not flabby like a lot of farmed salmon' (www.lochfyne.com). This is accomplished by putting priority on quality before quantity in the fish pens.

Underpinning the community. Loch Fyne's ownership structure, suppliers, production methods and marketing are all locally based, and this message runs through all the text on the website. When promoting sales worldwide, it is the local competence, skills, pride and environmental resources that constitute the unique selling position. All their product labels include the name of the place – Loch Fyne. This gives brand consistency across product categories and enhances the terroir qualities in their produce.

Discussion

The concept of terroir food reflects the complex relationship between environmental, social, cultural and institutional capital at a specific place (Amilien

2006). Together these forms of capital constitute symbolic capital that can be associated with the terroir. In brand management terms, this symbolic capital can be understood as the 'brand equity' of a place and its terroir produce. The three cases of terroir seafood products from Norway and Scotland share common features in how they present and document terroir features linked to their products on their websites. First, the cases adopt similar key concepts or attributes to describe their terroir food products. Second, the narratives focus on similar key themes that describe the interaction and interdependencies between different forms of terroir capital. Third, the three cases are all linked to international or national bodies of accreditation of terroir qualities, whose guarantees signal exclusivity and quality to consumers.

Key concepts

The websites use similar concepts and attributes to describe terroir qualities. Common concepts and phrases that occurred when describing the environment were, for example, *clean sea, beautiful scenery, good climate, rich fish grounds, biodiversity, and descriptions of space-specific animal habitat.* Needless to say, these attributes should be central in the branding process for any terroir product. However, on the Internet each of these concepts alone cannot enhance awareness of a terroir product. Typing any of these concepts as a search word on an Internet search engine will produce thousands, if not millions, of hits, and the specific terroir product will thus continue to live in web obscurity. Since terroir products are defined by their total package of attributes (Aurier *et al.*, 2005), promotion of terroir products requires Internet spaces where consumers can read the whole terroir story, as well as find external validation of this information. Consumers also need a virtual space where they can expect to find such material.

Terroir themes

One narrative theme was prominent in all of the cases examined, describing three forms of interdependencies or relationships: *people/man and the environment; culture and the environment; and production methods and the environment.* Descriptions of these relationships explain how each terroir product is developed over a long time in respectful interplay with the local environment. The terms sustainability, biodiversity and animal welfare link the terroir product not only to local but also to global environmental concerns. The narratives presented on the webpages explain that the attitudes of the fishermen and other parties involved in the production processes are built on long traditions dating back to times when respect for man's dependency on nature was more acknowledged. The cultural and institutional capital of the terroir place is typically explained as the result of long traditions and close interdependency between man and nature. The Loch Fyne presentation of their farmed salmon is interesting because salmon farming is a modern, high-tech, food production industry. To get around this conflict with terroir associations, the Loch Fyne story focuses on the role of the founders as *pioneers* in connecting principles for farmed salmon to local traditions, biodiversity and sustainability. Much of the narrative content on the Loch Fyne website is framed to explain their attitudes and efforts to harmonise production methods with the wild fish habitat.

National and international accreditation

The content of the Internet presentation of the three cases gives a rich, interesting and appealing portrait of the terroir products. However, the consumers would need to know of the products in advance in order to find their individual websites. To connect to target consumer groups, the three terroir brands are associated with different types of societies in the virtual space. Slow Food is an internationally fast-growing consumer and producer movement anchored both in real life and in the virtual world. The Slow Food concept has become a symbol of the rural and natural as opposed to the life on the fast lane in the cities (Featherstone and Lash, 1999). Slow Food and Slow Cities can be considered as brands of a lifestyle in harmony with nature and human needs. The Slow Food Presidia and membership in the Ark of Taste represent an exclusive accreditation scheme for terroir food. The local Slow Food Convivia suggest local producers of terroir food to the Slow Food international headquarters in Italy, which approves the terroir product to be catalogued in the Ark of Taste. This procedure gives the Presidia both local integrity and an internationally standardised status. As a global Internet community, Slow Food connects terroir food products to target consumer groups on a global scale.

The EatScotland case is an important link on the VisitScotland website. National/regional tourist boards all over the world promote their country or region through this standard web address format: www.VisitCountry/Regionname.com. These national/regional tourist portals officially represent the country or regions, and local food producers can benefit from a mention on such a site. Being linked to the national tourist-board portal raises expectations of quality and authenticity, and brings each individual producer in contact with the target audience on a global scale.

Loch Fyne Oysters is an individual website marketing the Loch Fyne brand. As such, it requires knowledge and awareness of the brand name in order to find the website. What makes Loch Fyne stand out on the Internet is its ability to document consistency of terroir values throughout its supply chain. By highlighting the names of suppliers such as Loch Duart and accreditation schemes such as Freedom Food, Loch Fyne can leverage its brand equity both through increased credibility and increased awareness by appearing on these organisations' websites. The approval of organisations such as the RSPCA has the potential to lend the brand a global presence since its agenda concerns the prominent topic of animal welfare and the politics of food (Bjørkum 1999).

Conclusion and marketing implications

There is increasing consumer demand for authentic, original food products, and the terroir concept offers rural areas the chance to capitalise on this demand by developing terroir brands for food products from their areas. The power of the Internet makes it much easier for rural areas to present themselves and their products to consumers all over the world. As this chapter aims to show, successful marketing of local, rural food products on the Internet can be linked to two factors: the development of a terroir brand, and a networking through information websites and portals and consumer communities.

Development of a terroir brand emphasising the characteristics of an area can enhance the commercial appeal and competitiveness of local food products, but this is not enough in itself. As the case analysis in this chapter illustrates, similar rural areas in different countries can present similar images of themselves. The difference with genuine terroir products is that they have a credibility that comes from external sources. This credibility engenders trust in consumers, and this is one of the important resources required for the formation and development of knowledge. A major source of credibility can come from being associated with organisations that by nature confirm the claims made by the terroir product, for example, the Freedom Food scheme and the Slow Food movement. Seeking to build credibility through co-branding, a terroir product with famous consumer community brands can reinforce the image and values of the core terroir brand. A terroir brand with credibility can achieve a real differentiation and value creation.

In order to reach a wider group of potential consumers, terroir products must establish a web presence (get connected) and become networked. By having links and references in the right places on the Internet, terroir products can reach far more potential consumers, in a much shorter timespan and, most likely, at a lower cost than traditional methods of marketing. They can also increase their credibility by association with websites and portals that can reinforce their core brand image. Moreover, using links strategically, companies can document consistency in terroir brand values along the value chain. Linking with other relevant websites and portals, and increasing the 'search-ability' of the terroir product's website, can also ensure access to consumers who are more likely to be interested in the product. In addition, the power of 'word of mouse' should not be underestimated, as consumers share their information, knowledge and experience with others who share similar interests. The Internet affords myriad opportunities for terroir products to build, develop and reinforce brand knowledge among a global pool of consumers.

The concept of terroir brands and the networking potential of the Internet allows rural areas to develop new, high-value markets for local food products at a potentially much lower cost than that of traditional marketing methods. They can also empower local people in rural areas to create new, exciting marketing concepts to bring additional income to these areas.

Notes

1 See definition of Internet terms after the reference list.
2 For a full list see http://ec.europa.eu/agriculture/qual/ en/1bbaa_en.htm.

References

Amilien, V. (2005) 'Preface: About Local Food', *Anthropology of Food* 4 (May) [online]. Available: www.aofood.org/JournalIssues/04/aof-local-sommaire.htm [10 August 2006].

Anon (2005) 'Power at Last – How the Internet Means the Consumer Really is King (and Queen)', *The Economist* – special supplement 2–8 April: 3–16.

Anon (2006) 'Twenty-five years of the IBM PC', *BBC News*, 11 August [online]. Available: http://news.bbc.co.uk/2/hi/technology/4780963.stm [11 August 2006].

Aurier, P., Fort, F. and Sirieix, L. (2005) 'Exploring Terroir Meanings for the Consumer', *Anthropology of Food* 4 (May) [online]. Available: www.aofood.org/JournalIssues/04/aof-local-sommaire.htm [10 August 2006].

Bjørkum, E. (1999) 'Opprinnelsesmerking av mat: En studie av forbrukernes syn på opprinnelsesmerking (Country of origin labelling of food)', Rapport nr. 3, Statens Institutt for forbruksforskning (SIFO), Lysaker, Norway.

Bolger, A. (2005) Research Style Helps Lift Noble, *Financial Times* 5 December 2005: 28.

Briscoe, B., Odlyzko, A. and Tilly, B. (2006) Metcalfe's Law Is Wrong, *IEEE Spectrum*, July [online]. Available: http://spectrum.ieee.org/print/4109 [11 August 2006].

Brown, S. (2000), Tradition on Tap: The Mysterious Case of Caffery's Irish Ale, *Marketing Review* 2000 (1): 137–63.

Cadot O., Estevadeordal, A., Suwa-Eisenmann, A. and Verdier, T. (eds) (2006) *The Origin of Goods*, Oxford: Oxford University Press.

Castells, E. (2001) *The Internet Galaxy-Reflections on the Internet, Business, and Society*, Oxford: Oxford University Press.

Dichter, E. (1962) 'The World Consumer', *Harvard Business Review* 40 (4): 112–13.

Dimara, E. and Skuras, D. (2003) Consumer Evaluations of Product Certification, Geographic Association and Traceability in Greece, *European Journal of Marketing* 37 (5/6): 690–705.

Dinnie, K. (2002) 'Implications of National Identity for Marketing Strategy', *Marketing Review* 2002 (2): 285–300.

EU (2006) From Council Regulation (EC) No. 510/2006 of 20 March 2006. Source: Official Journal of the European Union, 31 March 2006.

Featherstone, M. and Lash, S. (eds) (1999) *Spaces of Culture: City, Nation, World*, London: Sage Publications.

Goldberg, M.E. and Baumgartner, H. (2002) 'Cross-country Attraction as a Motivation for Product Consumption', *Journal of Business Research* 55: 901–6.

Homefjord, K. (2000) *Linking Products, Industries and Place*, Working paper No. 85/00, Foundation for research in economics and business administration, Bergen, Norway.

Keller, K.L. (2003) *Strategic Brand Management: Building Measuring and Managing Brand Equity* (International Edition), London: Prentice Hall.

Keller, K.L (1993) Conceptualising, Measuring and Managing Consumer-based Brand Equity, *Journal of Marketing* 57: 1–22.

Kelley, K. (1997) 'New Rules for the New Economy', *Wired* 5 (September) [online]. Available: www.wirednews.com/wired/5.09/newrules_pr.html [4 August 2006].

Kelley, K. (1998) 'New Economy? What New Economy?', *Wired* 6 (May) [online]. Available: www.wirednews.com/wired/archive/6.05/krugman_pr.html [4 August 2006].

Kleppe, I.A. and Mossberg, L.L. (2003) 'Company versus Country Branding: Same, Same, but Different', *Academy of Marketing Science, 2003 Conference Proceedings*, Developments in Marketing Science Series 26: 53–60.

Kleppe, I.A., Iversen, N.M. and Stensaker, I.G. (2002) Country Images in Marketing Strategies: Conceptual Issues and an Empirical Asian Illustration', *Journal of Brand Management* 10 (1): 61–74.

Kozinets, R. (1999) 'E-Tribalized Marketing?: The Strategic Implications of Virtual Communities of Consumption', *European Management Journal* 17 (3): 252–64.

Leiner, B.M., Gerf, V.C., Clark, D.D., Kahn, R.E., Kleinrock, L., Lynch, D.C., Postel, J., Roberts, L.G. and Wolf, S. (2003) *A Brief History of the Internet*, The Internet Society [online]. Available: www.isoc.org/Internet/history/brief.shtml [10 August 2006].

Loureiro, M.L. and McCluskey, J.J. (2000) Assessing Consumer Responses to Protected Geographical Identification Labelling', *Agribusiness* 16 (3): 309–20.

McGrouther, B. (2006) 'A Good Catch', *EatScotland: The Official Eating & Drinking Guide of VisitScotland*, [online]. Available: http://eatscotland.visitscotland.com/sitewide/feature_links/seafood-trail-featurelink/seafood-trail-page1/ [10 August 2006].

Nonaka, I. (1994) 'A Dynamic Theory of Organizational Knowledge Creation', *Organization Science* 5: 15–37.

Nonaka, I. and Takeuchi, H. (1995) *The Knowledge Creating Company: How Japanese Companies Create the Dynamics of Innovation*, New York: Oxford University Press.

Park, C.W., Sung, Y.J. and Schocker, A.D. (1996) 'Composite Branding Alliances: An Investigation of Extension and Feedback Effects', *Journal of Marketing Research* 33 (November): 453–66.

Reed, D.P. (2001) 'The Law of the Pack', *Harvard Business Review* 79 (2): 23–4.

Reiss, S. (2006) 'His Space', *Wired* July: 142–7.

Schuiling, I. and Kapferer, J.-N. (2004) 'Real Differences Between Local and International Brands: Strategic Implications for International Marketers', *Journal of International Marketing* 12 (4): 97–112.

Silverman, D. (2005) *Interpreting Qualitative Data, Methods for Analyzing Text and Interaction*, 2nd edn, London: Sage Publications.

Smith, D.C. and Park, C.W. (1992) 'The Effects of Brand Extensions on Market Share and Advertising Efficiency', *Journal of Marketing Research* 29 (August): 296–313.

Tregear, A.T., Kuznesof, S. and Moxey, A. (1998) 'Policy Initiatives for Regional Foods: Some Insights from Consumer Research', *Food Policy* 23 (5): 383–94.

Verlegh, P.W.J. and Steenkamp, J.-B.E.M. (1999) 'A Review and Meta Analysis of Country-of-Origin Research', *Journal of Economic Psychology* 20: 521–46.

Wellman, B. (1999) *Networks in the Global Village: Life in Contemporary Communities*, Boulder, CO: Westview Press.

Wellman, B. and Guilia, M. (1995) 'Net Surfers Don't Ride Alone: Virtual Communities as Communities', in P. Killock and M. Smith (eds) (1995) *Communities in Cyberspace*, Berkeley and Los Angeles: University of California Press.

Young, J.A., Brugere, C. and Muir, J.F. (1999) 'Green Grow the Fishes-oh: Environmental Attributes in Marketing Aquaculture Products', *Aquaculture Economics and Management* 3 (1): 7–17.

Websites

Cured and Smoked Herring from Sunnmøre. *Ark of Taste*, Slow Food Foundation for Biodiversity [online]. Available: www.slowfoodfoundation.com/eng/arca/dettaglio.lasso?cod=696&prs=PR_1220 [10 August 2006].

EatScotland: The Official Eating and Drinking Guide of Visit Scotland (2006) [online]. Available: www.eatscotland.com [10 August 2006].

Kristiansund Baccala. *Ark of Taste*, Slow Food Foundation for Biodiversity [online]. Available: www.slowfoodfoundation.com/eng/arca/dettaglio.lasso?cod=694&prs=0 [10 August 2006].

Loch Fyne Oysters [online]. Available: www.lochfyne.com [10 August 2006].

Royal Society for the Prevention of Cruelty to Animals [online]. Available: www.rspca.org.uk/servlet/Satellite?pagename=RSPCA/RSPCARedirect&pg=RSPCAHome [11 August 2006].

Slow Food [online]. Available: www.slowfood.com/ [10 August 2006].

Stockfish from the Isle of Sørøya. *Ark of Taste*, Slow Food Foundation for Biodiversity [online]. Available: www.slowfoodfoundation.com/eng/arca/dettaglio.lasso?cod=695&prs=PR_1221 [10 August 2006].

The Seafood Trail (2006) [online]. Available: www.theseafoodtrail.com/ [10 August 2006].

Definition of Internet terms

The Internet represents the technological infrastructure that enables a worldwide, publicly accessible network of interconnected computer networks. The web, on the other hand, is a global information space where users can both read and write information, and where text documents, images, multimedia and many other items are identified by short, unique, global identifiers so that each can be found, accessed and cross-referenced in the simplest possible way. The web is available via the Internet technology, although the terms are frequently used interchangeably. For consistency and ease, this chapter uses the term 'Internet' when referring to both the Internet and the world wide web.

With regard to the terminology used to describe elements of the Internet, the following definitions are taken from the online version of the Oxford English Dictionary (www.askoxford.com/):

link short form of hyperlink: a link from a hypertext document to another location, activated by clicking on a highlighted word or image.

portal an Internet site providing a directory of links to other sites.

search engine a program for the retrieval of data, files or documents from a database or network, especially the Internet.

webpage a hypertext document accessible via the Internet.

website a location connected to the Internet that maintains one or more webpages.

5 The persistence of place

The importance of shared participation environments when deploying ICTs in rural areas

Sarah Skerratt

Introduction

> A funny thing happened on the way to 2005: the digital revolution actually became real. Walk around any city or town and what do you see? You see young people text messaging; commuters jamming to their iPods; friends snapping photos on their camera phones. Look a bit further, and you see doctors' decisions aided by patient information called up on hand-held devices; teachers using wireless technology as tools; parents printing photos on cordless printers before leaving their children's football games.... It's a revolution in any sense of the word. But I have another name for it: a warm-up act. We are entering an era where everything is going digital. It's going to be the main event of our lives for decades to come.
>
> (Carly Fiorina, CEO Hewlett-Packard)

In rural areas of the UK, there are a number of ways in which individuals can become connected with the digital age: through owning a computer with dial-up or broadband connections in their own homes; through shared, communal computing and Internet facilities available through formal or informal channels; and through Internet-enabled phones (where 3G coverage permits).[1] This range of experience is also the case in the UK's urban areas, many of which have the added facility of Internet cafés, wifi hotspots which allow individuals with their wireless-enabled laptops to connect as they roam, and areas with strong 3G phone connectivity allowing individuals to 'web and walk'. However, rural areas have distinctive characteristics which mean that people's actual experiences of 'being connected' differ greatly from the apparent metropolitan mode of being 'totally digital'.

One is, rightly, reticent in accepting any generalisation of experience, either urban or rural. Therefore, there will be those who find Fiorina's picture of a connected urban populace to be futuristic even now. So I am not aiming to juxtapose 'rural' (disconnected) with 'urban' (connected). Rather, I intend to examine those characteristics of rurality which mean that people living and working in rural areas experience digital connectivity in specific ways. This is not to say that such experiences are *unique* to rural areas. Rather, they remain relatively *undiluted* in their impact, due to less provision (CA, 2002; Skerratt, 2005; Skerratt, 2003), and because of the mobility required for people to benefit from a wider range of access points away from the immediate locale.

Distinctive rural characteristics

Rural areas[2] of the UK possess a number of characteristics which contrast with urban areas: a physically dispersed population; dispersed (and thus often hidden) poverty; low population density; extended travel distance/time to hubs or centres and service outlets; a public living and learning environment; relatively weak communications infrastructure (roads and digital); lower adoption of Information and Communication Technologies (ICTs) in a range of rural jobs (MacLeod and Grimes, 2003); and an age profile skewed towards an ageing population. Although these characteristics vary across types of rurality (from 'remote rural' through to 'accessible rural', for example, SE, 2006), it has been argued that this list comprises recognised elements of rural life (CA, 2004, 2005, 2006). The extent to which these characteristics represent challenges to individuals is itself subject to variability, being dependent on a range of factors, including age, gender and individual assets (income, mobility, education, social and peer networks).

The relationship between these characteristics and communal rural digital experiences

This chapter aims to identify the ways in which informal, communal provision of ICTs is specifically experienced in rural areas; that is, to specify those elements of 'rural place' which are variously taken into account in rural provision, which mediate the experiences of such provision, and which are perceived to impact directly on people's engagement with ICTs in rural settings. Specifically, through reference to two case studies and the wider literature, I identify the ways in which communal ICT provision is embedded within highly localised social relationships (Ritchie and Brindley, 2005), which can variously help or hinder an individual's participation in the Information Society. Through examining people's experiences and perspectives, we will increase our understanding of the challenges and opportunities which these modes of intervention and provision represent.

Basis for the discussion

This chapter is based on six years of research into the ways in which the Information Society, or digital age, is being experienced by people in the rural areas of Scotland, England, Ireland, Finland, Norway and Sweden. Over this period, my research objectives have been to interrogate the evolution of policy and practice (both external interventions and bottom-up developments); to examine the feasibility of their implementation; to identify components of self-sustainability; and to incorporate people's own experiences as a component of ongoing policy dialogue. The motivation for this inquiry is the need to address the persistence of rural–urban digital divides, specifically examining the ways in which they are defined, and the extent to which they are therefore addressed and bridged.

The evidence base developed over this time comprises two main sources: desk research of digital policy and practice, and case study analyses of rurally based ICT-in-the-community initiatives (Skerratt, 2003, 2005, 2006).

The cases selected here comprise informal place-based activities and projects at rural community level, where ICT was/is seen as an enabler of learning and inclusion. I do not evaluate these initiatives (this has been done elsewhere; Skerratt and Warren, 2004a, 2004b) or present detailed methodological accounts, which have been published elsewhere (the reader is referred to Skerratt and Warren, 2003a, 2003b, 2003c; Skerratt *et al.*, 2004, 2005). This is because my role has been different in relation to each of the case studies – evaluator, researcher, observer, critical friend. This diversity of my interaction with the cases, and the range of individuals within them, means that I did not follow a standardised approach to the analysis of each, since this would not have been appropriate or possible.

Through the selected case studies, however, it is possible to identify the threads and themes which have emerged repeatedly over this time period. This has allowed me to clarify the elements of rural location which appear to affect individuals' experiences of these technologies; that is, how physical and social components of place impact on the opportunities and experiences.

The two cases cited below originate from externally funded ICT-in-the-community initiatives, part of the UK government's drive towards a 'smart successful society' (SE, 2004), one which is inclusive and progressive. In the next section, I present a summary of each of these cases and a synthesis of the main findings. This is then followed by a discussion of recurring themes within a wider research context. These examples, while illustrating externally driven provision opportunities, show how their design and implementation adaptations were formulated by the communities themselves, as they adhered to various principles and priorities relating to their locales.

Case study examples of communal ICT provision

Case study 1: Rural Broadband Community Network (RBCN)[3]

The original RBCN project proposal highlighted the lack of broadband services outside urban centres, stating that:

> Left to its own devices, it is unlikely that the free market model will stimulate the rollout of such services and therefore there is a need for a more creative approach to the building and financing of such networks. To take the specific example of our town, BT at this time have no plans to provide

> ADSL and the local Cable company recently by-passed the town in their cable expansion programme. The town is in danger of becoming a 'Digital Desert'.

RBCN is a project based in a small town (population 2,500) in a rural area of England. The project was instigated by local activists with assistance from their Regional Development Agency (RDA), the County Council (CC) and other partners, funded by the UK Department of Trade and Industry (Dti). The initial impetus for the project stemmed from the dissatisfaction of local people with dial-up access to the Internet, and with the low probability that the main infrastructure providers would support broadband Internet connection for the town in the foreseeable future. The project was funded from February 2002 to February 2004.

The expressed *objectives* of RBCN were 'to bring to a rural town community measurable social and economic benefits through the delivery of a series of broadband-enabled, locally based Action Programmes in the areas of *Education, Business, Healthcare, and Community*'. This would involve the creation of:

- A *broadband network* linking all the key public facilities – school; health centre; town hall; library, employing the latest broadband technologies.
- A *Marketing and Community Access Centre* in the High Street that would aim to promote broadband services to businesses and the wider community. This centre also offered training and a public Internet access point to such services, as well as a video-conferencing facility.
- A *Rollout Programme* to ensure maximum uptake of broadband services by commercial and non-commercial users. This was to encompass the town and its surrounding rural areas. In addition, lessons from the pilot would be made available to other rural communities.

The funding of the RBCN project ceased in February 2004. The Access Centre closed its doors at the end of December 2003, by which time the Action Programmes had also ceased.

Researching the RBCN

The overall aims of the research project were, first, to study the development process of RBCN over time, and to analyse its impact on the rural community (both the market town and surrounding villages and hamlets). Second, to produce guidelines for good operational practice, and to identify transferable processes and technologies which could benefit similar rural communities. Third, to produce guidance of benefit to policy-makers, funders, practitioners and the wider rural community.

The research approach comprised three phases: Pre-launch (June 2002), Action Programmes and Access Centre (February 2003), and Post-funding (February 2004). This comparative approach over time was designed to enable us to gather data relating to changes during the lifetime of the RBCN project.

Broadly, we applied the same tools for data collection in each of the three phases, in order to ensure that we generated data sets that could be compared. In addition, the topics and types of questions were structured in a similar way each time, while also allowing for the follow-up of pertinent issues at the time of interviewing. As far as was possible, we also tried to interview the same core individuals at each of the three phases, again to allow us to gather data which would help us to assess changes over time.

Case study 2: Rural cyberpubs[4]

This pilot project was launched in England in May 2003. The Countryside Agency, in its 2001 Report 'The Pub Is the Hub', described the rural pub as follows:

> Pubs have long been established at the heart of rural communities and are often important focal points for social interaction. Where there is no village hall, a pub may provide the only public meeting place. They have traditionally been involved in sports and recreation, playing host to local clubs and encouraging leisure facilities which are available to members of the community of all ages. Pubs also offer employment opportunities and contribute to the local tourist industry by providing overnight accommodation and running local events.
>
> (CA, 2001: 4)

This research showed the rural pub to be under the same threat of decline as other rural services, the main reasons being: greater observance of drink–drive laws, low incomes in rural areas, increasing customer expectations, and a shift from landlord to manager-run corporate premises which require higher profit margins. The implication of these trends for rural areas was highlighted: 'the loss of the local pub can often affect the quality of life as a focal point for the community disappears, as well as leaving a gap in the local economy' (p. 6). The Countryside Agency identified best practice relating to diversification of pubs, towards providing joint services, where two or more services operate from the same premises, for example, a pub, post office and shop all running from the same building. This enables running costs to be shared, and services to be retained on a smaller scale, thus preventing their loss altogether (p. 6).

In May 2003, a joint initiative between the Countryside Agency, the Department for Education and Skills, and Locals on Line, was launched to 'wire up country pubs', (i) as part of this diversification in provision of services, and (ii) to overcome elements of the identified rural–urban digital divide. This 12-month project had the objectives of: (a) providing a test-bed for establishing a network of well-used, sustainable community ICT centres, and (b) through Locals on Line, 'attract hesitant adults who have had little experience of using computer technology, to encourage lifelong learning and ensure that centres meet the needs and interests of the whole community' (CA News online, 02/06/03).

In May 2003, nine rural pubs were 'wired up', five in the county of Dorset, and four in the county of Northumberland. They were supplied with: free satellite broadband connection (asymmetrical), at least three high-spec PCs, two printers (one colour, one black and white) with paper and printer cartridges, support through a 'facilitator' who provided up to 12 hours per week onsite support, ad hoc training and advice. In Dorset, the five publicans were advised that this was to be a 12-month supported project and that, during that period, they were to create a local committee or group to take over, run, and find funding for, the ICT resource. In Northumberland, publicans were not advised in the same way, and Northumberland County Council was subsequently brought in during May 2004 to take over the public Internet access facility; therefore no such local committees or groups were formed in the four Northumberland villages.

Researching the rural cyberpubs

Our overall aim was to examine the phenomenon of rural cyberpubs in England, specifically assessing the extent to which they could creatively engage a diverse range of dispersed rural citizens within the Information Society. The research centred around five objectives, which also formed the basis for the interviews:

1 Examine the phenomenon of rural cyberpubs in England, addressing their extent, development and self-sustaining potential;
2 Investigate the range and spectrum of rural cyberpubs, and 'map' these according to emerging criteria;
3 Assess their potential to become viable channels of access to e-government provision, and for delivery of e-services, to a wide spectrum of rural inhabitants;
4 Identify, and produce an inventory of, characteristics of rural cyberpubs that ensure their survival as a self-sustaining community resource (i.e. beyond funding); and
5 Explore the implications for the local e-government strategies of local authorities and for economic and social policy at regional and sub-regional levels.

A combination of face-to-face semi-structured and structured questionnaire-based telephone interviews was used for the primary data collection, as follows:

1 Site visit and interview with nine original project public houses to explore developments and sustainability issues since the start of the project;
2 Telephone interview survey of broader random sample of 40 public houses identified from Yellow Pages in Dorset and Northumberland, to identify extent and patterns of ICT take-up in rural areas, reasons for non-adoption, and potential for future adoption;

3 Face-to-face interviews with key informants from stakeholder groups e.g. regional development agencies, the Countryside Agency, local authorities, pub owners, community and voluntary groups; and
4 Participant validation of findings with the original nine publicans in two group sessions.

Summary of findings: informal communal ICT provision

Case study 1: RBCN

The findings from the research show how people in the rural town valued the atmosphere in the Access Centre, and particularly its prime location on the High Street. It was felt to have created an upbeat buzz, with a 'metropolitan feel'. This was felt to be in large part due to decisions taken by those managing the project, as reported on various business technology webpages at the time, for example:

> She set out with some deliberately challenging ideas.... For a start, rather than trying to blend in with its surroundings, she decided to make the cafe look very different from the other shops in the street. She used an interior designer and ended up with a very modern and metropolitan look. Its five PCs and three iMacs sat on trendily curved coloured benches and tables with retro-styled chairs in white glass fibre and orange acrylic. 'Using people's curiosity and the gossip network is much quicker and more powerful [at promoting something] than virtually anything else,' she explained. She was keen that it should be available as a cafe, where people could nip in for good coffee, as well as an internet resource.
>
> (www.nvunet.com, 22 April 2004)

Interviewees described their experience of the Access Centre in extremely positive terms. Their comments focused on its welcoming and informal atmosphere, non-threatening and supportive approach, its value as a good informal meeting place, its constituting an asset to the High Street and its high-spec facilities.

It was seen as a friendly place to congregate, performing a positive social function as an informal networking hub, where people could interact socially, either at events or just by dropping in. It was thus perceived as having made a valuable contribution to the life and the centre of the small town, while increasing residents' computer literacy. Thus, it was seen not only to be raising awareness of the benefits of broadband, but of supplying the means by which people could overcome their fear of technology and the Internet.

When asked to distil those features of the Access Centre which were felt to be crucial to operating in a *rural* town, interviewees (both the managers and visitors to the centre) identified the following factors: a central location in the High Street; high visibility, its shop window making it easy to see inside and unthreatening to enter; a warm welcome and a social environment; user-centred,

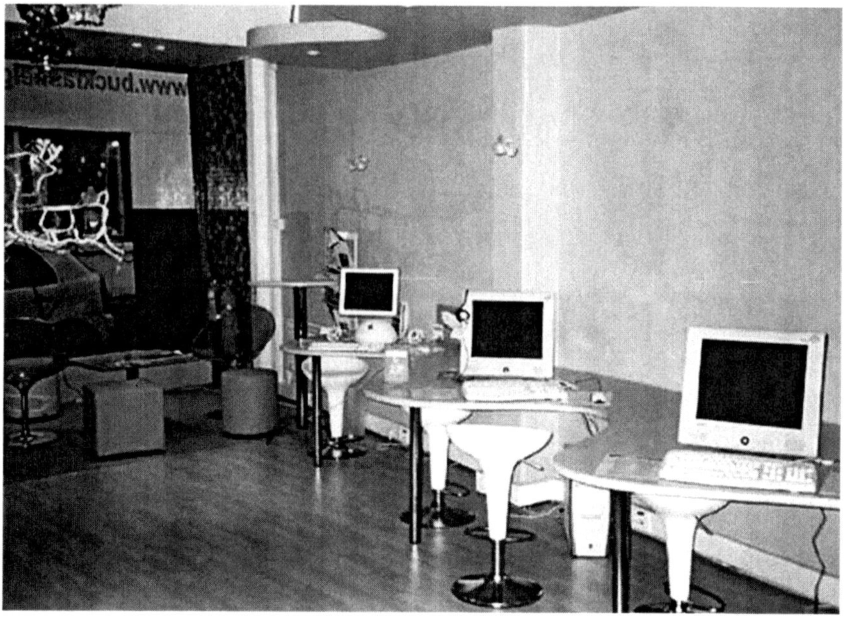

Figure 5.1 Up-to-date interior and high-spec computers in Access Centre.

unpatronising help and support, from 'people like us' rather than technicians; good, modern equipment coupled with fast broadband access; its catering for all ages, abilities, social groups; convenient opening hours, including some evenings; that it was something to be proud of, marking the town out as different, dynamic, special; that it represented evidence of regeneration, something happening for the community; an organised series of access programmes which acted as the catalyst for many people to start using the centre and broadband; a facility for professionals 'on the road' to drop in and work online; and high levels of technical user support.

Interviewees described those most likely to be excluded from RBCN as being: (i) those living on the main council housing estate in the town; (ii) the over-60s, and (iii) other economically and socially disadvantaged groups. The staff thus aimed to encourage greater inclusion, through group or club events, and through targeting these at the interests of potential users – to find a 'hook' to pull them in: 'The centre became widely used for a variety of activities, from people wanting to investigate their genealogy, to those keen to edit video, to groups of young parents on Surestart training schemes' (www.nvunet.com, 22 April 2004).

When the Access Centre closed at the end of the funding period in 2004, the majority of interviewees described the impact primarily in terms of losing a lively venue in a prime, High-Street location, and felt that its closure was symptomatic of a downturn for the town centre. They had lost not only a meeting place, but also of a sense of optimism and 'buzz' in their community.

Following closure, its relocation to a smaller venue was proposed. However, strong reservations were expressed because the alternative venue would only offer: restricted opening hours; voluntary staff as opposed to paid centre staff; poor technical backup; and a generally less conducive ambience. These features were felt to contrast negatively with the main positive characteristics of the old centre: its central location, modern and welcoming interior design, the visibility and open-ness created by the shop-window onto the street, and the constant presence of unpatronising, 'non-techie' helpers.

The interplay between rural context and communal ICT provision

This brief summary of findings reflects the ways in which the rural locale serves to emphasise the importance of certain features of the communal ICT provision. First, the positive impacts of the Access Centre remained 'undiluted' by other access points – it was the only such venue in the town, and moreover boasted a well-designed, chic, metropolitan interior, which set out to be welcoming and friendly. Indeed, it was the only such centre for several miles, anywhere else requiring a substantial round trip on infrequent public transport. Further, the social function of the centre was consistently highlighted by interviewees as its key attraction in the locality, since no other similar provision existed. Its subsequent closure, therefore, had a similarly undiluted impact, in that it was not replaced, and the property remained empty.

Second, the public nature of learning in a small rural community was addressed directly by the managers, through their emphasis on the centre being a social setting first and foremost. Thus, people were not necessarily publicly identified as 'learners' by others – rather, they could be using the café simply for coffee, or to meet and chat with others. The daytime and evening classes (including genealogy, salsa, and emailing photographs to family overseas) also served as 'hooks', which were particularly important in a small community for diffusing the emphasis on, and individual identification with, formal learning.

Third, the Access Centre was unique in the area in tailoring its opening hours to users, with staff shifts covering extended hours. This was considered to be particularly important (and is reflected in the second case study), since 'typical' outlets for public Internet facilities often offer very limited opening hours, sometimes requiring permission from a key-holder, or are focused around an organised class, thus formalising the arrangement and the experience. This can be off-putting for those lacking confidence in approaching ICTs.

Fourth, the fact that the computers were all up to date, that the interior was new and smart, were key to people in the rural town not feeling that they were inheriting secondhand equipment; rather, that they were on a par with the cities, particularly with regard to the high-speed broadband connectivity. This was coupled with a reported pride in the centre, which they felt marked the town out as different from others in the region, and caused it to stand out as 'go-ahead' in the area.

Finally, the Access Centre's high level of technical support proved a unique asset in this rural setting. As wider research shows, the proportion of employed people using ICTs in their jobs is lower in rural than in urban, areas, and thus the ICT-literate peer network is either non-existent or extremely dispersed (Skerratt, 2006). The centre therefore led to a reliable concentration of such expertise, coupled with a delivery style which was not overly technical, and thus remained accessible to a broader spectrum of users.

Case study 2: Rural cyberpubs

First, when reflecting on whether the pub as a village location allowed ICT access to a wider range of people than might otherwise have been catered for by a village hall or library, two sets of observations were noted: (i) the pub as compared with other facilities in the locale; and (ii) the attributes intrinsic to the rural pub.

When comparing the pub with other communal facilities in the area, interviewees stated that the library and village hall no longer exist, are too far away (and therefore not accessible), or are generally in a bad state of repair making them unwelcoming venues. Trips to such locations to access ICT required planning, often combined with journeys by public transport where available, checking opening times, or signing up for courses. Interviewees contrasted these aspects positively with the attributes of the rural pub, which they felt directly supported the easy access to computers and the Internet. These included their long opening hours (including evenings and weekends), thus allowing for casual as well as planned usage, their welcoming aspect to everyone, regardless of age or gender; the fact that they are heated, particularly important in the winter months and for locals on a lower income; and the setting facilitates socialising and relaxation as well as Internet/computer use, thus learning remained informal and often shared.

Second, interviewees found that the location of the computers within the pubs presented some difficulties, particularly in terms of privacy, an issue magnified within small communities. Overall, the findings showed that it is not really possible for individuals to look up their bank accounts, or search on sites concerning domestic abuse, drug abuse and other aspects of citizen's advice because: others can look over your shoulder or might come over to chat; and, given that they know you and your personal circumstances, they may also take an interest in your personal usage details. Therefore, the limited space available was felt to create real privacy problems. Also, the publicans had sited the computers where they could keep an eye on them, believing that this would discourage inappropriate use. They also had to trade this preference against the siting of the computers at the back of a room or in an annex, where they would lose the least amount of drinking and dining space.

The following photographs illustrate the ways in which publicans and local committees responsible for the ICTs attempted to resolve privacy issues, while still retaining space for other customers.

Third, a critical element for the sustainability of these rural ICT facilities was identified as technical back-up, both for the user (for example, when the system 'crashes') and for the equipment and software (updating operating systems,

Figure 5.2 Cyberpub showing computers situated in sight of bar man.

Figure 5.3 Cyberpub showing specially-erected screen to afford some privacy for local users.

resolving connectivity problems, virus protection, and ordering supplies of paper and inks), particularly given how rapidly such technology becomes obsolete, as new software and demands develop. The two counties where the cyberpubs were situated experienced different levels of technical back-up in the pilot project. Interviewees reported that, when they arranged their own back-up from a local person, this was more satisfactory. Where 'outsiders' were responsible for such support, the consistency of response times, and the regularity of tutoring, were both felt to be inferior to the local support. This issue led to significant concerns among landlords, who felt that they did not have the time or expertise to supply technical back-up. Once again, the sparsity of such technical expertise in rural areas was highlighted, and emphasised as a critical element in self-sustainability beyond the funded period.

Fourth, interviewees also focused on the issue of gender, which sparked a range of responses, although there was consensus around the 'comfort factor' associated with coming into the pub as an individual. Men were more accustomed to going into pubs on their own, finding it easy to chat with friends and the landlord while using the computers; also, businessmen tended to call in to check their email or their orders while on the road. Women, by contrast, reported that the presence of the computers made them more comfortable going into the pubs on their own. There was consensus that, for both men and women, those aged over 50 were more reluctant simply to call into the pub to go on a computer. The main factors here were felt to be fear of the technology and also feeling it to be irrelevant.

Fifth, interviewees consistently raised the issue of developing the local relevance of the ICT facility. Plans to encourage new/different usage at some of the pubs included: a webcam at the front door, so that visitors could see scenery in real time, and gauge the weather for walking; more courses and more training; greater marketing; a Learning Action Course (for the quieter winter months); and new courses, for husbands of some of the wives who first went on the courses (since husbands became interested). Publicans planned to put up physical noticeboards in the bar to find out what people wanted to use it for, what they needed, and how to develop locally relevant applications and content (such as for local sports teams, youth groups, historical societies, and seasonal activities).

A sixth point emphasised by publicans and managers of the ICT facilities in the pubs was the need for the skills and commitment of local people to be well integrated into the facility, in order to ensure it outlasts its initial funding period and maintains its usefulness to local people. The organisation of this effort and input was felt to be critical, particularly as support is otherwise typically drawn from the same small set of volunteers for most rural community initiatives. Local management of the ICT resource, on a day-to-day basis, was felt to be integral to its survival, as well as raising the locals' skills base to apply for further funding, produce business plans, and write application forms. The small population base in the immediate locale from which to draw people was felt to be a constant challenge.

Finally, interviewees stressed how the rural cyberpub facility directly addressed 'rural users'. They highlighted the ways in which it had overcome isolation for a number of people, particularly as the ICT facility enables them to keep in touch electronically with dispersed families. Further, publicans identified those who came in when their own Internet connection was down, or simply for recourse to a higher speed line. In addition, young mothers with children of school age took advantage of the facility at lunchtime; a number of parents in the areas studied were on low incomes, and the heat and light furnished by the pubs in wintertime were attractive to parents. A final point is that rural users in this sample felt that they were able to gain access to a valuable facility which they perceived to be largely taken for granted in urban settings. The computers and Internet in their local pub comprised the only such outlet for many miles around.

The interplay between rural context and communal ICT provision

First, as with the previous case study, the combination of learning and leisure was believed to have greater significance in small rural communities, where users do not necessarily want to enter a place of learning, or be identified as 'learners'. The fact that the pub also affords a context where informal peer support occurs, is seen as further diffusing a certain place-based self-consciousness associated with not knowing how to use computers or the Internet. This informal, often impromptu (for example, during a pub quiz) peer-to-peer exchange was identified as a significant asset. Further, where courses were organised, the pub setting led to participants feeling that they remained informal, though formalised to a limited degree.

Second, one drawback noted, based again on the fact that many of them know one another well, was the lack of privacy, which inhibited them from looking up certain websites. This could act as a disincentive to someone wishing to search for a support site.

Third, again as observed with the first case study, the absence of a high proportion of IT skills as a norm within rural communities was highlighted, together with the more limited choice of, and high call-out fees for, technical consultants in rural areas. Thus the importance of ongoing technical provision was identified as being particularly important.

A fourth aspect concerns the ways in which the place-based communities wanted to view, and then develop, content relating to their locale, their communities and activities. They particularly sought content which differentiated themselves from urban, metropolitan settings, and was also of value, such as information on local jobs, opportunities for lifts and car-sharing to towns and the local sale of skills and items. Again, although these content suggestions are not unique to rural settings, the fact that geographical (and mobility) distance is significant, and regularly prohibitive, makes place-based provision an ideal solution.

Further, the small human resource base from which support and management of the pub-based initiatives was drawn, presented an ongoing challenge. Within the immediate vicinity, a limited number of volunteers have the time and commitment to invest in the initiative. Interviewees felt this to be magnified in a rural context and it is a recurring issue in rural areas.

Finally, the pubs' Internet facilities were perceived as a chance to access a resource that was common in urban areas, so redressing an imbalance. This is based on the lack of broadband provision in many rural areas, and the fact that, even where broadband infrastructure exists, issues of relatively high cost and lower speeds compared with the cities, caused its users to feel left behind in a move within society towards near-ubiquitous connectivity. Thus, the cyberpubs were considered an opportunity to gain some ground in what, for some, is a rapidly changing world of communications and the associated required skills.

Discussion: implications for research

In discussing the findings from the two case studies, it must be emphasised that the aim is not to argue for an absolute uniqueness concerning rural attributes and their influence. Rather it is to identify those specific rural contextual characteristics which have a marked 'background effect' upon how people experience shared ICT facilities in small villages and outlying rural areas.

As is evident from the cases presented, ICTs are mediated through characteristics of place, locale and the nexus of social relations, where sparse population and limited infrastructure enabling ease of mobility and connectivity remain dominant. This being so, the implications for research are primarily twofold: the persistence of place, and the requirement for an enhanced definition of the digital divide.

The persistence of shared spaces

Within the wider literature, there is an ongoing debate concerning the persistence of place within the place-less world of the Internet. A 'utopian view' sees us all increasingly connected as 'networked individuals' (Wellman, 2002), free from the constraints of place-based identity, and from our gender/age/ethnic identities. Specifically, Wellman states that 'proximity continues to matter, but is losing its dominance' (p. 8). We can be (and are) therefore connected in a place-less way, without the negative attributes and ties of place-based community and identity. This implies the end of geography and the 'tyranny of location'. Thus, the Information Society comprises a highly individualised, mobile experience.

The associated demotion of place as a component of people's online experience is increasingly common currency. Within such a stance, 'the village' specifically is often considered as a term referring only to a bygone age (Cairncross, 2001), to a form of networking and exchange which is of the past, at best a romanticised notion of a bucolic idyll. For example, Wellman (2002) states that 'Place – in the form of households and work units does remain important – even if neighborhood or village does not' (p. 4), and claims that communities *have already changed* 'from densely-knit 'Little Boxes' (densely-knit, linking people door-to-door) to 'Glocalized' networks (sparsely knit but with clusters, linking households both locally and globally) to 'Networked Individualism' (sparsely-knit, linking individuals with little regard to space)' (2002: 1).

We therefore need to consider the extent to which this individualised version of experiencing the Information Society is appropriate, given the evidence presented in this chapter. For many, 'the village' persists as a component of lived experience, where, in spite of increased mobility for some, localised place and social relations continue to shape individuals' participation in the Information Society. We have seen how, for example, the undiluted public nature of being a learner, the lack of anonymity and privacy in computer use, the reliance on a single ICT setting as the only one for many miles, the paucity of local technical know-how, and the need to develop relevant applications, in order to increase usefulness and add value (McCown, 2002), are components of rural experience of shared ICTs. Thus, relegating 'rural/village' to a purely retrospective definition is not appropriate in the context of communal ICT provision in rural areas.

This is further supported by those who argue that community of place *is* critical to the appropriation of ICTs and to the integration of individuals and communities into the Information Society, a society which is inclusive and progressive. The debates and action research within Community Informatics in particular (Marshall *et al.*, 2004; Gurstein, 2000; Loader *et al.*, 2001) point to the place-based, and place-*defined*, social and cultural contexts as being integral to how people experience technology, and the extent to which it makes sense to them (Liff and Steward, 2001). The provision of informal communal ICTs within recognised public spaces (such as pubs and cafes) can lead to them being accessed by those unlikely to engage in formalised learning experiences (CA, 2002). Such environments often enable a shift from lower-level to higher-level participation, as appropriate (Richardson, 2002). Day and Harris (1997) highlight the importance of community-managed, non-threatening public places (p. 16), while Liff and Steward (2001) outline the social embeddedness of community e-gateways, and the importance of social networks in sustained public ICT access.

Further, analyses by Ritchie and Brindley (2005) show ways in which use of ICTs transforms relationships within rural SMEs, and they emphasise the need for these relationship components to be integrated within analyses of ICT use and non-use. Erumban and de Jong (2001) also point to social and relationship contexts as key explanatory variables in differences in ICT adoption between rural regions.

Enhanced definition of the digital divide

The urban–rural 'digital divide' – that is, between the haves and the have-nots – is primarily expressed in terms of the types of connectivity available in rural areas, and the implications that the 'rural broadband deficit' (CA, 2002) has for usage. I have summarised the key facets of rural life felt to affect the quality of digital experience in these areas, in the following table:

Table 5.1 Influence of rural topography and low population density on individual connectivity

Characteristics of rural infrastructural provision	
Topography	High (often prohibitive) cost of provision of high-speed digital connectivity infrastructure over distances of tens of kilometres Limited feasibility and resilience of line-of-sight wireless networks
Topography coupled with low population density	High cost of monthly online time, due to uncompetitive pricing for the provision of high-speed digital connectivity (due to small customer base remaining unattractive to Internet Service Providers) Paucity of connections/infrastructure/split copper wires: • Relatively slow/shared connections (contention issues) • Limited size of files; down-streaming speeds and thus limitations in moving from being a low-level to a high-level user

However, as illustrated through the case studies, the characteristics of rural areas not only affect the quality of Internet connectivity for *individuals*; they also affect the *shared* provision of Internet facilities, put in place either through bottom–up initiatives by local communities, or through government intervention, in direct response to a lack of affordable, individualised access. These effects in turn lead to distinctive rural experiences which are reflected within (i) scale, timeframe and technical support, and (ii) provision environments. Table 5.2 summarises the key elements.

Given this, it is therefore important to complement the existing analytical components of the digital divide (Servon, 2002; Hellawell, 2001) with a further dimension: that of the **'participation environments'** within rural areas. Our understanding of the components of that divide therefore require further coherent development through a collation of information and findings relating to *communally based rural ICT interventions and applications*, and the ways in which the rural environment and particular sociocultural contexts mediate people's experiences, both positively and negatively. There is the need for a consistent integration of the 'participation environment' within future definitions of the digital divide, and Figure 5.4 demonstrates how this complements analyses thus far.

Further, within the next phase, it is important to develop analyses which incorporate the concept of '*participatory* environment' whereby shared meaning, value, adaptation and applications are 'co-constructed' within and by the place-based rural community. The notion of co-construction builds on McCown's (2002) construction of the relevance component of initial and sustained ICT usage. I would suggest that *co*-construction further increases the probability that place-based, shared initiatives will be able to sustain themselves, adapting as need and opportunity evolves, and thus gain a greater communal

Table 5.2 Influence of rural demographic and social characteristics on shared connectivity

Characteristics of shared rural provision	
Scale, timeframe and technical support	Small-scale and uncertain due to small population numbers (equates with low critical mass), geographical distance between individuals, coupled with infrequent and inflexible public transport.
	Short-term and fragmented provision (often related to an external ICT-intervention project lifecycle; CA 2002), and often dependent on numbers of participants, and the increasing need for courses to provide accredited learning in order to secure local authority funding.
	Individual scale back-up due to costs of maintenance and upgrading (rapidly outdated technology, and technical support).
	High dispersal of any ICT-literate 'peers', therefore isolation.
Rural provision environments	The public nature of learning (within context of public way of life) in small rural communities.
	Appropriateness of places for ICT delivery (including gendered dimension, age dimension, neutrality of space, opening hours).
	Peer environment, specifically the legitimacy of outsiders as catalysts or 'teachers', as compared with locally-based peers.

meaning within their initial communities. The author has scoped this area of research, and explored how it might be incorporated within evaluation of ICT-in-the-community initiatives (Skerratt, 2006).

Discussion: implications for policy and practice

One could argue that, as broadband roll-out continues and as computers and mobile phones become relatively cheaper, the need for shared facilities is likely to decline. However, it is important to realise that individualised access is not simply related to being able to purchase the equipment and the online time. Rather, issues 'beyond access' (Hellawell, 2001), relating to ability and confidence in using the equipment, the relevance and added value of content (Servon, 2000; McCown, 2002), and increasingly the ability to produce one's own content (Web 2.0.), remain crucial reasons why individuals choose to become connected (Wilcox, 2005). It is currently argued, in UK policy and practice, and through voluntary and other initiatives, that communal shared acess to computers and the Internet allows the building of such confidence, competence and interest.[5] Further, there are those who argue that communal facilities not only furnish the technology, but also perform a social function and thus are likely to remain relevant to people's lives and ways of living and socialising (Gurstein, 2000). Finally, others argue for the provision of shared computers and Internet

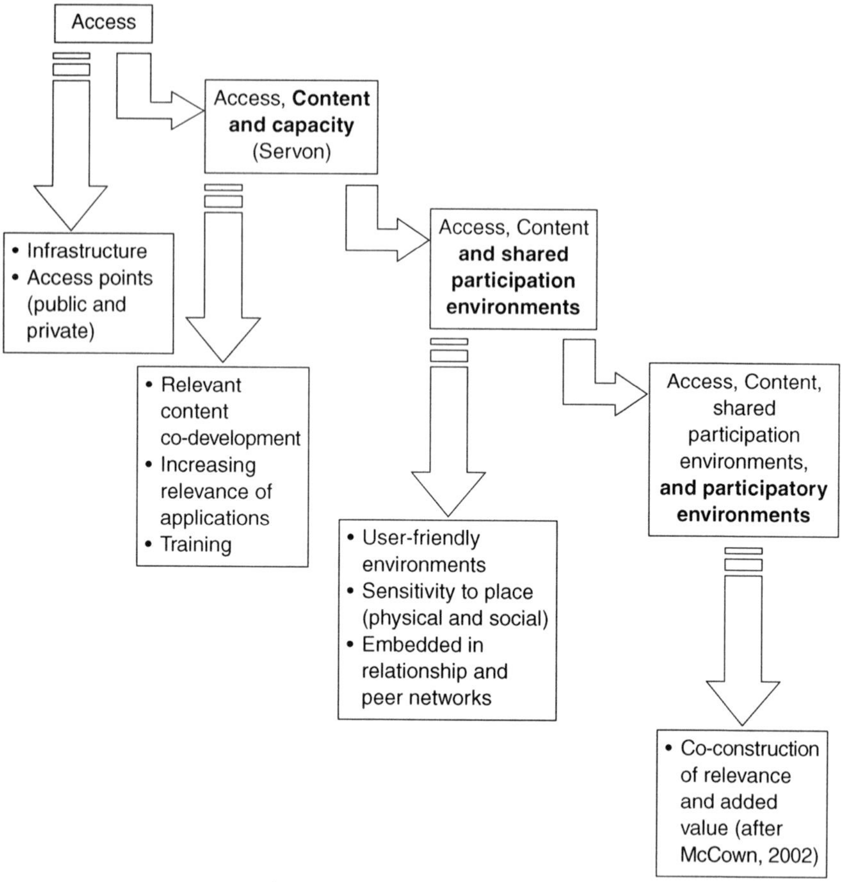

Figure 5.4 Progressing the digital divide definition to incorporate 'participation environments' and move towards co-constructed 'participatory environments'.

connectivity, in order to give everyone the chance to be part of the Information Society, regardless of personal means and location. It is this which drives much government rhetoric and intervention in the UK (in both urban and rural areas), since there is a recognition that costs still remain prohibitive and should not be the main cause of a persisting digital divide.

Further, when we consider rural-based ICT experiences in the range of rural areas of Europe, particularly in the new Member States and in parts of southern Europe, individualised Internet penetration remains low (see chapter 1 in this volume) and thus the issues identifiable within the rural UK have resonance within wider Europe, so gaining an added pertinence to debates concerning how the Information Society is variously experienced.

For these reasons, therefore, it is important to analyse how the provision of shared ICT facilities in rural areas reflects the specific characteristics of such physical and social environments. Although the communal provision experience is not unique to rural areas, rural contextual factors are arguably magnified in such settings due to the distinct characteristics of place and social networks.

Thus, evaluation of initiatives such as rural cyberpubs and broadband community networks, needs to include an increased understanding of how these rural hubs can – through an informal, inclusive environment – supply a vital entry-point for many otherwise isolated rural inhabitants. The role of the 'great good place' (Oldenburg, 1999) in enhancing opportunities to participate needs to be monitored and researched, together with the function of 'community e-gateways' into the Information Society (Liff and Steward, 2001; Richardson, 2002) – particularly since in rural areas 'public access points tend to be fewer and farther apart' (CA, 2000, p. 19). Further, ICT-in-the-community initiatives (bottom–up and external) are typically time-constrained in nature and limited in resources, with the associated need to ensure maximum leverage and added value for those resources across the widest spectrum of people in rural communities remaining a prime concern. Therefore, understanding *processes of co-construction* within communities of place would give further guidance.

Finally, as Cornford *et al.* (2000) state: 'The possible outcomes ... of non-participation and participation in the Information Society are not predetermined and are hence amenable to policy influence' (Cornford *et al.*, 2000: 23).

Acknowledgements

First, I would like to express my sincerest thanks to Professor David Preece, University of Teesside, for his support, interest in and significant contribution to the rural cyberpubs research. Also to the University of Newcastle Pump-priming Research Fund for providing fieldwork resources. Second, many thanks go to Martyn Warren, University of Plymouth, with whom I worked on the RBCN research over a period of two years; it was stimulating, productive and enjoyable, and I feel extremely privileged to have been able to work with him. In addition, the Countryside Agency furnished small grants enabling us to conduct the interviews, focus groups and observation. Third, I would like to say a very big thank you to Dr Rowena Murray, Reader, Strathclyde University, for her constructive and insightful feedback during earlier drafts of this chapter, and more importantly for building my confidence during the writing process. Finally, none of these observations or analyses would have been possible without the patience and openness of the range of interviewees with whom I worked in these two case-study locations, and over the past six years in the range of studies I have carried out in the UK and internationally. They have helped me greatly to critique and refine my ideas, and to test the robustness of the findings and their implications.

Notes

1 Digital television will be an increasing option for many UK rural households after 2008.
2 Using the Scottish Executive (2006) classification of rural, from 'remote rural' through to 'accessible rural'.
3 This research was carried out in partnership with Martyn Warren, University of Plymouth, and with funding from the Countryside Agency.
4 This research was undertaken in partnership with Professor David Preece, University of Teesside, with funding from the University of Newcastle upon Tyne.
5 Further, digital inclusion policy and practice continue to emphasise shared access and learning facilities as routes into participation, a most recent example in Scotland being the Learn Direct and Microsoft Adult Learning Initiative (Scotland, October 2006).

References

Cairncross, F. (2001) *The Death of Distance 2.0: How the Communications Revolution Will Change Our Lives*, New York: Texere.

Commission for Rural Communities (2005) *Beyond Digital Divides? The Future for ICT in Rural Areas*, Wetherby: Commission for Rural Communities.

Cornford, J.R., Gillespie, A. and Richardson, R. (2000) 'Regional Development in the Information Society', in K. Ducatel, J. Webster and W. Herrmann (eds) (2000) *The Information Society in Europe: Work and Life in an Age of Globalization*, Boulder, CO: Rowman and Littlefield, pp. 21–44.

Countryside Agency (2001) *The Pub Is the Hub*, Cheltenham: Countryside Agency.

Countryside Agency (2002) *ICT and Rural Inclusion*, Cheltenham: Countryside Agency.

Countryside Agency (2004) *The State of the Countryside 2004*, Cheltenham: Countryside Agency.

Countryside Agency (2005) *The State of the Countryside 2005*, Cheltenham: Countryside Agency.

Countryside Agency (2006) *The State of the Countryside 2006*, Cheltenham: Countryside Agency.

Day, P. and Harris, K. (1997) *Down to Earth Vision: Community Based IT Initiatives and Social Inclusion*, London: IBM.

Economist, The (2005) 'Totally Digital', C. Fiorina in *The Economist – The World in 2005*: 128.

Erumban, A.A. and de Jong, S.B. (2001) 'Cross-country Differences in ICT Adoption: A Consequence of Culture?', *Journal of World Business* 41: 302–14.

Gurstein, M. (2000) *Community Informatics: Enabling Communities with Information and Communications Technologies*, London: Idea Group Publishing.

Liff, S. and Steward, F. (2001) 'Community e-Gateways: Locating Networks and Learning for Social Inclusion', *Information, Communication and Society* 4 (3): 317–40.

Loader, B., Hague, B., Keeble, L. and Eagle, D. (2001) *Community Informatics: Shaping Computer-Mediated Social Networks*, London: Routledge.

MacLeod, M. and Grimes, S. (2003) 'Connecting Rural SMEs to the Digital Economy: Some Empirical Evidence from Ireland and Scotland', paper presented at ESRS, Sligo, Ireland.

Marshall, S., Taylor, W. and Xinghuo, Y. (2004) *Using Community Informatics to Transform Regions*, London: Idea Group Publishing.

McCown, R.L. (2002) 'Probing the Enigma of the Decision Support System for Farmers: Learning from Experience and from Theory', *Agricultural Systems* 74: 1–10.

NVUNET: www.nvunet.com, articles from 22 April 2004 (last viewed December 2006).

Oldenburg, R. (1999) *The Great Good Place*, New York: Marlowe and Company.

Richardson, R. (2002) *ICTs and Rural Inclusion*, Newcastle: University of Newcastle.

Ritchie, B. and Brindley, C. (2005) 'ICT Adoption by SMEs: Implications for Relationships and Management', *New Technology, Work and Employment* 20: 3.

Scottish Executive (2004) *Smart, Successful Scotland*: www.scotland.gov.uk/Publications/2004/11/20246/46555.

Scottish Executive (2006) *Urban Rural Classification 2005/2006*, Edinburgh: Scottish Executive, Office of the Chief Statistician.

Servon, L.S. (2002) *Bridging the Digital Divide: Technology, Community and Public Policy*, Oxford: Blackwell Publishing.

Skerratt, S. (2003) *The Implications for Rural and Regional Populations of the Irish Government's Provision of Broadband Communications Infrastructure*, National Institute of Regional and Spatial Analysis, report published by National University of Ireland.

Skerratt, S. (2005) 'Our Digital Futures: Policies for Broadband Connectivity in Remote and Rural Communities of Ireland and Scotland', *Scottish Affairs Journal* 53, autumn.

Skerratt, S. (2006) 'SME Behaviour and ICTs: Building Culture into Evaluation and Intervention', in A. Matilainen (ed.) (2006) *ICTs: Providing Information, Advice and Services to Rural SMEs?*, Helsinki: Ruralia Institute, University of Helsinki, pp. 57–73.

Skerratt, S. and Warren, M. (2003a) 'Rural Communities and Broadband: Local Appropriation of a Global Technology?', in P. Cunningham, M. Cunningham and P. Fatelnig (eds) (2003) *Building the Knowledge Economy: Issues, Applications, Case Studies*, Oxford: IOS Press, pp. 150–7.

Skerratt, S. and Warren, M. (2003b) 'Decision-mapping and Community Adoption Dynamics: Rural Broadband as the Focus', paper presented to E-Europe, Bologna, October.

Skerratt, S. and Warren, M. (2003c) 'Rural Communities and Broadband: Local Appropriation of a Global Technology?', paper presented to the Conference for Online Communities, Amsterdam, September.

Skerratt, S. and Warren, M.F. (2004a) 'Broadband in the Countryside: The New Digital Divide, *Farm Management Journal* 11 (12): 727–36.

Skerratt, S. and Warren, M.F. (2004b) *Buckfastleigh Broadband Community Network: Final Report*, prepared for the Countryside Agency and the SW Regional Development Agency.

Skerratt, S., Preece, D. and McLoughlin, I. (2004) 'Rural Cyberpubs: Promoting Wider Engagement in the Information Society?', paper presented to the International Rural Sociology Congress, Trondheim, July.

Skerratt, S., Preece, D. and McLoughlin, I. (2005) 'Rural CyberPubs: A Service Provision Initiative in the Changing Context of UK Public House Retailing', EURAM Conference, Munich, May.

Wellman, B. (2002) 'Little Boxes, Glocalization, and Networked Individualism', web-paper, www.chass.utoronto.ca/~wellman/publications/littleboxes/littlebox.PDF. Accessed January 2007.

Wilcox, M. (2005) 'Describing Networks: Joining Us, Joining in, or Joining up', paper for Partnerships Online Blog, 9 March. Accessed online at: www.partnershipsonline.org.uk/index.cfm?fuseaction=main.viewBlogEntry&intMTEntryID=2401.

Part III

The importance of social and cultural 'fit' of ICTs in rural areas

6 Digital divides within households

Rosemarie Gannon

Introduction

Much research suggests that information and communication technologies (ICTs) offer the potential to eliminate the 'friction of distance' in terms of location and social interaction (see Lægran, 2002; Valentine and Holloway, 2001; Graham, 1997). ICTs may be able to overcome the constraints that a remote location can impose on access to certain services and types of information. As a result, ICTs have particular relevance to rural areas, traditionally characterised in terms of their economic and social peripherality (Ward, 1990; Skerratt, 2003). Thus, it can be argued that ICTs have the scope to eliminate the importance of physical proximity to a whole host of economic, social, cultural and political activities, thereby making rural areas more attractive locations for businesses, services and people.

This chapter explores the adoption and use of ICTs (mobile phone, computer and the Internet) in everyday life in a rural Irish community. It examines the impact of ICTs on the 'friction of distance', and shows how this 'friction' can encourage ICT take-up. Moreover, it illustrates how the 'friction of distance' and other factors can discourage ICT use. It also shows how education, age and gender influence Internet use in some Irish rural households. Given that ICTs offer the scope to negate the 'friction of distance' (Lægran, 2002; Grimes, 2000; Valentine and Holloway, 2001; Graham, 1998; Gillespie *et al.*, 2001), the assumption is that distance is a constraint and that ICTs can present the solution to distance-related barriers (problems) specific to rural areas. On this basis, we would expect people to adopt and use ICTs because of their geographical location. Hence, the rural is regarded as a key motivator in ICT take-up and use by people living in such communities.

Little research has been done on this topic. Much of the research has focused on how ICTs can promote economic development in rural communities and how rural SMEs can better participate in the digital economy. Most studies conducted on domestic adoption and use of ICTs have focused on urban households. Very little *qualitative* research has been done on rural households and on what motivates people living in a rural area to adopt and use ICTs.

This chapter reports on some findings from a qualitative study for my PhD carried out in a rural community in the northwest of Ireland in 2004/5, (Gannon, forthcoming). The purpose of the research was to examine how ICTs (computer, Internet and mobile phone) have an impact on the 'friction of distance' and what this means for adults and teenagers living in a rural Irish community (Lirmara)[1] in terms of their social contact, information acquisition and leisure activities. Interviews with household members and focus groups were undertaken in order to collect the necessary data. Households selected had to have a computer and Internet access. A snowball technique was employed to build the sample. In this way, people interviewed in the early stages of the data collection recommended other people in the community whom they thought would be suitable for the research. These people were subsequently asked to participate in the study. Only adults and teenagers were invited to participate in the household interviews. In total, 57 people were interviewed. This involved 22 household interviews and four focus-group interviews. Two of the focus groups were with household members previously interviewed, one focus group with those who did not have computers and the Internet at home and the fourth focus group was with members of the local youth club. The data was collected between May 2004 and January 2005. Through my findings, I explore the emergence of digital divides within some households in Lirmara. I now turn to explore the 'friction of distance' in more detail.

'Friction of distance'

In terms of examining relations between ICTs and space and place, it has been primarily researchers in geography and urban studies who have explored the 'spatial' criteria of the Information Society, by examining space, telematics and social change, and hence, the impact of ICTs on rural development and on people living in rural areas. Graham (1998) identifies three broad dominating perspectives: substitution and transcendence (drawing on technological utopianism), co-evolution (drawing on political economy and cultural studies) and recombination (drawing on actor-network theory). The first perspective 'substitution and transcendence' is the most dominant perspective in the discourse on ICT and space and place. It examines the impact of ICTs on space and place and such discourse refers to the 'death of distance' (Cairncross, 2001) or the 'end of geography' and 'dissolution of the city' (Gillespie, 1992; Graham, 1997). 'Distance effectively dies as a constraint on social, economic and cultural life' (*The Economist*, 1995, as quoted in Graham, 1998: 168). ICTs can serve to eliminate the 'friction of distance' in terms of location and social interaction (see Lægran, 2002; Graham, 1998). Information becomes accessible everywhere. With such emphasis on the potential of new communication technologies for all parts of society in the new emerging 'Information Society', it is therefore not surprising that the substitution and transcendence perspective has been the most dominant one in terms of understanding ICT and space and place relations. In terms of the other two perspectives proposed by geographers and urban-studies writers: 'co-evolution' and 'recombination', the co-evolution perspective tries to explain

ICTs and space and place by referring to urban areas and emphasising how urban spaces and technological networks are co-evolving (Castells, 2000a, 2000b; Swyngedouw, 1993). Moreover, the recombination perspective argues for a fully relational view of the links between technology, time, space and social life (Harvey, 1996; Thrift, 1996; Graham, 1998). Space and place are emphasised in the above three perspectives and such models suggest space (geographical location) plays a key role in terms of understanding ICTs and space and place.

Graham and Marvin (1996) suggest that, with the introduction of ICTs, human life becomes 'liberated' from the constraints of space and the 'friction of distance'. Various definitions of the term 'friction of distance' exist. Economic definitions stress the potential that ICTs have to help diminish regional imbalance and alleviate rural marginality (Cornford *et al.*, 2000; Gillespie *et al.*, 2001). Human geographers define 'friction of distance' as the inhibiting effect of distance on human activity (Case, 2000). In this study, the 'friction' is seen as the inhibiting effect of distance on social and cultural activities in everyday life. In rural areas, the assumption is that distance is a constraint to socio-economic and cultural activity. ICT is viewed as a way to overcome distance-related barriers, often problems specific to rural areas. With the advent of ICTs, distance is no longer a constraint to social, economic and cultural life in rural areas. Hence, we would expect people living in rural areas to adopt and use ICT differently to people living in urban areas. Furthermore, it is assumed that the rural is a key motivator to ICT adoption and use by people living in rural areas. I now turn to examine the impact of ICTs on the 'friction of distance' in some everyday activities of people in a rural Irish community.

ICTs' impact on the 'friction of distance'

While some evidence from my study suggests that the 'friction of distance' encourages ICT take-up and use, many of the reasons given by interviewees for ICT could be common to all, irrespective of geographical location. Hence the 'friction of distance', or physical distance is not their primary motivator in accessing ICTs. It appears that ICTs can have an impact on everyday life activities when interviewees identify a *need*, be it to get in contact with somebody or access a particular type of information or product. On occasion, such a need will necessitate use of the mobile phone and Internet. In other instances, there will be no recourse to the Internet, in particular, thereby showing how computers have had little impact on some interviewees. It could be argued that interviewees' need for social contact is greater than some of their information needs or leisure activities, because social contact is at the heart of everyday activities, whereas information needs change over time, thus explaining the greater and faster integration of the mobile phone into interviewees' lives.

More detailed exploration of whether people interviewed are using ICTs because of their geographical location revealed that a lot of the reasons for mobile phone and Internet use are reasons common to all. For example, they choose the Internet because it is cheaper, more convenient and efficient, easier and quicker to access information online than by going to a public library, with more information available online, etc. Moreover, mobile phones are perceived as handy, convenient for peace of mind and privacy issues and the main mode of communication among young people interviewed. Some examples indicate how geographical location can promote ICT use, i.e. to access types of medical information or buy specific products online. These examples show how ICTs help to overcome the 'friction of distance' experienced by some interviewees in some everyday activities. Overall, my findings show that the 'friction of distance' is an influencing factor among other factors and plays a secondary rather than a key role in ICT adoption and use in everyday life in Lirmara. On the basis of my findings, a *need* in one's life, be it an information or communication need or a need for a product or service, appears to be the main motivator behind domestic ICT adoption in Lirmara. I now present some examples which show how the 'friction of distance' encourages ICT use.

Examples showing how the 'friction of distance' promotes ICT use

Some evidence from the study suggests that ICT is employed on occasion to purchase certain products and access particular information not available locally, in addition to fulfilling some communication needs which are more acute because of interviewees' geographical location. Many found mobile phones essential to enable them to keep in constant contact with other people. The majority left their phones switched on all the time. Being contactable made them feel more secure and lent them a certain *peace of mind*. In addition, my findings show that some female interviewees had to call their husbands on their mobiles, because they were not accessible via a landline during the day. This was in part due to the type of work they did, i.e. it was not office-based and involved more mobility. For example, their occupations included a fitter/mechanic (HH2),[2] part-time farmer and self-employed supplier of mechanical parts (HH4), builder (HH6) and part-time farmer and self-employed oil distributor (HH16) (see tables in Appendix for more information). Several men living in Lirmara worked in the trades and this type of occupation was more common than others in the community. Hence, it could be suggested that the lack of office jobs in Lirmara meant that the mobile phone played a more important role in fulfilling residents' communication needs. In contrast, people living in urban areas may be able to contact their spouses on their landlines during the day as they are more likely to have office jobs.

Furthermore, several of the older female interviewees were housewives or worked part-time. This is similar to data relating to women's employment in Europe which shows that 28 per cent of women in the EU have part-time jobs in comparison to only 4 per cent of men. Unemployment was higher among women (12 per cent) than men (9 per cent) in the EU.[3] In the fourth quarter of 2005, 64 per cent of the working-age population (15–64 years of age) in the EU-25 had a job. More men (71.5 per cent) than women (56.6 per cent) had jobs at that time. Ireland was slightly higher than the EU-25 average with 67.8 per cent of the working-age population having a job at that time. More men (77 per cent) than women (58.4 per cent) aged 15 to 64 years were employed in Ireland (Romans and Hardarson, 2006). This lack of employment could explain why some female interviewees felt lonely at times, with a greater *need* for social contact during the day than a person who is out working and meeting people or living in a city boasting more leisure activities for adults. The lack of childcare facilities in Lirmara made it difficult for women with small children to work outside the home. The greater availability of childcare facilities in an urban area may lead to increased employment opportunities outside the home. Hence, women living in an urban area may feel less isolated or lonely, than, for example, some of the female interviewees in Lirmara. Such findings are similar to those from Moyal's study (1989) on use of the telephone at home in Australia, which found rural women had a stronger motivation for using the phone than women living in urban areas because these women often live in some degree of isolation, with less chance of travelling to visit friends and family.

The 'mobility' aspect attached to the mobile phone was seen as very advantageous by several of the interviewees. For example, some (the sisters in HH17 publican in HH22) said that they no longer had to stay at home and wait for a call. The publican in HH22, whose pub was closed during the day, found his mobile convenient as it allowed him to spend the day outdoors but remain in touch with suppliers, other family members and friends. Such an example shows how on occasion the 'friction of distance' encourages mobile phone use among some interviewees, as it enables them to contact others and be contacted whenever and wherever. This also highlights the benefits of the mobile phone to some people in Lirmara because they are no longer constrained by some of their everyday activities, in terms of fulfilling their communication needs.

With regard to educational information, it could be argued that the *need* for this experienced by a teenager living in Lirmara may on occasion be more acute than that felt by a teenager living in a city, because fewer resources are available in Lirmara. Hence it is important to have domestic Internet access, as there is no Internet cafe or public library in Lirmara offering such access. Despite the lack of public points of Internet access in rural communities in Ireland, the highest levels of computer ownership in Irish households are found in the Mid-East (53.8 per cent) and Dublin (50.5 per cent) regions, according to Central Statistics Office (CSO) statistics from 2003. The Border and West regions reported penetration rates of home computers at 34.3 per cent and 32.3 per cent respectively. Internet access was also highest in Dublin (41.9 per cent) and Mid-East (40.2 per cent). In contrast, households enjoying access in the Border region amounted to 27.2 per cent and in the West (26.3 per cent). It should be noted that the Border and West regions are less urbanised than Dublin and Mid-East regions; hence, have got a higher proportion of rural areas. Apart from CSO data on ICT use in households in different regions in Ireland, e.g. the West, Border, Mid-East regions etc., which make no distinction between *urban* and *rural* areas, there is no publicly available data on ICT use in Irish households in *urban* and *rural* areas.

Some teenagers interviewed (girl in HH13 and boy in FG4)[4] felt that their school assignments benefited when they were able to access relevant information online; hence, the importance of this access. This was further reiterated in the interviews with adults attending third-level courses, who stressed the importance of Internet access at home because of their geographical location. Third-level students emphasised the importance of the Internet in obtaining the necessary information to complete assignments. Some third-level students in Lirmara may be constrained by the physical distance between their home and college, the lack of public transport and the lack of childcare facilities. For example, the poor childcare provision made it difficult for the mother in HH16 with four children under the age of 12 to physically go and spend time in a college library. In addition, the poor public transport impeded Lirmara teenagers from visiting the local public library in the nearest big town during the week. This could be why parents buy a computer and procure Internet access at home for their children, so that they are not missing out on something and can find additional information for their schoolwork.

In terms of health information, there are very limited resources for health information and health promotion in Lirmara. There is no general practitioner (GP) or health centre. The mother in HH16, who moved to the community from an urban area, said people living in Lirmara are very limited and isolated in terms of health information. 'I think, particularly in rural areas, is that there is very poor, you know, health promotion or health information. I think it is very difficult to access it if you don't know where to look.' She believed that health promotion in rural communities needed to be improved by, for example, arranging medical talks and distributing more leaflets and booklets. Moreover, she said very limited information is available to pregnant women in Lirmara. Not surprisingly, two interviewees (mothers in HH5 and HH17), who had recently had babies, looked up material regarding motherhood on the web. In HH5, the mother found this particularly helpful, as it was her first pregnancy and all very new to her. She said she got more information on the Internet than from her doctor. Furthermore, the mother in HH11 sought information on varicose veins on the web. She was interested in having her veins removed and said that there was no other way she could obtain this information before visiting her surgeon. Other types of health issues searched for online because it was not available locally include e-numbers and food additives (father in HH7) and skin disorders (adult female interviewee in HH13). These examples show how the 'friction of distance' encouraged some interviewees to access health information online.

In terms of online shopping, interviewees (members in HH1, HH10, HH16, HH22) bought items online because they could not find them locally or did not know where else they could buy them. For example, the male interviewees in HH1 bought Status Quo videotapes and a Status Quo CD, in addition to computer games online because there was no other place he could buy them. Examples of other items purchased online which interviewees could not buy locally include: CDs of jazz music, DVD of the film *Dangerous Liaisons*, book of poetry and a lock for a horsebox (male interviewee in HH22), seven Hornby trainsets and a damp meter (male interviewee in HH10), Liverpool FC wallpaper (mother in HH16) and hair extensions (members in HH18). People living in urban areas have access to a wider variety of shops, in comparison to people in Lirmara. Hence, they may be able to purchase such products in person in a store, if so desired, or else online. However, the main point is that urban areas offer more choice and options than Lirmara can.

Apart from shopping online, some interviewees also accessed information online for some offline leisure activities because it was hard to access this information locally. For example, the father in HH1, who has an interest in music, regularly visited the Status Quo website, claiming that it would otherwise be difficult to find out about this band. Furthermore, the male interviewee in HH22 described how he looked up a famous jazz bassist, Jaco Pastorius, as this is not a mainstream artist and, given the fact that the artist is no longer living, it could be very hard to get information on this artist in any other way. These examples show us how the 'friction of distance' motivated these interviewees to pursue their music interests via the web.

In terms of other leisure activities, the father in HH12 sometimes visited the website of the Chicago Bears to get information on the club and its activities, finding it otherwise impossible to learn news about American football teams because, up until very recently, American football magazines were not sold in the nearest big town. This example once again highlighted the fact that Lirmara is a *rural* community and shows how its residents had less access to newsagents and bookstores selling a large variety of magazines. In contrast, people living in an urban area may be able to go to one of several chains of newsagents or bookstores carrying numerous categories of magazines. I now turn to examine some factors which discouraged ICT use and contributed towards digital divides within the households interviewed.

Examples showing the 'friction of distance' and other factors discouraging ICT use

While I have described above examples of how the 'friction of distance' appeared to encourage some interviewees to adopt and use the mobile phone and Internet, several interviewees chose not to use the computer and Internet, in particular, in their everyday life. This shows that this technology was having little or no impact on these interviewees' lives. It also emphasises the fact that the 'friction of distance' did not encourage some interviewees to turn to the Internet to fulfil their information needs. Instead, some were happy to fulfil these needs by recourse to other sources.

Lack of interest appears to be the main reason why some interviewees (mother in HH7, fathers in HH3, HH8, married couples in HH2, HH4, HH6, HH9 and members of FG2)[5] did not use the computer and Internet at home. Furthermore, some of these interviewees (married couples in HH2, HH6 and HH9, mother in HH4, father in HH8 and members of FG2) felt that they had no need, or were too busy with no time to use the technology at home (married couple in HH4, father in HH6 and mother in HH7). Others could not be bothered as this technology was not around when they were younger (mothers in HH2, HH4 and members of FG2). In terms of leisure activities, several of the interviewees (mothers in HH2, HH4, HH11, HH12, HH14, HH17, HH18, HH21, couple in HH5 and father in HH21) said they had no interest in using the technology for such purposes, appearing happy with their existing leisure activities, be it walking, set dancing, watching television with no need to go online for leisure purposes.

Lack of skills was another reason given by the mothers in HH4, HH6, HH14 and married couple in HH21, and lack of awareness of the amount and different types of information available online (members in FG2). The mother in HH7 said that she had a fear of technology and was wary about the Internet and disclosing creditcard details online. Reluctance to disclose creditcard details online is one of the main reasons why respondents did not shop online. This is similar to findings from the CSO surveys in 2003 and 2004 (CSO 2003, 2004), which suggest that some Irish people do not purchase online due to security concerns. Another reason is that some households (HH8, HH9, HH13) do not own creditcards and are therefore unable to book flights. The non-users in FG2 had made no purchases online and seemed unaware of the type of products available online.

Some interviewees (mothers in HH8, HH11, HH15 and couples in HH5 and HH12) said it was too much hassle and required too much effort to connect the computer to the Internet, boot up the PC, log onto the web, etc. Some interviewees (fathers in HH1, HH5 and HH12, female interviewee in HH10 and mothers in HH11 and HH19) used the computer and Internet at work everyday, hence had little need for the technology at home in the evening. These interviewees were the only ones who used the computer and Internet at work. Many adults interviewed either did not work outside the home or did not use a computer in their job, perhaps explaining why they remained unaware of the technology's potential benefits. Reasons given by teenagers interviewed in FG4 as to why they use the computer and Internet so little at home included the assertion that there was nothing for them to do on it, it was boring, too slow, and surprisingly, one of the 15-year-old boys in FG4 said that the computer is too complex to use. Interestingly, cost does not appear to be an inhibiting factor to computer and Internet use at home. The only mention of cost was by some interviewees (the fathers in HH1 and HH5 and mothers in HH6 and HH12) who limited Internet use at home during the day, believing it expensive to go online at this time.

Poor mobile-phone coverage in the community is one reason cited by interviewees (HH3, HH9, HH10, HH12 and HH22) as to why they employed the mobile phone less when at home, with some preferring their landline (female interviewees in HH2, HH12, HH15 and HH16). This finding shows how the geographical location of Lirmara has a negative effect on mobile-phone use in the community. In general, mobile coverage is very good in urban areas of

Ireland. In addition, some interviewees tried to reduce the number of calls they make from their mobile due to its cost compared to the landline. Many found the mobile phone expensive and tended to keep calls very short. Some interviewees also limited the number of calls made on their mobile and the time of day they call. Some interviewees were concerned about the potential health risks of mobile phones, for example, the father in HH2 disliked using the mobile phone, feeling the radiation to be harmful.

While downloading music is considered to be a popular music-related Internet activity, many interviewees in HH1, HH15, HH17, HH21 expressing an interest in this, respondents in HH1 and HH15's Internet connections were too slow to download music, as broadband is not available in Lirmara. This demonstrates how the lack of an adequate technical infrastructure hindered some people from pursuing certain online activities. This lack of broadband is more of a problem in Lirmara than in an urban area. While the Irish Government has in recent years launched various schemes to promote the roll-out of broadband Internet access in the regions and rural communities of Ireland, up until the time of writing (August 2006), Lirmara had not received any funding for this purpose, even with regard to the local primary school. I now present some examples which show how other factors, such as age, gender and education influence Internet take-up and use in Lirmara and contribute towards digital divides within households interviewed.

Other factors influencing Internet use in rural households

On the basis of my findings, occupation and education appear to be influencing factors in terms of computer and Internet use at home. For example, in the focus group with non-users (FG2), five members were housewives and one a care assistant. With regard to education, three have completed Intermediate (Junior) Certificate,[6] two Leaving Certificate[7] and one has a Third-Level Certificate. Therefore, because five of these six interviewees did not work outside the home and the other interviewee did not use a PC in her job, they were not computer-literate. In addition, because these interviewees had never applied or experienced this technology in the workplace, they were unaware of its potential benefits. In a similar vein, parents in HH2, HH4, HH6 and HH9 had no experience of computers in the workplace (see Appendices A and B for a list of their occupations) or at home. However, some of their children used the computer and Internet for educational purposes. Moreover, the older male in HH21 who had primary-school education lacked computer skills. In a similar vein, the fathers in HH4, HH13 and HH20 only had primary-school education (see Table 6.1). According to members of these households, these fathers did not use PCs at home.

Some reasons given for non-use are related to age. It appears that younger interviewees were more inclined to access educational information online than their elders because they were still at school and had a greater need for this material. Hence, such a finding shows how age influences Internet use. In the focus group with non-users, I learned how they might be interested in learning to use the computer and Internet in the future, if they thought it was important for them to know what their children were doing on the web. In a way, their children would be the main reason why they would learn to do this. This is in contrast to the thinking behind the 'friction of distance' where physical distance and the associated disadvantage due to remoteness are seen to be the core reasons behind adoption and use of ICTs by people living in a rural community.

Furthermore, gender differences were also apparent, with adult male interviewees generally more interested in listening to music than adult females. They thus carried out more music-related activities on the Internet than female interviewees. One wonders why the women were less interested in visiting band websites and copying CDs? It could be that they preferred to watch television or go for a walk in the evening rather than listen to music or check out music websites online. Indeed, the most popular hobbies among adult female interviewees were walking, reading, watching television and set dancing. Moreover, it could be suggested that men preferred to spend time by themselves in the evening, having been out working all day, whereas some women who had been at home all day may have preferred to go for a walk with friends and have a chat.

Conclusion

The chapter described how some people interviewed use ICTs on occasion because of their geographical location. It showed how ICTs can solve some rural problems, such as overcoming the dearth of local shops and/or the long distance required to travel to shops in cities by purchasing some products online, or by accessing information online not available locally. Such examples illustrate the impact of ICTs on the 'friction of distance'. It also examined some factors which discouraged ICT use and contributed towards digital divides within households. In addition, it showed how other factors, such as age, gender and education influenced Internet adoption and use in Lirmara and contributed towards digital divides within households.

By and large, the findings show that interviewees chose to use the Internet because it is cheaper, faster and more convenient, etc. Such benefits represent benefits experienced by all ICT users and not just those living in a rural community. In a similar vein, some interviewees resorted to mobile phones because of their geographical location, but also for other reasons, such as convenience, peace of mind, privacy issues and/or its popularity among young people. Overall, the findings show us that, while the 'friction of distance' is an influencing factor, it is not the primary motivator behind ICT adoption and use in everyday life by interviewees in Lirmara. In terms of the theoretical models proposed by geographers and urban-studies writers: substitution and transcendence, co-evolution and recombination, these models suggest that space (geographical location) plays a key role in terms of understanding ICTs and space and place. My findings show that geographical location is very much a secondary factor in regard to this in rural areas. Hence my findings do not support these models.

My study highlights some limitations of technology and how at times it fails to live up to the expectations of interviewees. For example, some interviewees find it too much hassle to log onto the Internet, or for example, wait for a slow connection, which emphasises the lack of broadband in Lirmara, and highlights the need for such access in rural areas. Urban areas benefit from the greater availability of broadband. In addition, the findings show how poor mobile-phone coverage in Lirmara encourages some interviewees to choose to make more calls from their landlines. Therefore, there is a need for better mobile-phone coverage in rural areas. In contrast, this coverage is very good in urban areas thanks to the predominance of telecommunication masts.

There can be great variation in technology take-up even within such a small rural community, and this needs to be remembered when discussing ICT adoption and use in rural households. The findings emphasise the heterogeneity of people living in a rural community. Some interviewees went on the Internet a lot to access travel information and purchase flights online, etc., whereas others used the Internet very little (mothers in HH2, HH4, HH5, HH7, fathers in HH6, HH8 and HH21). Such findings show the existence of a digital divide within some households in Lirmara. The limitations of the technology discussed above, can potentially widen rather than bridge this existing digital divide within some Irish rural households.

Appendix

Table 6.1 Information on participants in household interviews

Household code	*Household member*	*Age*	*Level of education*	*Occupation*
HH1	Father	44 years	Third level diploma	Civil engineering technician in third level college
	Mother	39 years	Leaving certificate	Supervisor in pharmaceutical company
HH2	Father	45 years	Inter (junior) certificate	School receptionist and housewife
	Son no. 1	26 years	Leaving certificate and apprenticeship	Mechanic
HH3	Mother	55–64 category	Leaving certificate	Housewife
	Daughter	25–34 category	Undergraduate degree	Environment, health and safety officer
HH4	Mother	55–64 category	Undergraduate degree	Housewife and helps husband in business
	Daughter	21 years	Undergraduate degree	Third level student
HH5	Father	25–34 category	Leaving certificate	Civil servant
	Mother	25–34 category	Leaving certificate	Civil servant
HH6	Father	35–44 category	Leaving certificate	Builder
	Mother	35–44 category	Leaving certificate and Hairdressing course	Hairdresser
HH7	Father	35–44 category	Inter (junior) certificate	Self-employed butcher
	Mother	35–44 category	Third level diploma	Childcare worker
HH8	Father	35–44 category	Inter (junior) certificate	Workshop administrator in garage
	Mother	35–44 category	Inter (junior) certificate and Catering college cert	Carer
	Daughter (no. 1)	17 years	Junior certificate	At school
	Daughter (no. 2)	15 years		At school
HH9	Daughter	15 years		At school
HH10	Husband	25–34 category	Postgraduate degree	Engineer and town planner
	Wife	25–34 category	Postgraduate degree	Medical scientist

HH11	Father	45–54 category	Inter (junior) certificate and trades certificate	Electrician
	Mother	45–54 category	Leaving certificate	Works in sales
HH12	Father	42 years	Leaving certificate	Works in HR in telecoms company
	Mother	39 years	Leaving certificate	Housewife
HH13	Grandmother (female adult)	55–64 category	Primary school education only	Housewife
	Granddaughter 14 years		At school	
	Grandson	13 years		At school
HH14	Mother	35–44 years	Third level certificate	Housewife
HH15	Mother	35–44 category	O levels (junior certificate)	Housewife
HH16	Mother	35–44 category	Leaving certificate and nursing course	Part-time nurse and third level student
HH17	Daughter (no. 1) (and mother)	28 years	Third level diploma	Nurse
	Daughter (no. 2)	21 years	Third level certificate	Legal secretary
HH18	Mother	35–44 category	Inter (junior) certificate	Catering assistant
	Daughter	17 years	Junior certificate	At school
HH19	Mother	35–44 category	Undergraduate degree	Community development worker
	Daughter	15 years	Junior certificate	At school
HH20	Daughter	21 years	Third level diploma	Third level student
	Son (no. 1)	19 years	Third level certificate	Third level student (both college students work part-time in supermarket)
HH21	Father	45–54 category	Primary school education only	Maintenance work in hospital
	Mother	35–44 category	Leaving certificate	Machine operator in healthcare company
	Son (no. 1)	16 years	Junior certificate	At school
	Son (no. 2)	13 years		At school
HH22	Adult male	25–34 category	Third level diploma	Self-employed publican and third level student

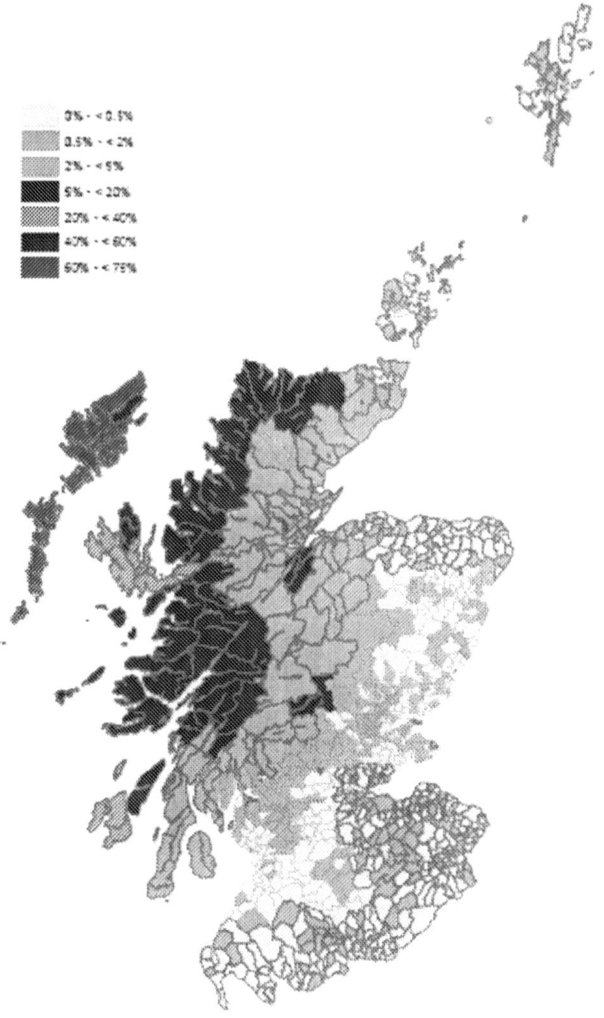

Figure 7.2 Parishes in Scotland by the percentage of people aged three and over who speak Gaelic, 2001 (source: General Registrar of Scotland, © Crown copyright 2005).

decreasing level of intergenerational transmission of Gaelic in the family. On the other hand, there is an increase in Gaelic speakers in more urban and central, 'Lowland' Scotland, explained by a growth in migrant speakers, second-language learning and, in the case of the younger age-cohorts, in Gaelic medium education.

However, whereas Gaelic was once the 'bedfellow of poverty and underprivilege' (Crofters Commission, 1937, quoted in Hunter, 1976: 218) and was sym-

Table 6.2 Information on other household members who did not participate in interviews

Household code	*Household member*	*Age*	*Level of education*	*Occupation*
HH1	Daughter	10.5 years		At school
	Sons	4.5 years		
HH2	Father	48 years	Inter (junior) certificate	Fitter/mechanic
	Son (no. 2)	23 years	Leaving certificate and apprenticeship	Mechanic
	Daughter	22 years	Leaving certificate	Third level student
HH3	Father	55–64 category	Leaving certificate	Retired police officer
HH4	Father	55–64 category	Primary school education only	Part-time farmer and self employed: supplies mechanical parts for cars and tractors
	Son	15 years	Junior certificate	At school
HH5	Baby daughter	5 months		
HH6	Daughter	12 years		At school
	Son	10 years		At school
HH7	Son	5.5 years		At school
	Daughter	3 years		
HH8	Son (no. 1)	12 years		At school
	Son (no. 2)	9 years		At school
	Daughter (no. 3)	4 years		
HH9	Father	45–54 category	Inter (junior) certificate	Porter in hospital
	Mother	45–54 category	Inter (junior) certificate	Carer
HH11	Son	17 years	Leaving certificate	Trainee electrician
HH12	Son	8 years		At school
	Daughter (no. 1)	6 years		At school
	Daughter (no. 2)	3 years		
HH13	Grandfather (husband)	55–64 category	Primary school education only	Unemployed lorry driver

HH14	Father	35–44 years	Third level diploma	Company director (company based in one of business units in Lirmara)
	Son (no. 1)	7 years		At school
	Son (no. 2)	4 years		At school
	Son (no. 3)	2 years		
HH15	Father	35–44 category	O levels and apprenticeship	Building site manager
	Son (no. 1)	10 years		At school
	Son (no. 2)	2 years		
HH16	Father	35–44 category	Inter (junior) certificate	Part-time farmer and self-employed oil distributor
	Son (no. 1)	11 years		At school
	Son (no. 2)	9 years		At school
	Daughter (no. 1)	8 years		At school
	Daughter (no. 2)	2.5 years		
HH17	Father	55–64 category	Third level certificate	Part-time farmer and retired psychiatric nurse
	Mother	55–64 category	Leaving certificate	Carer
	Older daughter's partner	25–34 category	Third level diploma	Police officer
	Older daughter and partner's baby	4 months		
HH18	Father	35–44 category	Inter (junior) certificate	Carpenter
	Son	19 years	Leaving certificate	Third level student
HH19	Father	45–54 category	Inter (junior) certificate	County Council employee (outdoor work)
	Daughter (no. 2)	13 years		At school
HH20	Father	45–54 category	Primary school education only	Warehouse supervisor
	Mother	45–54 category	Leaving certificate	Post office employee
	Son (no. 2)	16 years	Junior certificate	At school
	Son (no. 3)	13 years		At school
HH22	Mother (of adult male interviewee)	55–64 category	Third level diploma	Nurse

Table 6.3 Information on participants in two of the focus groups

Focus group code	*Gender*	*Age*	*Level of education*	*Occupation*
FG2 (non-users of the computer and Internet)	Female No. 1 (F1)	35–44 category	Inter (junior) certificate	Housewife
	Female No. 2 (F2)	35–44 category	Leaving certificate	Care assistant
	Female No. 3 (F3)	35–44 category	Leaving certificate	Housewife
	Female No. 4 (F4)	45–54 category	Inter (junior) certificate	Housewife
	Female No. 5 (F5)	45–54 category	Leaving certificate	Housewife
FG4 (youth club members)	Male No. 1 (M1)	13 years	–	2nd year at school
	Male No. 2 (M2)	15 years	Junior certificate	4th year at school
	Male No. 3 (M3)	15 years	Junior certificate	4th year at school
	Male No. 4 (M4)	15 years	Junior certificate	4th year at school
	Male No. 5 (M5)	16 years	Junior certificate	4th year at school
	Male No. 6 (M6)	17 years	Leaving certificate	Trainee electrician
	Female No. 1 (F1)	14 years	–	3rd year at school
	Female No. 2 (F2)	16 years	Junior certificate	4th year at school

Notes

1 A rural community in the northwest of Ireland, which is referred to as 'Lirmara', was selected for my case study. Accepting the census definition of 'rural' in Ireland as all areas outside towns of more than 1,500 inhabitants, Lirmara, with a population of 814 inhabitants, can be described as a rural community.
2 HH2 denotes household 2, HH4 refers to household 4, etc.
3 Source: Statistical Information on Women's Employment and Gender Equality in Europe www.women-employment.lt/statistics.htm (viewed on 5 September 2006).
4 FG4 denotes Focus Group 4: Focus Group with teenagers in local youth club. See Table 6.3 for more information on participants.
5 FG2 denotes Focus Group 2: Focus Group with non-users of the computer and Internet at home. See Table 6.3 for more information on participants.
6 'Junior Certificate', formerly known as the 'Intermediate Certificate' sat at 15 years (approx.) is the first state examination in secondary school.
7 'Leaving Certificate' sat at 17/18 years (approx.) is the final examination in secondary school and determines entry into Third-Level institutions.

References

Cairncross, F. (2001) *The Death of Distance 2.0: How the Communications Revolution Will Change Our Lives*, London: Texere Publishing.

Case, N. (2000) 'Friction of Distance and Population Growth in the United States' presentation to Geography Department, University of St Thomas, USA, www.stthomas.edu/geog/All%20Projects/StudentProjects/Nate%20final.ppt (viewed on 5 September 2006).

Castells, M. (2000a) *The Rise of the Network Society*, 2nd edn, Vol. 1 of *The Information Age: Economy, Society and Culture*, Oxford: Blackwell.

Castells, M. (2000b) *End of Millennium*, 2nd edn, Vol. 3 of *The Information Age: Economy, Society and Culture*, Oxford: Blackwell.

Central Statistics Office (CSO) (2003) *Quarterly National Household Survey: Information and Communication Technology (ICT), June 2003*, Dublin and Cork: CSO.

Central Statistics Office (CSO) (2004) 'Use of ICT by Households', in *Information Society Statistics – Ireland 2004* [ICT module of the Quarterly National Household Survey, June 2004], Dublin and Cork: CSO, pp. 15–26.

Cornford, J., Gillespie, A. and Richardson, R. (2000) 'Regional Development in the Information Society', in K. Ducatel, J. Webster and W. Herrmann (eds) *The Information Society in Europe: Work and Life in an Age of Globalization*, Lanham, MD: Rowan & Littlefield.

Economist, The (1995) 'Telecommunications Survey', 30 September–6 October.

Gannon, R. (forthcoming) *Exploring the 'Spatial' Dimension of an 'Information Society': An Investigation of the 'Friction of Distance' in a Rural Irish Community*, unpublished PhD thesis: University College Dublin, Ireland.

Gillespie, A. (1992) 'Communications Technologies and the Future of the City', in M. Breheny (ed.) *Sustainable Development and Urban Form*, London: Pion, pp. 67–77.

Gillespie, A., Richardson, R. and Cornford, J. (2001) 'Regional Development and the New Economy', *European Investment Bank Papers* 6 (1): 109–31.

Graham, S. (1997) 'Cities in the Real-time Age: Telecommunications as a Paradigm Challenge to the Conception and Planning of Urban Space', *Environment and Planning* A 29: 105–27.

Graham, S. (1998) 'The End of Geography or the Explosion of Place? Conceptualizing Space, Place and Information Technology', *Progress in Human Geography* 22 (2): 165–85.

Graham, S. and Marvin, S. (1996) *Telecommunications and the City: Electronic Spaces, Urban Place*, London: Routledge.

Grimes, S. (2000) 'Rural Areas in the Information Society: Diminishing Distance or Increasing Learning Capacity?', *Journal of Rural Studies* 16: 13–21.

Harvey, D. (1996) *Justice, Nature and the Geography of Difference*, Oxford: Blackwell.

Lægran, A. (2002) 'The Petrol Station and the Internet Café: Rural Technospaces for Youth', *Journal of Rural Studies* 18: 157–68.

Moyal, A. (1989) 'The Feminine Culture of the Telephone: People, Patterns and Policy', *Prometheus* 7 (1): 5–31.

Romans, F. and Hardarson, Ó. (2006) 'Labour Market Latest Trends – 4th Quarter 2005 Data – Increasing Trend for the Employment Rate', *Statistics in focus – Population and social conditions*, Issue no. 11/2006, Luxembourg: Eurostat.

Skerratt, S. (2003) *The Implications for Rural and Regional Populations of the Irish Government's Provision of Broadband Communications Infrastructure*, National Institute of Regional and Spatial Analysis, Maynooth: National University of Ireland.

Swyngedouw, E. (1993) 'Communication, Mobility and the Struggle for Power over Space', in G. Giannopoulos and A. Gillespie (eds) *Transport and Communications in the New Europe*, London: Belhaven, pp. 305–25.

Thrift, N. (1996) 'New Urban Eras and Old Technological Fears: Reconfiguring the Goodwill of Electronic Things', *Urban Studies* 33: 1463–93.

Valentine, G. and Holloway, S. (2001) 'A Window on the Wider World? Rural Children's Use of Information and Communication Technologies', *Journal of Rural Studies* 17: 383–94.

Ward, C. (1990) *The Child in the Country*, London: Bedford Square Press.

7 Revitalising rural Europe's indigenous languages

'Technologisation' and the Gaelic language

Marsaili Macleod

Introduction

The eminent linguist David Crystal (2002) contends, 'an endangered language will progress if its speakers can make use of electronic technology' (2002: 142). While acknowledging that this is largely a hypothetical statement, Crystal claims to be 'sufficiently convinced' that information technology, and the Internet in particular, is one of six postulates for progress in minority-language (ML) revitalisation (2002: 143). In the context of rural Europe, this is significant because, for the most part, not only are autochthonous minority languages so identified due to the limited numbers of speakers, but also because they are largely synonymous with underdeveloped, peripheral rural regions of the European community (Keane *et al.*, 1993: 399). Think of the Irish Gaeltacht (*Gaeilge*), the Basque Country (*Euskara*), Brittany (*Breton*), the Highlands and Islands of Scotland (*Gàidhlig*), the Dolomites (*Ladin*), west and Northwest Wales (*Cymraeg*), the northern periphery of the Nordic countries (*Saami*) and Galicia (*Galician*). Further to the latest accessions to the EU, an estimated 40 million citizens regularly use a regional or ML: 'a language traditionally used by part of the population of a state that are not dialects of official languages of the state, languages of migrants or artificially created languages' (European Commission, 2006).

Rural areas, which have traditionally been the minority-language heartlands, continue to be subject to major demographic changes. Sustained out-migration of ML-speaking populations from rural areas to urban centres has been succeeded by in-migration of majority-language speakers in the second half of the twentieth century. More recently, this historic growth in urban immigrant-language communities is being paralleled by the establishment of rural immigrant-language communities in minority-language regions, such as the Western Isles in Scotland, as a direct result of Eastern European accession to the European Union (De Lima *et al.*, 2005). These processes of demographic change, together with other outcomes of social and economic integration of rural areas, are challenging the survival of minority languages and their normalised use in the modern context.

In this chapter I wish to consider how digital technologies, and in particular the Internet, are being appropriated by ML speakers in rural areas, and question their potential for supporting minority-language revitalisation and maintenance in recognition of language diversity's contribution to societal well-being, and as an asset for socio-economic development. To explore this embryonic research area, I wish to draw upon the case of the Gaelic language in Scotland, which has recently gained legislative support for its protection through the Gaelic Language (Scotland) Act 2005. It is also 'protected and promoted' under the 1992 treaty of the European Charter of Regional and Minority Languages.

The 'technologisation' of language

The 'technologising of language' refers here, broadly, to the convergence of language and technology (Halliday 1993: 68). There are a variety of different aspects to this relationship. First, those writing from a linguistic perspective understand this process as pertaining to the technologisation of common discourse. Examples include the plethora of neologisms created in relation to the medium of 'netspeak'; the blurring of boundaries of speech and written forms through chatrooms and instant messaging; and new linguistic conventions for expressing feelings and emotions such as the ubiquitous 'smileys' (for a fuller analysis, see Crystal, 2001). Second, the technologisation of language serves to describe, broadly, the appropriation of technologies in the development and delivery of language resources as part of the emerging knowledge economy. This refers to electronic support tools such as online dictionaries, data banks, text-processing software, translation equipment and other business products. Third, we can add to these conceptualisations the use of technology in creating new ways of communicating, thereby transforming the social structures of production and exchange and personal relations (Scanlon and Singh, 2006). A key component of all these aspects of technologisation is the use of Internet applications.

The communicative power of the Internet, and its social potential, has however, given rise to serious concern among both linguists and minority-language supporters. While the former are alarmed by its effects on literacy, and on the technologisation of common discourse as mentioned above, the latter are apprehensive about its capacity to enhance English as the homogenising medium of the 'global village', a tool of cultural imperialism which can potentially contribute to the demise of lesser-used, minority languages. For example, Erikson, writing in 1998 and referring to the frequently touted statistic of 80 per cent of online content being Anglophonic, argued that, rather than foster cultural diversity, the net was hastening the shift to an already dominant language (Erikson, 1998).

Current estimates suggest that 32 perc ent of Internet users are English first-language speakers (Figure 7.1, OECD, 2006), whereas approximately 70 per cent of content is in the English language (OECD, 2006). As such, there is a large pool of English second-language speakers who access the net through English. The corollary of this is that the Internet is growing increasingly multilingual, both in terms of its users thanks to penetration of affordable broadband technology, and more significantly in relation to minority-language mainte-

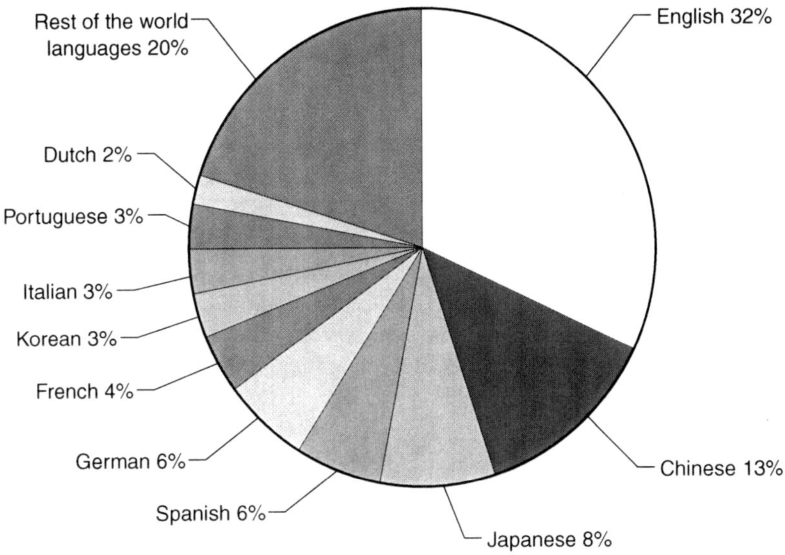

Figure 7.1 Internet users per language (source: adapted from OECD 2006b:13).

nance, in content. The latter is occurring through two parallel processes: first, through more formal and hierarchical structures characterised by Web 1.0 development and including publishing of minority-language literature and the translation of web material into other languages as part of the growth in global e-commerce; second, through a growth in informal, populist activity where users actively participate in creating new content and developing new software. While these types of activity are commonly regarded as part of Web 2.0 developments (O'Reilly, 2005), they were prevalent in the historical origins of the Internet prior to the onset of commercialisation. Facilities for user-generated content include blogging, podcasting and digital video as exemplified by websites such as MySpace and YouTube, in addition to user-generated content platforms such as the Wikipedia encyclopaedia. Collectively, these kinds of interaction have been attributed the label, 'participative web' (OECD, 2006).

The role of the Internet in enhancing linguistic diversity

The increase in the diversity of languages online, and the significance of Internet communication in societal relations today, has stimulated debate among linguists and minority-language planners on the scope of the Internet to support minority-language maintenance and indeed, to challenge the supremacy of dominant languages in particular contexts. Indeed, social theorists Scanlon and Singh (2006) argue that, unless MLs can operate at the level of abstract social integration characterised by relations mediated through a range of technologies, they are destined to decline further. At a perfunctory level, it seems valid to reason that the dynamic growth of the Information and Communications Technology (ICT) industry and the globalisation of ICT-enabled services have the potential to support the maintenance of minority languages in a myriad of ways, 'notwithstanding the limited role it has been able to play in this domain hitherto' (Crystal 2002: 143).

Crystal's (2002) argument hinges on two main axes. First, he contends that the Internet provides an 'even playing field' for languages, overcoming what were previously unequal power relations between minority languages and majority languages over print, the media and public literature. The relative cheapness of producing bi- or multilingual web content has increased the presence of smaller language groups on the web, and has been employed by private organisations to promote a multicultural corporate identity and expand into new language markets. Crystal writes:

> The crucial point is that languages are out there, even if represented by a sprinkling of sites. It is the ideal medium for minority languages, given the relative cheapness and ease of creating a Web page, compared with the cost and difficulty of obtaining a newspaper page, or a programme or advertisement on radio or television.
>
> (Crystal, 2001: 221)

Crystal goes on to argue that, second, the Internet proffers an opportunity to generate (virtual) communities of interest and, in doing so, potentially nullifies the negative impact of out-migration from (rural) minority-language (place-based) communities. That is to say, Crystal is suggesting that virtual online communication can in some way substitute place-based networks, not only by enabling out-migrants to maintain their ML usage but through creation of a new kind of language community incorporating both first-language and second-language users.

Clearly, the rise of the 'participative web' over recent years strengthens the potentiality of the Internet to network ML speakers. Real-time communication through online chatrooms and discussion forums create options not only for network-building and information exchange but, along with interactive web material, for generating opportunities to increase literacy in ML Internet users. This is particularly the case where occasion to exercise writing skills are infrequent or isolated, as is often the case where the ML has limited legislative protection and therefore, limited formal or official use.

In addition to liberalising spatial barriers of social interaction, the net enables minority languages to be more accessible to second-language learners through online resources, thereby expanding the size of, what is likely to be, an otherwise shrinking speech community. The creation of web-based language resources is not relevant to second-language learners alone. Rather, the digitisation, documentation and archiving of language materials online create a cultural resource for future generations of ML speakers. Above all, an increase of an ML in information technology in general, will have the effect of increasing the language's status in society and therefore the propensity of ML speakers to use the language, and transmit it to their children.

Crystal's perspective is based on the notion that the Internet is releasing ML speakers from the constraints of place-based community and the particular identity that this cultivates. Whether, however, the increasing pervasiveness of the Internet can fulfil this utopian vision is questioned by other linguists and commentators. There are, it would seem, significant challenges for minority languages in cyberspace.

While the Internet may foster the growth of an online ML-speaking community, Grenoble and Whaley (2006) are sceptical of conceptualising the web as a new language domain – a setting or function.[1] Although acknowledging that the Internet might potentially supply a 'creative way to increase local language use' (Grenoble and Whaley, 2006: 10) they don't feel it merits co-option as a new language domain, on the grounds that:

> the fact remains that the internet, at this point, is overwhelmingly dominated by a handful of languages even if some web sites arise which employ a local language, speakers of the local language will make greater use of the Internet in a non-local language.
>
> (Grenoble and Whaley, 2006: 10)

Grenoble and Whaley do not qualify this statement with any empirical evidence; however, research by Gandal (2006) into the language of home Internet use by Quebecois supports this assertion. Gandal's results suggested that the majority of native French speakers accessed the web in English, with the younger age cohort more likely to visit English language URL domains than older age cohorts. The study was unable, however, to distinguish whether there was a choice of language or identify which type of websites were visited.

Grenoble and Whaley's (2006) basis for the dismissal of the Internet as a new language domain eludes to the subtle distinction between the volumes of ML online content and the potential for the Internet to foster language vitality and active language use through, for example, interactive web functions. That is to say, one cannot simply equate volume of ML web content with language vitality due to the interplay of sociolinguistic factors that affect interactive web activity in variable ML contexts. An additional but related clause concerns the socio-economic position of ML speakers, and their linguistic situation. The potentiality of technology and the net cannot be isolated from issues of ICT accessibility and user capacity, and the ML's level of fragility – an absolute ML with a small and diffuse language community, and with limited access to computers will engage with ICTs in a more limited way than a close-knit ML community that speaks a language which is an ML elsewhere, and with access to high-speed Internet connections, for example.

Contrary to the belief that computers and the net can support the profile, learning and dissemination of MLs, some analysts believe that the Internet could continue to pose a significant threat to minority languages in the European context. While the net may be growing increasingly multilingual, with a demand for multilingual websites, data retrieval, machine translation and voice-recognition systems, there are concerns that such developments will not extend beyond the principal languages of the world. Thomas *et al.* (2000) comment:

> We find that the threat to linguistic diversity on the Internet will not in the future come from the dominance of one language but from the uneven development of language technology and resources, which given present trends, will privilege half a dozen world languages.
>
> (Thomas *et al.*, 2000: 2)

We might say, therefore, that in the same way that adoption of information technologies by small and medium enterprises (SMEs) is essential in rural Europe in order to maintain competitiveness with urban counterparts, the adoption of information technology, and net applications in particular, are critical for minority-language communities to avoid 'losing ground' in relation to English and other majority languages. The concern is that MLs, which lack modern language resources, run the risk of being excluded from the Internet and their use of a dominant language for Internet-based processes and transactions becomes normalised:

> The weakest language-groups in the EU – both very small state languages and regional and minority languages, inhabit an IT environment that marginalises them through an absence of word-processors, spell-checkers, Internet browsers, IT manuals in their language. There is a danger here that an Internet culture – indeed a computer culture – develops in which people either come to accept it as natural to use a language other than their own when using the Internet, or else feel excluded because of lack of fluency in another language.
>
> (Thomas *et al.*, 2000: 3)

In many ML cases, it is unlikely that the market will be able to provide these bilingual services: minority-language groups are numerically too small to make such developments commercially viable. Unless public funding can be mobilised in support of the development of digital ML resources, either on the grounds of language rights or equal opportunity, then MLs run the risk of being increasingly marginalised from the digital age.

In addition to being disadvantaged by limited size and a lack of critical mass to enable the commercial development of online applications, MLs are affected by a range of locational factors related to their concentration in rural and peripheral regions, which disadvantages their progress relative to majority-language groups. These interrelated factors include (Millard: 2005):

- a less developed and less competitive ICT network infrastructure;
- lower organisational and entrepreneurial capacity;

- lack of knowledge clusters due to small and distributed networks;
- lower levels of ICT knowledge for ICT diffusion, and;
- lower household incomes.

We might add to these a range of associated factors including an older age profile and lower deployment of ICTs in the worksphere due to the economic structure of rural areas.

One issue, which remains to be addressed in the scant literature on MLs and digital technologies, is the extent to which participative web innovations – in software applications and collaborative online ventures – can overcome gaps in digital ML resource provision and can foster and support the use of MLs in virtual space. In the remainder of this chapter I wish to undertake a case-study example of the Gaelic language in Scotland, to examine in more depth how the technologisation of Gaelic can contribute to language revitalisation and sustainable development in ML rural areas from a social and economic perspective. In doing so, I wish to explore in more detail Crystal's thesis, that an endangered language will make progress if its speakers make use of technology, in the context of the (former) Gaidhealtachd, through focusing in particular, on participative web activity.

Reimagining the rural Gaidhealtachd

The rural–urban divide in Gaelic Scotland

In the eleventh century Gaelic was the primary language for most of Scotland; however, over the centuries it has 'retracted' both demographically and geographically.[2] Processes of social and economic integration of previously Gaelic-speaking communities into the modern-state system from the thirteenth century onwards, have resulted in a continued northward retreat of the 'Gaidhealtachd' area – the district where Gaelic is an autochthonous language and passed orally from generation to generation – so that today, Gaelic is a majority community language only in the Western Isles and in northern pockets of the Isle of Skye[3] (see Figure 7.2).

The 2001 Census indicated that 58,652 people in Scotland (1.16 per cent of the population) speak some level of Gaelic of which approximately 55 per cent live in the 'Highlands' (the former 'Gaidhealtachd' local authority areas of Argyll and Bute, Highland Council and *Comhairle nan Eilean Siar* (the Western Isles Council) and 45 per cent in the 'Lowlands' of Scotland (all other local authority areas) (Registrar General for Scotland, 2005). This represents a decennial decrease of 11 per cent, continuing a persistent trend of language decline since the 1891 Census.[4]

Two parallel linguistic trends are occurring. On the one hand, the territorial maintenance of Gaelic is being weakened by increasing fragmentation and attrition of 'native' speakers in the heartlands as a result of natural deaths of Gaelic speakers, continued net loss of Gaelic speakers through migration, and a

bolic of an outmoded and 'backward' lifestyle connected to the croft and the creel of the Gaidhealtachd areas, a combination of improved economic conditions in the Gaidhealtachd areas and relative growth of a Lowland Gaelic-speaking population is challenging these categorisations. Since the 1980s, there has been a resurgence of interest in Gaelic, or a so-called 'Gaelic renaissance' (MacDonald, 1997), which has been driven by the growth of a middle class, urban-based revivalist movement (MacDonald, 1997). Paradoxically, however, there persists, it would seem, a chasm between what have been referred to as the 'urban, intellectual, educated elites' (Chapman, 1978, quoted in MacDonald, 1997) and native Gaelic speakers in what are, or were until recently, Gaelic-speaking communities in the rural Highland periphery.

In general, the language suffers from having a low status, and continues to be viewed by many in the Gaelic heartlands as being old-fashioned and irrelevant, thus the place of Gaelic in the cultural identity of people in the Gaidhealtachd areas continues to weaken. While numerically, an increase of speakers in non-heartland areas may exceed those in the traditional heartlands in the near future, there is a widespread consensus that the revitalisation of Gaelic in Scotland is dependent upon the maintenance of Gaelic in the rural heartlands as a living and working everyday language, embedded in local cultural practices.

The infrastructure: Gaelic language technology

Charalabopoulou *et al.* (2005) argue that the development of language technologies is essential for European languages from the perspective of citizenship and equal opportunity in the new information society. They conceive of languages being differentiated on the basis of being language-technology-poor or language-technology-rich, with the latter as linguistically secure.

The convergence of technology and the Gaelic language has a very short history. The earliest technological developments were concentrated in the broadcasting and media sector when the Gaelic Department of the BBC was established in Glasgow in the 1930s to produce occasional radio broadcasts. It expanded during the 1960s to produce Gaelic television programmes and established offices in Inverness and Stornoway, principal settlements of the Highland mainland and Western Isles respectively, in the 1970s.[5] Whereas some Gaelic speakers had campaigned vociferously for an expanded BBC media service from the streets of Glasgow, not all welcomed this. In 1972 James Shaw Grant, then editor of the *Stornoway Gazette*, commented in a speech at the National Mod:

> The value of Gaelic lies precisely in the fact that it is not the language of commerce and technology, it is not the language of the mass media. It is the language into which one can retire from the hurly-burly of an over-busy world.... It is a folk language, in which people still make their own songs and write their own poetry ... Gaelic has no material value whatsoever and thank God for it. It is not the language of the rat race. That is its supreme value.
>
> (quoted in Hutchinson, 2005: 99)

Hutchinson himself goes on to comment, 'This definitively reactionary view of the language as a docile relic of prelapsarian rural Scotland was unlikely to win friends on the campaigning, radical missionary wing of the late-twentieth-century Gaelic world' (Hutchinson, 2005: 100). Indeed, a range of technological developments was to emerge to enable contemporary expression of Gaelic from the 1980s onwards. While the initial developments stemmed from the Lowland, Anglo-speaking central belt, the next major technological developments related to Gaelic took place at the newly formed national Gaelic College of Scotland in the Isle of Skye.

In 1983 *Sabhal Mòr Ostaig* commenced tertiary courses through the medium of Gaelic. The first course in business and Gaidhealtachd studies was succeeded the following year by an HNC in information technology and office technology which, in keeping with its policy, was delivered through the medium of Gaelic. The visionaries at *Sabhal Mòr Ostaig*, far from seeing Gaelic as a traditional medium of communication, were of the opinion that if Gaelic were to continue to be used in the twenty-first century, it had to be the language of business, commerce and technology. From small seeds sown in the early 1980s, *Sabhal Mòr Ostaig* has been a significant adopter of ICTs in its teaching practices, while educating students to be competent in working in the media, commerce and administration through the medium of Gaelic.

Despite the relatively early ambitions at *Sabhal Mòr Ostaig*, it was some time before language technology tools and resources were developed that could support graduates from *Sabhal Mòr Ostaig* to use Gaelic in more public domains such as the workplace. It was *Sabhal Mòr Ostaig* itself that initiated the first 'content creation' tool. The online Gaelic dictionary, the *Stòr Data*, commenced in 1986 with funding support from no less than 24 organisations. In conjunction with the IT team at *Sabhal Mòr Ostaig*, Gaelic enthusiast Roy Wentworth produced a Gaelic custom dictionary compatible with MS Windows which was, for many years, a fairly rudimentary solution to a Gaelic spell-checker and available to download from the college website.

In 2003 IleTec, a computer solutions company now based in Inverness produced the first Gaelic keyboard. Continuing its commitment to supporting Gaelic's use in 'modern and relevant ways' (IleTec, online: 2006), IleTec launched a Gaelic word-processor in 2005, which, together with the Gaelic keyboard, provides a comprehensive Gaelic desktop for retail at approximately £200. The parallel development of an office suite in Gaelic, Open Office Gàidhlig, for distribution in schools, represents a significant step forward in Gaelic language tools (see Box 7.1).

In 2006 the first nationally agreed spell-checker was produced, with substantial public funding, by the European Language Initiative. Microsoft Corporation donated the search engine, which had been developed for use by the Irish equivalent. Developed through a national partnership, it is both wider in content and in scope than its predecessor. Its purpose is to provide a nationally agreed standard of Gaelic, and as such, it is available to download free from a governmental education website.[6] In this sense, the spell-checker is not simply a tool to

The market for specialised minority-language software is small. Minority-language groups have turned to 'open-source' software to develop customised software in order to address gaps, both through incremental development by individual programmers and collaborative partnerships. 'Open source' describes software for which the source code is made available (online) to the general public for modification and redistribution with limited intellectual property restrictions. Accessibility and affordability make the development and linguistic customisation (part of the process of 'localisation') of open-source software the most practical means of addressing small language-group provision. In Gaelic Scotland, open-source software has been employed to create a Gaelic web-browser (Opera), word-processor (Abiword) and office suite (Open Office 1.1.1). While the voluntary efforts of individuals in the Gaelic open-source community are ongoing, government intervention to stimulate partnership collaborations are recognised as being imperative for the sustainable and significant development of software for educational, commercial and governmental application. The 'localisation' of the Opera web-browser in 2000 formed part of a cross-country, EU-funded initiative under the 'DART' project. *Sabhal Mòr Ostaig*, in its capacity as Scottish partner, undertook the Gaelic localisation process and, in doing so, produced the technical Gaelic terminology which has acted as a foundation for later projects. A more ambitious localisation initiative has been funded through the Scottish government's Education Department in order to produce a word-processor for Gaelic in education. The contract, which was won by Cànan – an offshoot of *Sabhal Mòr Ostaig* – proposed localising the Open Office suite to produce a word-processor, spreadsheet, presentation package and drawing software in Gaelic. Open-office Gàidhlig 1.1.1 was launched in 2005, and distributed to Gaelic Medium Schools. The licence conditions do, however, enable the product to be distributed to anybody and the product will be released shortly along with the source code. In parallel, a private software company localised AbiWord source code to produce the Gaelic word-processor, Sgrìobh. Despite expectations, Sgrìobh, which retails at £200 along with a Gaelic keyboard, has had limited take-up and future modifications are uncertain. However, as Henderson *et al.* comment 'it is important that the development is not treated as an isolated event' (2005: 176). Despite voluntary work to maintain the Opera web-browser in Gàidhlig, the software has not kept up with more recent versions of the Opera web-browser. Ongoing development of Open Office Gàidhlig is hoped to be realised through the Open Office community.

Box 7.1 Localisation of open-source software

enhance the production of written documentation in Gaelic, but a means of standardising local variations, through consistency with the Gaelic Orthographic Conventions (GOC).

While the original GOC, established in 1981, were designed to ensure consistency for Scottish Qualifications examinations, the expansion of Gaelic into other areas of public life in Scotland means that the 2005 GOC has much wider relevance. The development of linguistic conventions, and their application in print, media and public literature, form part of an ongoing process of 'corpus cultivation' – involving terminology unification, lexical modernisation and stylistic simplification – to extend Gaelic's functional use. The adoption of these conventions is enabled through publication and dissemination on the Internet, and the public literature which is distributed on the net in accordance with the conventions. These conventions help to modernise Gaelic's lexicon and standardise its writing system thereby making it more practical. The launch of an inter-university project to produce a comprehensive online historical dictionary of Gaelic (*Faclair na Gàidhlig*/Dictionary of the Scottish Gaelic Language) in 2006 will, it is hoped, supply the basis for more systematic and coordinated corpus development in the future. On the other hand, the language still lacks a comprehensive electronic linguistic corpus, which could act as a basis for a range of more sophisticated language technologies (see Box. 7.2).

Dissemination and adoption of these content-creation tools outside of the educational community are critical for Gaelic's normalised use in a PC culture, and a key challenge for the Gaelic community. The recent announcement of a joint venture between *Bòrd na Gàidhlig*, the Gaelic development agency established in 2005, the University of Strathclyde, Learning and Teaching Scotland and Microsoft to develop support for Gaelic in Windows Vista and Office 2007 packages will provide a significant boost in this direction. The localisation of Microsoft Vista and

> In 2002 Lancaster University led a research partnership to examine the development of corpus text and annotation for Britain's indigenous languages, including Gaelic in partnership with *Sabhal Mòr Ostaig*. The project, entitled 'Language Engineering Resources for the British Isles Indigenous Minority Languages', aimed to investigate the practical and technical issues that indigenous languages, including Gaelic, raise for language engineering resource development, especially in terms of spoken corpus collection, transcription and annotation. The project outcomes included a small annotated Gaelic corpus. This research could act as the foundation for expansion to a wider electronic lexical database, to underpin machine translation and speech technology and grammatical aids. There has not as yet, however, been any software developed to deal with the syntactic or grammatical issues in Gaelic.

Box 7.2 Corpus development

Office stemmed from the demand for bilingual computing from teaching staff in Gaelic Medium Education. Translation of Vista, the new operating system from Microsoft, into Gaelic will furnish an integrated Gaelic interface, web-browser and e-mail client while Office will supply a suite of productivity software (press release, 16 February, 2007). The translation of approximately 600,000 words into Gaelic is anticipated to be completed by September 2007 and will address what have been to date key gaps in the infrastructure (press release, 16 February, 2007). There remain, however, no grammatical aids for Gaelic, although localisation ports of the open-source grammar-checker *An Gramadóir*, are underway.[7]

The development of Gaelic educational software and digital content development has been fragmented and led by a mixture of the education sector, central government and international language software companies. The majority of material is based on CD-ROMs or multimedia learning modules, such as the CD-ROM for Gaelic learners produced by *Cànan*, the multimedia and communications company at the Gaelic college on the Isle of Skye. Co-funded by the Education Department, the European Commission, the Scottish Council for Education and Technology, the Gaelic Broadcasting Committee and *Cànan* itself, the CD was distributed free to secondary schools and is available for sale to the general public. The launch of '*Gàidhlig-air-loidhne*' (Gaelic-online) as part of the Education Department's funded organisation, Learning and Teaching Scotland (LTS), in 2004, along with the establishment of a Gaelic and ICT Implementation Group for education, have driven computer-based learning initiatives in Gaelic medium teaching. Outside of the educational sector, and in some instances in partnership with it, the BBC has developed a range of online interactive learning materials for schools and for wider language learning (Figure 7.3). While some mainstream multilingual language packages incorporate speech recognition and processing technology, no applications have been developed to enable automatic speech recognition and speech synthesis for Gaelic to date.

To date, it might be concluded that the Gaelic language has come some way in the development of language-technology tools, through a combination of localised initiatives driven by impassioned individuals, and more recently, nationally supported ventures as Gaelic gains increased recognition in the political system. However, little is known about either the extent or the nature of adoption of any of the content-creation tools or digital resources for Gaelic. Without extensive research, the only means of gaining an insight into how embedded ICTs are within Gaelic speakers' social and informational networks is through an examination of the evidence of Gaelic's presence online.

The Gaelic Internet revolution

The 'Gaelicisation' of the Internet, as in other ML situations, is occurring through both formal organisational use of Gaelic and translation of organisational material into Gaelic, and through informal, interactive web developments. A review of the linguistic content of 60 websites with Gaelic material was undertaken in order to examine the nature of Gaelic online, and to deduce both

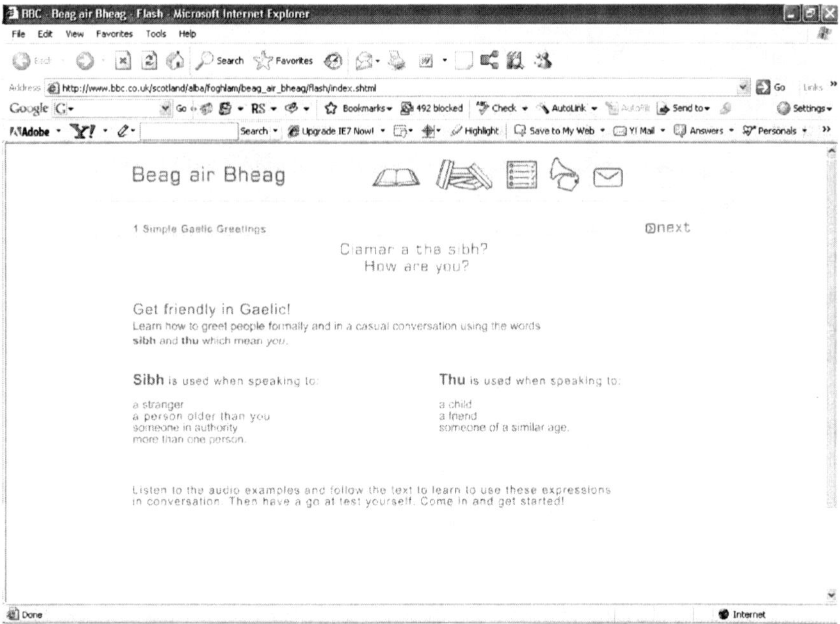

Figure 7.3 The BBC's interactive website 'Beag air Bheag' (Little by Little) which gives a taste of Scottish Gaelic for beginners (source: www.bbc.co.uk/scotland/alba/foghlam/beag_air_bhead (accessed 12 February, 2007)).

the scope of engagement of the language online through formal organisational websites, and the nature of user-generated content. The 'snapshot' review did not aim to be statistically representative; rather, it strove to capture the diversity of Gaelic online through a random sample of websites with Gaelic content, stratified on the basis of authorship. Personal authorship was treated as 'participative web' content, whereas commercial, voluntary organisation or public organisation content was treated as 'formal' web content.

Gaelic and the formal web

Unlike in some other ML situations, historically there has been no legislative framework to protect and promote the use of the Gaelic language through statutory bilingual provision in public or commercial organisations. This is not the case, for example, in the neighbouring Celtic country Wales, where a statutory language scheme requires equal prominence to be given to both Welsh and English by public bodies in service provision. As such, the development of Gaelic-English bilingualism online has occurred at the discretion of individual organisations, and has evolved without statutory guidance. A review of Gaelic on organisations' website interfaces reveals a mixed picture. The homepage is the typical entry-point to a website for users. It reveals whether Gaelic forms part of an organisation's corporate identity, and commonly directs the visitor to any Gaelic content. Five different types of homepages are identified for organisations that feature some Gaelic material online (see Table 7.1).

The first four types of homepage are 'gateways' to a bilingual website, where content is presented both in Gaelic and English to some extent. Type 1, which gives precedence to English on the homepage but which offers a Gaelic version (with equivalent or non-equivalent content), is typical of significant public-sector organisations that are likely to have adopted a language policy. Examples include the Crofters' Commission, a regulatory body for croft (land) holdings which are principally within the former Gaidhealtachd area, and Scottish Natural Heritage, the agency responsible for caring for Scotland's natural heritage. Both organisations have interests in the cultural and natural heritage, and have a strong presence in the Gaelic-speaking heartlands. An animation company that 'promotes the Gaelic language and culture to a wider audience through the medium of animation and interactivity' (West Highland Animations, online, 2007) is the only example of Type 1 from the private sector. Additional examples include the Royal Family and Prince of Wales websites, which on the basis of a language policy centred on a linguistic-rights perspective, offer a reduced level of Gaelic content through a Gaelic web version.

Type 2, which gives precedence to Gaelic on the homepage and offer an equivalent English version, is provided by 'Gaelic organisations', whose remit is to promote and develop the Gaelic language in the media, educational, and Gaelic-language development sectors. Type 3, a homepage designed solely to offer a language choice, was only revealed by one example: *Faclair na Gàidhlig*,[8] a project to develop a historical dictionary of Gaelic. Whereas this type of homepage is common in for example, Welsh and Catalonian public-sector organisations and valued for its language equality, it is rare in Gaelic Scotland as it requires equivalent information to be available in both languages. Close in ethos, though not in design, is Type 4 where the homepage contains both English and Gaelic material.

The fifth type of homepage contains no Gaelic version despite the organisation providing some Gaelic content – such as key organisational documents and Gaelic learning resources – online. Surprisingly, the website of the local authority for the Western Isles, *Comhairle nan Eilean Siar* (Western Isles Council),[9] falls into this category, along with the government-funded development agency for the Highlands and Islands, Highlands and Islands Enterprise.[10]

Table 7.1 Gaelic organisational content online: types of homepage

Type	*Description*
Type 1	Monolingual English with 'button' to Gaelic version
Type 2	Monolingual Gaelic with 'button' to English version
Type 3	Homepage designed solely to offer language choice
Type 4	Entirely bilingual
Type 5	No Gaelic version or Gaelic content given

The prominence of bilingualism on organisations' homepages is closely related to the extent and nature of bilingual content. Where an English version is offered (Type 2), then the content is equivalent to that of the Gaelic. The contrary does not apply, however, to Type 1 homepages. Whereas the earlier example of the Crofters' Commission homepage leads to an entirely equivalent version of this small and relatively 'static' site, in the case of SNH, the Gaelic button directs the user to a Gaelic 'contents' list which is offered within the English interface (Figure 7.4).

The organisation's Gaelic language policy, an overview of the concern's remit and objectives, along with key documents are available in Gaelic. In stark contrast is the Gaelic web version of the local authority website for the Highland area which, at the time of writing, only features a bilingual statement on its statutory obligation to prepare a Gaelic Language Plan. On the other hand, when organisations are offering services tailored to the Gaelic-speaking community in addition to English mainstream services, the Gaelic version of the website may contain content that is available in Gaelic only. Examples include the Gaelic webpages of the BBC[11] and of *Gàidhlig-air-loidhne* (Gaelic online), a subgroup of the national educational body Learning and Teaching Scotland.[12]

Whereas public concerns are most likely to offer a language choice in the viewing of web content to cater for the needs of its bilingual customer base, there is a notable absence of online Gaelic content in the private sector. Given the limited Gaelic-speaking market, the economic rationale for web translation

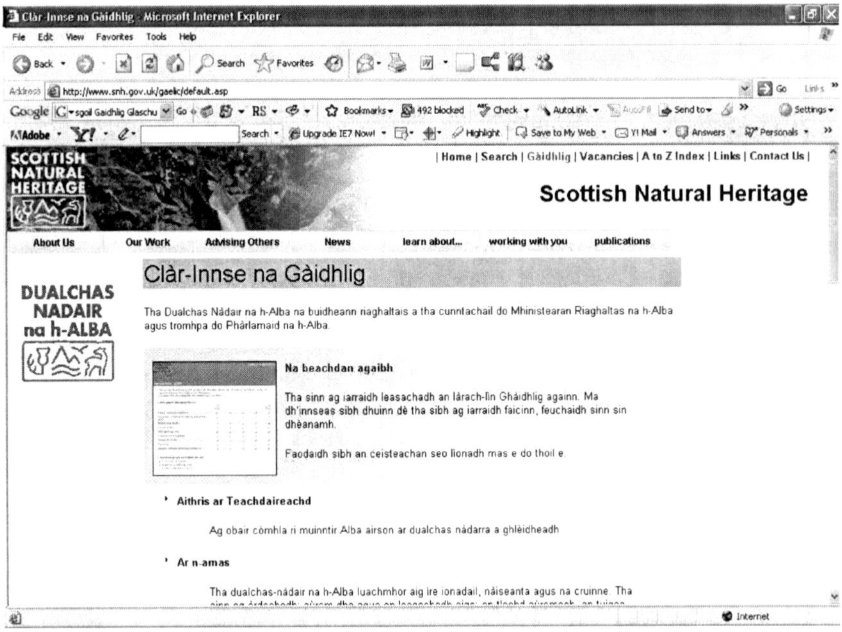

Figure 7.4 The Gaelic 'contents' (clàr-innse na Gàidhlig) in the Gaelic version of the Scottish Natural Heritage website (source: www.snh.gov.uk/Gaelic/ (accessed 12 February, 2007)).

and (Gaelic–English) bilingual commercial services is weak – particularly given that all Gaelic speakers are fluent English speakers. Notwithstanding Gaelic-specific companies and organisations, previous research into the use of Gaelic in the marketing and selling of business products and services revealed that few businesses employ Gaelic in order to gain, for example, customer loyalty, niche marketing, or a competitive edge even within localised, Gaelic-speaking markets (Chalmers, 2003). Indeed, the potential for customers to engage in the world of e-commerce through the medium of Gaelic would appear to be very rare: the organisation *Comhairle nan Leabraichean* (the Gaelic Books Council) sells its Gaelic products online through its bilingual website yet when the user navigates to the online marketplace – to checkout, payment and delivery options – the content is in English only.[13]

Furthermore, an examination of voluntary bodies and local websites reveals a very limited array of Gaelic material. Cultural concerns, such as the *Ceòlas* music festival,[14] promote a Gaelic identity and feature a predominantly bilingual websites, yet local community websites are typically in English only, even in areas where Gaelic is still a community language. This remains the case when the site is targeted as much at locals as at non-locals, such as *Comunn Eachdraidh an Toabh Siar* (West Side Historical Society) in the Isle of Lewis.[15] Explanations for these language choices requires further investigation but might include low literacy skills, a lack of resources for translation, or simply not perceiving language choice as a (political) issue.

Explanations for the differing levels of online Gaelic content in the public sector would appear to be related to the breadth of content of organisations' websites (and therefore the cost of translation); the type of services offered through Gaelic; the presence or absence of a Gaelic language policy, and the degree to which Gaelic has been 'mainstreamed' into service provision. While the 'geographical reach' of an organisation might be considered an explanatory factor in the presence or absence of bilingual content online, this does not seem to hold given that major public organisations in the former Gaidhealtachd area do not offer a Gaelic version of their websites.

This brief review of Gaelic in organisations' websites suggests that to date, the development of Gaelic service provision in the public, voluntary and private sectors – with the exception of 'Gaelic organisations' and the BBC – is fragmented, with many reticent in producing Gaelic interfaces and content. The appearance of Gaelic in formal sites frequently appears tokenistic and unplanned, and rarely as comprehensive in provision as the English equivalent content. Poor navigation between English and Gaelic versions of websites, inconsistency between the languages of the web domain name and organisation name, and between the domain name and email addresses, further exacerbate the image of Gaelic as being a poor relation to English, and concomitantly, such factors are unlikely to instil trust in a user wishing to view Gaelic content. Whether, however, the demand for online Gaelic services exists and whether speakers have the skills and inclination to take advantage of the web to access information, networks, and services and products, needs to be investigated.

Gaelic and the 'participative web'

Whereas the growth in the volume of Gaelic in more formal web structures has been fairly timid, and organisations somewhat reticent in producing Gaelic content – and therefore, in driving developments in Gaelic-language technologies – the development of informal activity in the form of virtual language communities and blogs has been relatively more expedient. As suggested above, the net's potential to foster language vitality through active engagement and usage is where the significance of the technology to support the maintenance and growth of ML communities lies.

Aside from the emergence of a plethora of individual Gaelic blogs, online chatrooms and forums have allowed individuals to engage with other Gaelic speakers in the online community, with several online discussion groups developing in Yahoo!, Google and MSN. Unsurprisingly, the majority of members of such groups form an international community. A Manchester-based Gaelic speaker established the blog-portal '*Tìr nam Blòg*' (Land of the Blog) in December 2005 (Figure 7.5). It is modelled on the Welsh equivalent and acts as a central point for locating Gaelic blogs – with the governing rule that all material is in Gaelic only. With links to approximately 30 individuals' blogs, *Tìr nam Blòg* claims to be more than just a portal, but a meeting place for Gaelic speakers. Yet, while Crystal envisages the net as enabling out-migrants to communicate with fellow ML speakers, in the case of Gaelic, the virtual web community is dominated by Gaelic learners.

Figure 7.5 The Gaelic blog-portal, Tìr nam Blòg (Land of the Blog) (source; www.tirnamblog.com (accessed 12 February, 2007)).

The MSN group '*an t-Seòmar-Chòmhraidh Gàidhlig*' (the Gaelic Conversation Room) was established by a German learner of Gaelic, and the *Fòram na Gàidhlig* moderator is a learner of Gaelic from southwest Scotland. While, without further analysis, it is not possible to identify the origins of contributors or their method of language acquisition, the forums clearly help to generate Gaelic-language networks to support learners who are often living in areas with limited opportunities to speak Gaelic locally.

Of the 104 (of 199) members who disclose their location on *Fòram na Gàidhlig*, the majority are located in North America with less than 8 per cent of members based in the Gaelic heartlands (see Table 7.2). This particular webgroup is divided into three sections: a 'general' section which comprises issues of interest to learners, including grammar, word of the day, Gaelic lessons, Gaelic news and a bilingual section (where contributors supply an English translation); a 'Gaelic only' section incorporating Gaelic news and politics, science and technology, poetry and music, and general conversation; and finally, an 'other languages' section for those learning Gaelic through a medium other than English. Similarly, the MSN group is targeted at learners, providing support materials and links, in addition to the chance to use Gaelic in a supportive environment.

There are several online developments whose purpose is more targeted towards campaigning and lobbying for the Gaelic language in general. The Yahoo group, *Iomairtean Gàidhlig*, was established and is moderated by the Edinburgh-based campaign group *Fàs*. Its purpose is to supply 'Information, news and views about Gaelic development, Gaelic campaigns and the Gaelic campaign group Fàs' (*Iomairtean Gàidhlig*, online, 2006). Founded in 2002, this group has 202 members and, through email notifications, web-based postings, and a file-uploading service, it acts as a knowledge network, aiming to stimulate debate and action on Gaelic matters among Gaelic-language activists. Highly political in its content, and active in debating and responding to localised issues and consultations over, for example bilingual road signage and Gaelic medium education, the membership comprises speakers from the international Gaelic (often second-language learners) community.

Table 7.2 Fòram na Gàidhlig – geographical membership

Member location	*Membership*	
	No.	*%*
Skye and the Western Isles	8	7.69
Rest of Scotland	24	23.08
Rest of the UK	13	12.50
Rest of EU	15	14.42
North America	39	37.50
Other	5	4.81
Total members (specifying location)	104	100.00

Source: http://31.freebb.com/gaidhlig/gaidhlig.html (accessed 30 November 2006).

A parallel online development is the establishment of the campaigning website 'SaveGaelic.org'. While criticised by activists on the above forum for both its English title and predominantly English-language content, SaveGaelic.org describes itself as 'a living project that has been set up to help preserve what is left of the Scottish Gaelic language and to promote its use where possible to help this language survive' (SaveGaelic.org, 2006). It was founded in 2003 and receives all its funding and web support from an Australian web-hosting firm. It is not the only net-based Gaelic-language initiative to have originated overseas. Gaeldom's only podcast is produced in Washington, DC by two Gaelic-learning enthusiasts. Podcast on a fortnightly basis, 'Gaelcast' features interviews, news and features intended for both learners and fluent speakers of Gaelic.

The evidence suggests that those who organise and voice their opinions on the Internet on topics of importance to Gaelic and minority-language issues are in fact, typically second-language speakers in the international rather than the (indigenous) Gaidhealtachd community. This has not escaped observation and comment by the online Gaelic community. Scholes (2006), himself a learner of Gaelic and active contributor to *Tìr nam Blòg* and other online Gaelic groups, comments:

> Up until now, there are only two bloggers who are native Gaelic speakers that are putting their material on *Tìr nam Blòg* and that has started a debate amongst bloggers.... A Blogger from Massachusetts said that he was concerned that this was portraying the views on the Gaelic language to the world from the perspective of learners only. Is this a good or a bad thing or is there perhaps even a touch of arrogance in this?
>
> (Scholes, 2006: 36 translated from the Gaelic original)[16]

He refers here to the legitimacy of learners to speak on behalf of the (entire) Gaelic community and indeed, goes on to claim that online networks are not a substitute for, but a support to, place-based networks and face-to-face interaction within the learner community. While the net may be helping to break down vertical barriers, allowing ML speakers to engage with other, previously unavailable ML speakers, and to access information on ML issues, the net does not appear to be supporting horizontal networks among the place-based, indigenous Gaelic community, or what might in developmental terms, be regarded as 'bottom-up' development.

There are two notable exceptions to this trend. The first exception is *Fòram Gàidhlig Inbhir Nis* (Inverness Gaelic Forum), a community-based organisation located in the predominantly English-speaking capital of the Highlands.[17] Formed to represent the views of the Gaelic community in their locality, the *Fòram* website states:

> Fòram Gàidhlig Inbhir Nis ... looks to provide a regular open forum raising issues in areas such as education, broadcasting, bilingual signage, culture,

> and more, ensuring that 'an Guth na Coimhearsnachd' (the voice of the community) is heard by officials and organisations at this time of unprecedented growth and change in the city.
>
> (*Fòram Gàidhlig Inbhir Nis*, online, 2006)

The *Fòram* has utilised its network of Gaelic supporters to lobby and campaign for Gaelic in the city, using email as a tool to encourage people to act and write in support of local and national Gaelic developments. With an emphasis on being inclusive, all of the *Fòram*'s electronic literature is bilingual and the URL of the website is in Gaelic, reflecting the focused objectives of the organisation. The website contains a discussion forum, with 47 participating members, to support the *Fòram*'s social networking function (Figure 7.6).

The second exception is in the southern peninsula of the Isle of Skye. In December 2005, a local authority released a contentious proposal, instigated by the local Gaelic Parents Group *Comunn nam Pàrant Shlèite*, to designate the primary school in Sleat, Skye as a dedicated Gaelic school.[18] This led to the establishment of an opposition group named 'Sleat Primary School for All' in January 2006, at an inaugural meeting instigated and chaired by a 'returner' resident, Neil Robertson. Shortly thereafter, 'Sleat Primary School for All' had established a professional website in support of their cause.[19] The bilingual website has a file-sharing service, enables visitors to register to receive updates, links to press coverage, in addition to information on membership; the campaign; dates for the

Figure 7.6 The website of Fòram Gàidhlig Inbhir Nis (source: www.inbhirnis.org/ (accessed 12 February, 2007).

diary; how to help the campaign; write to the Council; and meeting minutes. Its purpose is to engender support through the 'networked community' for their cause and, more importantly, to facilitate enactment of this support through following the 'write to the Council' and 'how you can help' webpages.

It was some weeks later that the pre-existing group, *Comunn nam Pàrant Shlèite* launched its website which, rather than focusing on the wider constitution and objectives of the group, was created solely to engender support for the proposal to designate Sleat Primary School as a dedicated Gaelic school.[20] This somewhat less professional bilingual website contains the following features: information about the committee; how to help; links both to Gaelic organisations and to information to inform readers' opinions; open letters (in support of the proposals), and a link to an online petition and standard letter of support (Figure 7.7).

While the topic of education delivery might usually be of interest to members of this rural community alone, emotive debates on Gaelic minority-language concerns meant that the future of Sleat Primary School became a national – and even international – issue. Both campaigning groups made selective use of the Internet to engage with the wider Gaelic-speaking community and with those with an interest in matters relating to Gaelic.

That two opposing bodies deployed the net to empower their organisations in this rural community, and to engage in international debate is at first surprising: there are no other examples of such public campaigning on Gaelic-related issues

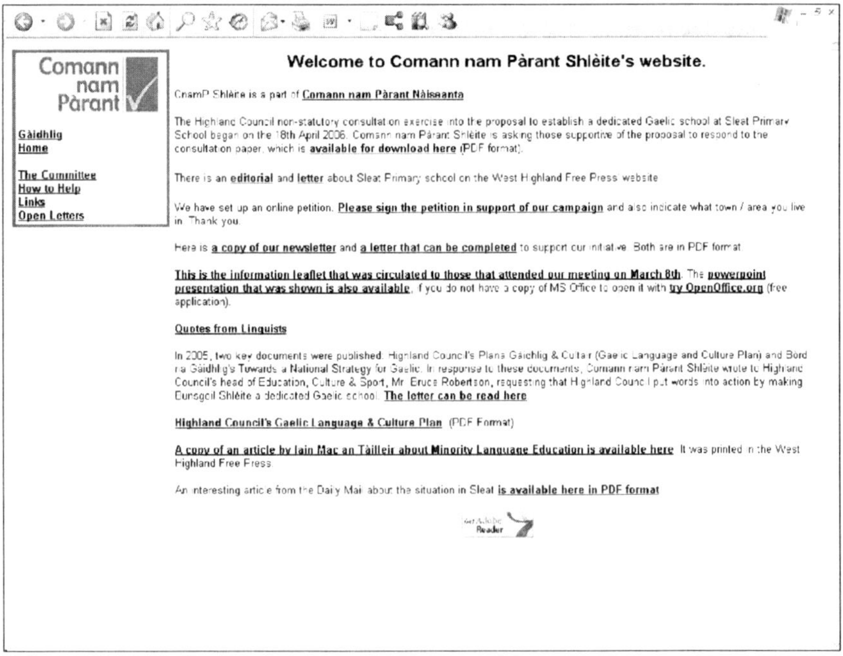

Figure 7.7 The website of Comann nam Pàrant Shlèite (source: www.cnampshleite.org.uk (accessed 14D ecember, 2006)).

despite similar circumstances occurring in the Western Isles in response to the local-authority proposals for designation of Gaelic schools. However, unlike the majority of rural Highland communities with significant proportions of Gaelic speakers, Sleat benefits from a generally younger population, and in particular a younger Gaelic-speaking population, and access to a technologically advanced college in *Sabhal Mòr Ostaig*. The college has not only played a part in developing the local technological infrastructure (in high-speed broadband connectivity) but has skilled the population in its capacity as both a public learning environment, and as the area's foremost employer – and by implication, resulting in higher than average application of ICTs in the occupational workforce and ICT-enabled peer networks.

These features make Sleat stand apart from the majority of Gaelic-speaking, rural communities in the Highlands and Islands. The growth in a range of ICT-enabled projects at *Sabhal Mòr Ostaig* further exemplifies the capacity of a previously dying Gaelic-language community to be regenerated through Internet-based activities. A good example is the *Tobar an Dualchais* (Kist o Riches) project, a collaborative venture to digitise the Gaelic audio archive, which had previously been collected, maintained and managed by the School of Scottish Studies in Edinburgh.[21] The project manager states, 'We thought it was important from a cultural point of view that this material should be returned in some way to the communities where it was gathered' (Martin MacIntyre in BBC news release, 1999). Could the Internet be enabling, therefore, indigenous Gaelic communities to reclaim their linguistic heritage from urban centres of industry and commerce and, in doing so, enhancing their own capacity to participate in the digital age?

Conclusion

While ICT in general and the Internet in particular have the potential to foster multilingualism and to empower minority-language cultures, there would appear to be a set of challenges that need to be overcome in order to realise this potential.

The premise that the development of an ML community of interest online can support ML maintenance by co-joining an otherwise disparate or weakening community is not unproblematic. There is little foundation to the assertion that international learners and local native speakers can unite online to form one language community in support of an ML's maintenance and/or revitalisation, as suggested by Crystal (2002). Indeed, as evidenced by an examination of this online Gaelic community, it might be argued that a digital divide is emerging: between a learner community comprising (younger) language activists with an ability and capacity to engage in new technologies, and an older, native, Gaelic-speaking group in the rural periphery less able to benefit from new technologies. While it may be overly simplistic to apply the rural–urban distinction, the extent to which rurality is contributing to Gaelic speakers in the heartland being under-represented online is worthy of further investigation: that is to say, are causal and associative locational features inhibiting native Gaelic speakers' participation in the digital age?

The case of Sleat Primary School illustrates the potential use of the net to debate local ML issues in an international arena. However, a tendency of native Gaelic speakers to shy away from sensitive issues relating to Gaelic and language rights has meant that the Internet, rather than empowering local Gaelic-speaking communities, is enabling non-indigenous speakers to appropriate the Gaelic culture and its identity into the national and international arena. At the same time, individuals, community organisations and even the public sector in the rural heartlands are typically reticent in representing Gaelic online, thereby reinforcing Gaelic's lack of utility in the modern context in the autochthonous language area. This raises research questions related to rural Gaelic speakers' perceptions of 'authenticity' and 'legitimacy' of Gaelic learner- (and by implication non-local)-led interactive webgroups and 'cool technologies', such as the Gaelic podcast.

Should Internet applications and services, and ICT-associated language resources, be excluded from everyday language practices in areas where Gaelic survives as a community language, the symbolic relationship between the language and an outmoded lifestyle will be reinforced, and will offer little incentive for intergenerational transmission of the language and second-language learning either in youth or adulthood. Only through continued development of language technologies which enable speakers to comfortably live through Gaelic on the Internet and ICT-enabled applications, will technology be truly positioned to support, rather than diminish, minority languages in the European context.

Notes

1 Generally speaking, the greater the range of language domains, the 'stronger' a language is in maintaining itself.
2 For a comprehensive overview of the history of Gaelic in Scotland, see Withers (1984) or MacKinnon (1991).
3 In modern-day speech, 'the Gaidhealtachd' is commonly used synonymously with the historically Gaelic-speaking geographical area of the Highlands and Islands of Scotland. As noted by Herd and Jentsch (2006), however, the label 'the Gaidhealtachd' is not truly interchangeable with 'the Highlands', referring as it does to the language and culture of Gaelic-speaking communities, rather than the geography itself.
4 There is one exception to this trend. The 1971 Census recorded a small increase in Gaelic speakers, attributed to the rephrasing of the question on Gaelic. In 1891 there were 254, 415 Gaelic speakers accounting for 6.84 per cent of the Scottish population (MacKinnon, 2006).
5 In 1976 BBC Radio Highland was established with a Gaelic-friendly remit and morning Gaelic news bulletins. *Radio nan Eilean* in Stornoway also produced Gaelic output. In 1985 BBC *Radio nan Gàidheal* was launched, subsuming the Gaelic content of Radio Highland and *Radio nan Eilean*.
6 The spell-checker is available to download from www.ltscotland.org.uk/gaidhlig/.
7 *An Gramadóir*, along with a range of additional language tools developed by Kevin P. Scannell can be viewed at http://borel.slu.edu/gramadoir/index.html (accessed 23 January 2007).
8 The URL for *Faclair na Gàidhlig* is www.faclair.ac.uk.
9 The URL for *Comhairle nan Eilean Siar* is www.cne-siar.gov.uk.
10 The URL for Highlands and Islands Enterprise is www.hie.co.uk.

11 The URL for the BBC Gaelic website is www.bbc.co.uk/alba.
12 The URL for Learning and Teaching Scotland's Gaelic project pages is www.ltscotland.org.uk/Gaidhlig.
13 The URL for *Comhairle nan Leabhraichean* is www.gaelicbooks.net.
14 The URL for *Ceòlas* is www.ceolas.co.uk.
15 The URL for *Comann Eachdraidh an Toabh Siar* is www.ceats.org.uk.
16 Gu ruige seo, chan eil ann ach dithis bhlogair aig an robh Gàidhlig bho thùs a tha a' cur an cuid sgriòbhadh air Tìr nam Blòg agus tha sin air deasbad a thòiseachadh am measg nam blogairean … Thuirt Blogair bho Mhassacheusetts gun robh eagal air gun robh sin a' toirt seallaidh air a' Ghàidhlig dhan t-saoghal bho shùilean luchd-ionnsachaidh a-mhàin. An e rud math no dona a th'ann an sin no a bheil fiù 's boinne dànadais na lùib?
17 At the time of the 2001 Census, only 4.6 per cent of the total population of Inverness had any oral Gaelic competence.
18 In Scotland, Gaelic medium education units are situated within English medium primary schools. In Sleat Primary School, the school role in the Gaelic medium unit was higher than in the English medium unit prompting a proposal from *Comunn nam Pàrant Shlèite* to designate the school as a dedicated Gaelic school. Glasgow Gaelic Primary School is currently the only dedicated Gaelic primary school in Scotland. It opened in August 2006.
19 The URL for Sleat Primary School for All is www.sleatprimaryforall.org.
20 The URL for *Comann nam Pàrant Shlèite* is www.cnampshleite.org.uk.
21 The URL for *Tobar an Dualchais* is www.smo.uhi.ac.uk/dualchas/.

References

BBC news eelease (1999) *Gaelic Makes Sound Use of the Internet*, Friday 19 November 1999.

Chalmers, D. (2003) *The Economic Impact of Gaelic Arts and Culture*, unpublished PhD thesis, Glasgow Caledonian University.

Charalabopoulou, F., Carayannis, G. and Steinhauer, G (2005) *Deploying ICT to Empower Linguistic Diversity*, paper presented at the 7th Hellenic-European Conference on Computer Mathematics and Its Applications, September 2005, Athens. Online. Available online at: www.aueb.gr/pympe/hercma/proceedings2005/H05-FULL-PAPERS-1/CHARALABOPOULOU-CARAYANNIS-STEINHAUER-1.pdf (accessed 5 November 2006).

Coupland, N. (2003) 'Introduction: Sociolinguistics and Globalisation', *Journal of Sociolinguistics* 7 (4): 465–472.

Crystal, D. (2001; 2nd edn 2004) *Language and the Internet*, Cambridge: Cambridge University Press.

De Lima, P., Jentsch, B. and Whelton, R. (2005) 'Migrant Workers in the Highlands and Islands', Report to Highlands and Islands Enterprise by UHI PolicyWeb and National Centre for Migration Studies. Online. Available online at: www.hie.co.uk/migrant-workers-2005.html (accessed 12 October 2006).

Erikson, Jim (1998) 'Cyberspeak: The Death of Diversity: Will the English-dominated Internet Spell the End of Other Tongues?', *Asiaweek* 3 July 1998: 15. Online. Available online at: www.asiaweek.com/asiaweek/98/0703/feat_7_millenium.html (accessed 4 November 2006).

European Commission (2006) *Regional and Minority Languages of the European Union*. Online. Available online at: http://ec.europa.eu/education/policies/lang/languages/langmin/regmin_en.html (accessed 14 October 2006)

Fòram Gàidhlig Inbhir Nis (2006) Online. Available online at: www.inbhirnis.org (accessed 3 November 2006).

Gandal, N. (2006) 'Native Language and Internet Usage', *International Journal of the Sociology of Language* 182: 25–40.

Global Reach (2006) *Global Internet Statistics (by Language)*. Online. Available online at: http://global-reach.biz/globstats/index.php3 (accessed 5 November 2006).

Grenoble, L.A. and Whaley, L.J. (2006) *Saving Languages: An Introduction to Language Revitalization*, Cambridge: Cambridge University Press.

Halliday, M.A.K. (1993) 'Language in a Changing World', in R.B. Baldauf, Jr (ed.) *Occasional Paper Number 13*, Deakin, ACT, Australia: Applied Linguistics Association of Australia.

Henderson, J., Brown, E. and Mitchel, C. (2005) 'Adapting Open Source Software for Education: Challenges, Methodologies and Result', paper presented at Open Source for Education in Europe: Research and Practise, Open University of Netherlands, Heerlen, Netherlands 14–15 November 2005. Online. Available online at: www.openconference.net/viewabstract.php?id=18&cf=3 (accessed 23 January 2007).

Herd, G.P. and Jentsch, B.E. (2006) '"Social Security" and the *Gaidhealtachd*: Migrants as Pandora's Box or Panacea?' paper presented at Rannsachadh na Gàidhlig 4, Sabhal Mòr Ostaig, Isle of Skye, July 2006.

Hunter, J. (1976) *The Making of the Crofting Community*, Edinburgh: John Donald Publishers Ltd.

Hutchinson, R. (2005) *A Waxing Moon – the Modern Gaelic Revival*, Edinburgh: Mainstream Publishing.

IleTec (2006) Online. Available HTTP: www.iletec.co.uk (accessed 2 November 2006).

Iomairtean Gàidhlig (2006) Online. Available online at: http://groups.yahoo.com/group/Iomairtean_Gaidhlig/ (accessed 29 November 2006).

Jenkins, G.H. and Williams, M.A. (eds) (2000) *'Let's Do Our Best for the Ancient Tongue': The Welsh Language in the Twentieth Century*, Cardiff: University of Wales Press.

Keane, M.J., Griffith, B. and Dunn, J.W. (1993) 'Regional Development and Language Maintenance', *Environment and Planning A* 25 (3): 399–408.

MacDonald, S. (1997) *Reimagining Culture: Histories, Identities and the Gaelic Renaissance*, Oxford: Oxford International Publishers Ltd.

MacKinnon, K. (1991) *Gaelic: A Past and Future Prospect*, Edinburgh: Saltire.

MacKinnon, K. (2006) 'Migration, Family and Education in Gaelic Policy Perspective', paper presented at Rannsachadh na Gàidhlig 4, Sabhal Mòr Ostaig, Isle of Skye, July 2006.

Microsoft (2007) 'New Vista for Gaelic – Microsoft Supports Language Development', press release, 16 February.

Millard, J. (2005) 'Rural Areas in the Digital Economy', in D. Schmied (ed.) *Winning and Losing: The Changing Geography of Europe's Rural Areas*, Aldershot: Ashgate, pp. 90–123.

O'Reilly (2005) *What Is Web 2.0: Design Patterns and Business Models for the Next Generation of Software*. Online. Available online at: www.oreillynet.com/pub/a/oreilly/tim/news/2005/09/30/what-is-web-20.html (accessed 15 September 2006).

Organisation for Economic Development (OECD) (2006) *OECD Information Technology Outlook 2006*, Paris: OECD Publishing.

Registrar General for Scotland (2005) *Scotland's Census 2001: Gaelic Report*, Edinburgh: General Register Office for Scotland (GROS).

SaveGaelic.org (2006) Online. Available online at: www.savegaelic.org (accessed 3 November 2006).

Scanlon, C. and Singh, M. (2006) 'Theorizing the Decline of Linguistic Diversity', *International Journal of the Sociology of Language* 182: 1–24.

Scholes, D. (2006) Conaltradh Air-loidhne: dè am feum a th'ann? Online Conversation – Of What Use Is It?, in R. Cox (ed.) *Gath*, 5, Berwick-upon-Tweed: Foillseachaidhean Ghath Earranta.

Thomas, N., King, A. and Gruffydd Jones, E.H. (2000) *Linguistic Diversity on the Internet: Assessment of the Contribution of Machine Translation*, European Parliament: Stoa Publications. Online. Available online at: www.serv-inf.deusto.es/ABAITUA/konzeptu/ta/EuroParlament.html (accessed 5 November 2006).

West Highland Animations (2007) Online. Available online at: www.westhighlandanimation.co.uk/ (accessed 23 January 2007).

Williams, C.H. (1991) 'Linguistic Minorities: West European and Canadian Perspectives', in C.H. Williams (ed.) *Linguistic Minorities, Society and Territory*, Clevedon: Multilingual Matters, pp. 1–43.

Williams, G. (2005) *Sustaining Language Diversity in Europe*, Basingstoke: Palgrave Macmillan.

Withers, Charles W.J. (1984) *Gaelic in Scotland, 1698–1981*, Edinburgh: John Donald.

Part IV

Implications for the feasibility and trajectory of Information-Society policies

8 Policy and the rural Information Society

Hilary Talbot and Andrew Gillespie

Introduction

The shift in thinking in the last decade or so about the advantages that ICTs would bring to rural areas is well summed up as 'from dream to reality'. The dream was that the distance-transcending attributes of the technologies would bring specific, additional benefits to rural areas; the reality was a worry that many were being left behind by their more urban counterparts in adopting the trappings of the 'Information Society'. The concern was particularly for those rural areas already struggling to maintain an adequate economy and quality of life – typically those with low GDP, sparse and dispersed populations, difficult topologies, and/or those remote from major centres of population and markets. Such areas would frequently have a European or national designation as a rural deprived region, or as a rural area in a mixed deprived region. Any lack in terms of ICT provision and use could exacerbate their existing deprived status.

In discussing policy and the rural Information Society in this chapter, the focus is on such regions and areas. They are linked by notions of their rurality, but this masks the diversity between areas, and even within them. Some are islands, others are mountainous; some attract many visitors, others are very isolated or their landscapes bear the scars of heavy industry; some are agricultural societies, but others might be based around a range of alternative industries; some are still in decline, but others are turning this around; and so on. Even the discourse of rurality varies greatly across rural Europe. In some countries or regions it is tied firmly to agricultural production, in others it is the type (and quality) of the landscape that is important, and in others notions of rural community and society are prominent.

This chapter explores the thinking behind rural Information-Society policies and the policies themselves, and discusses the issues that might act as barriers to the entry of more deprived rural areas into the Information Society.

The death of distance

The new ICT technologies of the late twentieth century were initially heralded by many (e.g. McLuhan, 1964; Toffler, 1980) as of particular benefit to rural areas because of their ability to transcend distances. Of particular interest for remote and/or declining rural districts was Toffler's vision of decentralised business structures with people working from 'electronic cottages' or 'neighbourhood work centers', which in turn, would lead to the 'home-centred society'; and McLuhan's claim that the 'very nature of the city as a form of major dimensions must inevitably dissolve like a fading shot in a movie' (McLuhan, 1964: 366).

The discourse of the death of distance brought with it a utopianism about the power of ICTs to bring more advantages to rural areas than to their urban counterparts, an inevitability about the power of the technology per se to influence change, and the assumption that physical distance was the root of rural development problems. As such, it was very attractive to policy-makers at all levels who were grappling with the problems of rural regions, representing something of a panacea, seemingly without the need for any great amount of investment of time or money.

Some policy-makers, such as the High Level Group on the Information Society (Bangemann, 1994), fully embraced such utopian visions for rural areas, describing how the technology would facilitate the re-integration of home, work, education and leisure (in local places). Coupled with their neoliberal approach, this potential cure-all for rural regions meant that the European Union and Member States could apply light-touch policy and effect major changes – their approach was simply to encourage and enable the market to function efficiently.

Other policy-makers were less convinced that the telecommunications infrastructure would roll-out to more peripheral areas without some policy interventions to encourage this, but still saw the technology, once in place, as inevitably yielding major benefits to such areas. Studies in the 1980s and early 1990s showed a positive correlation between the existence of an advanced telecommunications infrastructure and a strong economy, and the causality was thought by some to be in both directions. This, coupled with the identification of a 'substantial telecommunications gap between the prosperous core and the poorer periphery of the EU' (Cornford, 2003: 18) supplied the justification for the EU to invest in telecommunications infrastructure 'ahead of demand' in these 'at risk' regions. An example of this approach was the EU STAR programme (Special Telecommunications Action for Regional Development) of the late 1980s.

By the end of the 1990s, it was becoming clear that simply providing these 'death-of-distance' technologies had not, in general, redressed the balance between rural and urban areas, nor indeed between the core and peripheral regions of Europe. Thus by 1997 the Commission was sounding a more circumspect tone, and recognising the need for more active policy intervention beyond liberalisation:

> The opportunities offered by the emerging information society are huge.... Making these opportunities available throughout Europe is one of the central objectives of the gradual liberalisation of telecommunications

> markets. However, not all European regions, citizens or firms are equally well equipped to enjoy these benefits because of geographic, social and economic reasons. Thus the development of the information society needs to be complemented, where necessary, by policy action in order to close the existing gaps and ensure that the information society develops at the desired rate throughout the Union.
>
> (European Commission, 1997)

The 'gaps' which troubled European policy-makers a decade ago clearly still persist. A 2005 Commission staff working document (European Commission, 2005c: 21) still found 'big disparities between [European] regions – especially among central and peripheral ones'. Rather than bringing rural advantage, 'urban areas come first … and rural areas and small towns considerably lag behind in their access to the new medium, in a blatant denial of the futurologists' image of the electronic cottage' (Castells, 2001: 212). Various reasons are put forward as to why the 'death of distance' has failed to materialise.

Policy-makers have, for some time, accepted that market forces alone will not necessarily furnish the necessary telecommunications infrastructure in rural areas. For example, the EU document, *Bridging the Broadband Gap* (European Commission, 2006) identifies that DSL 'broadband' at 1.2005 was available to 62 per cent of rural households, compared to 85 per cent of households overall; that it was common for rural connection speeds to be less than 512 kbps while average speeds in urban areas were higher than 512 kbps; and that only 8 per cent of rural households were subscribing to broadband, compared with 18 per cent in urban areas. Since the millennium, EU Information-Society policy has consistently encouraged interventions to support the development of telecommunications infrastructure in remoter areas (European Commission, 2002; European Commission, 2005b) – this is discussed in detail in the next section.

The technological deterministic assumption in the 'death-of-distance' discourse is something that has been counter-argued more and more during the 1990s and 2000s. The idea that technology comes first and impacts on the economy and society in 'inevitable' ways (McLuhan, 1964) that people have subsequently to respond to has been largely refuted by much of the work on the social shaping of technologies (e.g. Bijker *et al.*, 1987; MacKenzie and Wajcman, 1999; Williams and Edge, 1996). People's interests, institutions, politics and so on are all seen to influence the development of technologies, from their design stage through to their application. Grimes (2002), for example, critiques one of the EU Framework Programme IV Telematics Application Programme projects, the IRDSS project, for its expectation that technology will have major impacts on the economy and society. He explains how

> through the provision of user-friendly multi-media kiosks in libraries and community centres, [it] sought to help marginalised communities to do business with cross-border regions, to bring these communities more into

> the development process and to bring about a decentralisation of work to the local level. Such high-minded rhetoric is unlikely to be fulfilled merely by providing access to information through such kiosks.
>
> (Grimes, 2002: 979)

Policy-makers have become aware of the need not only to provide the technologies, but also to address the demand-side issues: 'there is a large gap between coverage and take-up of broadband in all areas' (European Commission, 2006: 6). Initiatives to encourage take-up and effective use include the development of online public services as 'a powerful instrument to drive broadband demand' (p. 10). Certain societal groups have been identified as being the most 'at risk' of not making effective use of ICTs: the elderly, people with low levels of education, the unemployed and disabled people (e.g. EU/AT, 2006); many of the problems of take-up in less developed areas will be due to such characteristics as much as to issues of rurality (European Commission, 2006).

Gillespie *et al.* (2001) identify how much of the forecasted explosions of new ways of living, working and doing business, especially in less favoured regions, had failed to materialise. They point to the mis-specification of 'the problem of remoteness' as the reason: 'geographic distance is not the main barrier facing peripherally located SMEs wishing to gain access to core markets, rather it is their inability to compete in these markets' (p. 122). The inability of most peripherally located SMEs to compete beyond their local markets is, it is true, in part a consequence of remoteness, but in rather complex and path-dependent ways. Further, transcending the distance barrier through new technologies would in many cases simply expose such firms to much more vigorous competition from external firms in local markets, previously protected by these same distance barriers.

The over-simplicity of conceiving of exclusion in rural areas as directly related to the physical distance from a central point is something also picked up upon in the rural-society literature – for example, Woodward (1998) talks about its complexity and, rather than highlighting distance, talks instead about 'poor transport provision (lack of public transport, prohibitive cost of owning and running a car, inability to drive)' (p. 1). Distance, per se, is not the problem; people are only socially excluded when they are unable to transcend the necessary distance to access services, find employment and so on.

This critique of the 'death-of-distance' discourse is not comprehensive, but rather serves to indicate the areas that the rest of this chapter explores. The technology will not necessarily be made available to rural areas without public-sector intervention, but such provision is only a prerequisite for its take-up and effective application. There is a need to understand better what constrains people and businesses in rural areas exploiting broadband provision. There is no simple technological fix for rural areas but rather it is part of the society-wide 'multidimensional transformation ... [which] is the outcome of an interactive process between technology, economic strategies, social interests, cultural values and power struggles' (Castells, 1999: 27).

Rural Information-Society policies

Introduction

'Death-of-Distance' rhetoric, with reference to rural or remoter areas, is now not prominent in Information-Society policy. Not only has the promise failed to materialise, there is now much evidence that rural and remoter regions lag behind their more urban counterparts in terms of the availability of broadband and its take-up. The main thrust of current policy insofar as it focuses on rurality is to address this territorial 'gap' or 'digital divide' between rural and urban areas. There is no policy domain specifically for 'rural Information Society'; this section explores rural aspects of European Information Society and regional policies, and the Information-Society aspects of European rural policy.

EU policy is driven by discourses of liberalisation and competitiveness, as set out most recently in the revised Lisbon Agenda (European Commission, 2005a). However, it also has a commitment to 'cohesion' between Member States and to support the 'less favoured regions'. Although the liberalisation discourse has tended to dominate EU policy, politics has ensured that economic and social cohesion between territories has always been kept somewhat on the agenda. At some points in time, EU Information-Society policy as specified by DG Information Society and Media has been almost exclusively driven by notions of liberalisation and competitiveness (such as during the 'Bangemann' era in the mid-1990s (European Commission, 1994)) with social and economic cohesion aims being relegated and consigned to the EU's regional policy; at others the two policy domains accommodate and to an extent integrate both agendas. The subject matter of this book – the *rural* Information Society – introduces a third relevant policy domain: rural development policy. All three have an input into what is ultimately delivered to rural areas to support the development of the local Information Society, as do individual Member States.

This section investigates in turn the relevant recent and current EU policies: 'Information-Society' policy, regional policy and rural development policy. It then discusses the role of the Member States both in defining these EU-level policies, and in acting independently to support their rural areas.

EU Information-Society policy

Recent EU Information-Society policy is set out in *eEurope 2005* (European Commission, 2002) which ran from 2002 to 2005 (succeeding eEurope 2002) and *i2010 'A European Information Society for Growth and Employment'* (European Commission, 2005b). These are both pan-European policies within which rural issues are specified or inferred as a small component of the overall policies.

The objective of *eEurope 2005* was to 'provide a favourable environment for private investment and for the creation of new jobs, to boost productivity, to modernise public services, and to give everyone the opportunity to participate in the global information society' (European Commission, 2002: 2). 'Actions' centred around modernising online public services (e-government, e-learning, and e-health), supporting a dynamic business environment, developing secure information and extending broadband coverage. Only the last of these had a territorial focus. While most broadband investment was to be supplied by the market, there was a commitment to public policy focusing on areas of market failure, and on political objectives such as territorial coverage for cohesion purposes. Supporting broadband access in less favoured regions, including outermost regions, was an explicit component of this policy.

The current *i2010* policy (European Commission, 2005b) is explicitly based on the renewed Lisbon strategy (European Commission, 2005a) goals of growth and jobs, and sets out three priorities: creating a single European information space where systems, regulations, security and so on, would be converged to allow interoperability; innovation and investment in research; and inclusion in the European Information Society. The last of these is about 'reinforcing social, economic and territorial cohesion by *making ICT products and services more accessible, including in regions lagging behind*' (emphasis in original) (p. 9). European Commission measures for this priority include a European initiative on e-inclusion in 2008 which will address a number of issues including regional divides, and three quality-of-life ICT flagship initiatives: the needs of an ageing society, clean transport and cultural diversity. The Commission was tasked to give 'guidance to extend the geographical coverage of broadband in under-served areas and will review the scope of the Universal Service Directive' (p. 10).

Although *i2010* inclusion measures are not exclusively for rural areas, commitments to 'regions lagging behind', and to 'under-served areas' are highly relevant. Various policy-related documents have since been produced to reinforce this commitment. The most important to this discussion of Information-Society policy and rurality is 'Bridging the Broadband Gap' (European Commission, 2006) which is focused on the territorial divide for broadband access, and states that 'the availability of broadband services is one critical element in assisting local communities in attracting businesses, in enabling telework, providing healthcare, improving education and government services' (p. 4). It proposes encouraging further broadband coverage through the development of technologies that are particularly suited to rural areas – new wireless platforms in association with sufficient radio spectrum, and/or a combination of technologies; it suggests, however, that demand may be inhibited by 'structural characteristics such as lower income and education' (p. 6). In order to address the demand-side constraints, it highlights the need for local planning, drawing on the Commission staff working document on the local dimension of the Information Society (European Commission, 2005c). The provision of appropriate infrastructure and public Internet access points (PIAPs) to rural regions is seen as an essential precondition to a 'context-based approach' at the regional or local level in order to foster economic growth, quality of life, social equity and environmental sustainability with local, endogenous developments being crucial to successful adoption of ICTs in rural areas.

The Riga Ministerial Declaration (EU/AT, 2006) on ICT for an inclusive society also reinforces the commitment to tackling the geographical digital divide, along with a commitment to the 'at-risk' social groups identified by the e-inclusion agenda. There was agreement to focus on five areas of work, with one being a reduction in the geographical digital divide. This was to be effected through a number of measures which included increasing the availability of broadband to under-served locations with a target minimum coverage of 90 per cent of the population by 2010, and support to PIAPs where appropriate. This included a specific target of remote and rural areas, lagging regions and small settlements.

There is clearly recognition in EU Information-Society policy that an unacceptable rural broadband gap exists, and that actions are needed to address this. However, with its emphasis on liberalisation and competitiveness, this policy domain is not oriented towards direct implementation, and has a very limited budget. Where intervention is deemed appropriate, this usually takes the form of enabling or encouraging 'others' to take action: other silos of European government, state governments, regional government, the voluntary sector, civil society or self-help. Taking the *eEurope 2005* policy (European Commission, 2002) as an example, the commitment to providing easy access to everyone through the development of PIAPs was to be resourced by the EU structural funds (described in more detail below), by private-sector and voluntary-sector investment; an increase in broadband access was to be achieved by reducing barriers to deployment, and by allowing Member States to support access in less favoured regions through appropriate use of the EU structural funds or individual state investments.

EU regional policy and the structural funds

In part because of this complex relationship between the different EU discourses, EU regional policy has also paid considerable attention to telecommunications (Gillespie, 1999). The main responsibility of this policy domain is to support the 'less favoured regions' in Europe, and the persistent gap in telecommunications provision and usage between the less developed regions and countries in the Union and their more affluent counterparts has been a concern since the first formulation of EU telecommunications policies in the early/mid-1980s.

At times there has been congruence between the aims of EU telecommunications and regional policies, and associatedly integrated and joint programmes have developed, such as the Special Telecommunications Actions for Regions (STAR) programme in 1987. However, in a later phase of policy development, the STAR programme

> came to be seen by the telecommunications policymakers as increasingly anachronistic, in that it continued to operate in an exclusively public-sector monopoly context. At best it was seen as rather an irrelevance to the main thrust of policy development; at worst, it conflicted with this main thrust [liberalisation and competitiveness].
>
> (Gillespie, 1999: 11)

During the last decade, the relationship has become more harmonious, with the discourse of an Information Society (rather than a more narrow 'Information Economy') making it important for legitimacy reasons that membership is available to all regions of the EU.

DG Regional Policy, unlike DG Information Society and Media, has major funds at its disposal to aid least prosperous countries and regions in the EU, and support for Information-Society initiatives has been available for 20 or more years. Some of the funding in the past was for specific telecommunications programmes initiated by the Commission – STAR and Telematique in the late 1980s and early 1990s – but all Member States also have the opportunity to fund Information-Society projects through their individual Strategic Frameworks agreed with DG Regional Policy as their structural fund allocations. However, in 1997, the Commission described the Member States' commitment of structural funding through their Community Support Frameworks to Information-Society issues as 'modest and insufficient' (European Commission, 1997: 6). As a result, from the mid-1990s onwards, DG Regional Policy attempted to stimulate the Member States, and the individual regions within them, to prioritise the Information Society more strongly within their structural fund programmes. One of the mechanisms for doing this comprised 'innovative pilot actions' initiated by the Commission, such as the Regional Information Society Initiative (RISI), which provided funding for regions to develop Information-Society strategies and action plans, which could then be implemented through the 'mainstream' structural funds.

In the 2000–6 period, EU Information-Society policy and regional policy share a number of key aims: the provision of telecommunications, particularly where the market fails to provide; stimulating new electronic services and innovative ICT applications; and developing skills and capabilities (European Commission, no date a).

In this planning period, support for Information-Society initiatives from DG Regional Policy is almost exclusively supplied via the mainstream structural funds, and Member States have been steered towards the inclusion of such initiatives in their Community Support Frameworks (Technopolis, 2002). The estimated spend by the EU on Information-Society initiatives via the structural funds 2000–6 is €10 billion, with Member States match-funding a further €6 billion. This amounts to between 4–4.5 per cent of the total structural funds budget from the EU (Technopolis, 2002), compared with about 2 per cent in the previous planning period (1994–2000) (European Commission, 1997).

In the planning period 2000–6, 94 per cent of the structural funds is concentrated on three 'objectives' (European Commission, 2003). Objective 1 aids regions behind in development, targeting those with a GDP per capita of less than 75 per cent of the EU average. Objective 2 helps regions with structural difficulties; and Objective 3 focuses on modernising systems of education and training and promoting employment. Only the regions that meet the EU's criteria and are designated as such are eligible for the 'objective' funding. A small proportion (less than 6 per cent) of the structural funds provides support to four 'community initiatives', one of which is focused on innovative sustainable development initiatives in rural areas (LEADER). Four EU funds contribute to the structural funds, two of which are particularly pertinent to this exploration of rural Information-Society measures: the European Regional Development Fund (ERDF) which invests in infrastructure, job creation, local development projects and small firms; and the European Agricultural Guidance and Guarantee Fund (EAGGF) which finances rural development measures and aid for farmers.

In 2007, regional policy entered a new planning phase, and one which is likely to be substantially influenced by the enlargement of the EU from 15 in 2004 to 27 in 2007. A total of €308 billion has been allocated to the structural funds for the period 2007 to 2013, which will be allocated to designated 'objective' states and regions using similar criteria to the previous planning period; there is also a new European Territorial Co-operation Objective to promote integrated territorial co-operation across borders (European Parliament and European Council, 2006). The overall aim of the structural funds is very similar: 'reducing the disparities between the levels of development of the various regions and the backwardness of the least favoured regions or islands, including rural areas' (p. 25). 'Information Society' still features under a high-level priority of promoting competitiveness and creating jobs, associated with well over half of the budget (European Commission Directorate-General Regional Policy, 2006).

At the time of writing, the 2007–13 programming had not started, and nor had the 2000–6 programme ended. DG Regional Policy states that '2007 will be an overlapping year of two programming periods' (European Commission Directorate-General Regional Policy, 2006: p. 7), with their main focus being to complete the finalisation of the 27 National Strategic Reference Frameworks. Of specific rural interest is the fact that EAGGF ceases to contribute to the structural fund in the 2007–13 programme.

The last decade or so of regional policy/structural funds has seen a marked change in the way rural areas have been managed. Before the millennium, specific programmes addressed rural areas and issues, with certain 'objectives' of regional policy being dedicated to rural regions. Objective 5(b), for example, designated areas that had low population densities, high rates of emigration, job losses, overdependence on and vulnerability to decline in the agricultural sector and the disappearance of enterprises and services (Lowe *et al.*, 1998). A specifically rural funding stream (EAGGF) contributed to the structural funds available for the rural 'objective' regions. The LEADER community initiative, introduced in 1991, was concerned with rural participatory development at the local level (less than 100,000 population) in Objective 1 and 5b areas. In the programme planning period 2000–6, no 'objectives' were dedicated to rural areas, although EAGGF continued to contribute to the structural funds available to the generalised 'objective' regions; LEADER was continued as a new programme that was decoupled from 'objective' regions. The new phase of regional policy we are now entering completes the transition: there are no dedicated rural 'objective' regions and EAGGF no longer contributes to the structural funds.

However, this does not mean that regional policy has been gradually excluding rural areas from its responsibilities. Since 2000, rural regions have been eligible to be designated as Objective 1 or 2 regions, and all the funding streams of the structural funds (not just EAGGF) have been available to them subject to the same criteria as more urban areas. Many rural areas are also part of a wider designated 'objective' region, with rural-specific issues written into the region's programming document. Although from 2007 EAGGF will not contribute to the structural funds, rural areas will continue to be eligible to be 'objective' regions, or to be part of a wider designated region, and to draw from the other funding streams (ERDF and ESF), as in the 2000–6 programming period. The withdrawal of EAGGF from the structural funds has also to be seen as complemented by the burgeoning of EU rural development policy (see next section), in the context of a growing emphasis in EU regional policy document statements concerning their responsibilities and commitment to rural areas, such as:

> the assistance will support sustainable *urban development* and the *renewal of rural areas and of areas dependent on fisheries* through economic diversification. The assistance will also *support areas affected by geographical or natural handicaps* ... particularly the outermost regions as well as the northern areas with very low population density, certain islands and island Member States, and mountainous areas.
>
> (European Commission Directorate-General Regional Policy, 2006: 7, emphasis in original)

EU rural development policy

European rural development policy was first identifiable as such in 2000, when the reform of the common agricultural policy (CAP) introduced the 'second pillar' of the CAP (Lowe and Ward, 1998). However, although having a European rural policy in 2000 was

> a novel departure, it incorporates several existing CAP measures, including: structural adjustment of the farming sector (investment in agricultural holdings, establishment of young farmers, training, early retirement); support for farming in less favoured areas; remuneration for agri-environmental activities; support for investments in processing and marketing facilities; and forestry measures.
>
> (p. 2)

Only one set of measures was distinctly new: Article 33 of the Council Regulation made provision for 'promoting the adaptation and development of rural areas' (European Council, 1999). Along with the rest of the CAP, these new measures had a very land-based notion of rural development, and were inclined towards supporting farmers and farming.

The first programming period of rural development policy was for seven years from 2000. At the beginning of the period, no additional funding was allocated for the new Article 33, or for the new 'rural policy' generally; the existing level of EAGGF fund continued to resource this. The later CAP reform of 2003/4, however, saw the decoupling of direct aids for agricultural production and a transfer of these funds into rural development measures (European Commission, 2004). In association with these reforms, a new fund, the European Agricultural Fund for Rural Development (EAFRD) was created, and the LEADER programme became mainstreamed in European rural development policy programming (European Council, 2005).

A long list of measures were identified under Article 33 of Council Regulation 1257/1999 (European Council, 1999) (introducing EU rural development policy) which were mainly targeted at farms, farming and/or farmers, but which included (of specific interest to this investigation of rural Information-Society policy) 'basic services for the rural economy and population' and 'the development and improvement of infrastructure connected with the development of agriculture'. The measures were described by an EU website as 'relatively small-scale' (European Commission, no date b) but cross-refer to the significant EU structural funds for infrastructure (including telecommunications), how they can be capitalised via EU rural development measures for supporting the diversification and development of the agricultural and food sector, and identify how the funds can contribute to 'encouraging the take-up and use of ICT'. The later regulation introducing EAFRD (European Council, 2005) widened provision for contributions to 'local access to Information and Communications Technologies (ICTs)' (p. 5) to include the non-agricultural sector.

We are now entering a new programming period (2007–13). This phase of the EU rural development policy is in the context of an enlarged EU. Its main features were set out in Council Decision 2006/144/EC (European Council, 2006). The policy has four axes (p. 22):

1 improving the competitiveness of the agricultural and forestry sector;
2 improving the environment and the countryside;
3 improving the quality of life in rural areas and diversification of the rural economy;
4 developing the principles of the LEADER programme.

Of most relevance to our interests in this chapter are axes 3 and 4. Axis 3 includes reference to: upgrading local infrastructure (including telecommunications), particularly in the new Member States; encouraging the take-up and diffusion of ICT; and 'putting the heart back into villages', including infrastructure for local services. Axis 4 is a crosscutting theme to the other three, aimed at 'improving governance and mobilising the endogenous development potential of rural areas' (p. 27). An ICT-specific example under this axis is that co-operation and innovation could be helped by online communities.

The principle of subsidiarity was, and is, prominent within EU rural development policy, with each Member State developing its programme of activities – national strategy plans – within the strategic guidelines set out in the EU legislation for the relevant planning period (European Council, 1999; European Council, 2006). In the first planning period (2000–6) Member States were to draw up rural development plans at the geographical level deemed to be the most appropriate (1257/1999); in the new planning period the implication of the fourth axis (LEADER) is that actions will develop in the context of community-led local development strategies (European Council, 2006). The funding furnished by the EU is enhanced by the contribution made by each Member State, with some making a more significant donation than others.

The role of Member States

All three policies described above devolve much of the decision-making about what gets priority and funding to the Member State or regional level. In terms of EU Information-Society policy, Member States are now required to define, and update annually, their Information-Society priorities in line with the Lisbon priorities of growth and jobs, stressing ICT uptake, ICT infrastructure and ICT for jobs and education (European Commission, 2005b). Under regional policy, states work in partnership with the EU to define the regions which will be eligible for structural funds, and each of these regions produces its own programming document identifying the priorities for funding applications. Likewise each country produces its own rural development programme, as described above.

The EU's Information-Society policy has very few funds at its disposal; in terms of the interests of this chapter, most of its priorities are cross-referred to the structural funds and/or the rural development funds for resources. The Information-Society policies described here make regular reference to the other two policies mainly in terms of resourcing; regional policy and rural development policy cross-refer to each other (and to other EU policies) as part of a more comprehensive effort towards the co-ordination and consistency of policy. This is more marked in the most recent documents, which all take the Lisbon strategy (European Commission, 2003) as their starting point, and explicitly discuss complementary sources of funding. For example, rural development policy 2007–13 (European Council, 2006) states:

> The synergy between structural, employment and rural development policies needs to be encouraged. In this context, Member States should ensure complementarity and coherence between actions to be financed by the European Regional Development Fund, the Cohesion Fund, the European Social Fund, the European Fisheries Fund and the EAFRD on a given territory and in a given field of activity.... For infrastructure investments, the scale of intervention could be a guiding principle. For example, for investments in transport and other infrastructure at Member State, regional or subregional level, cohesion policy instruments would be used, while at the local level the basic services measure under axis 3 could be used, ensuring a link between local and regional levels.
>
> (p. 29)

Funding for rural Information-Society policy implementation is thus made available to 'eligible areas' via two separate policy domains, in accordance with the national or regional programming documents of the Member States. Member-State funding contributions enlarge the amount available to local projects. In rural development policy, Member States increase, within limits, the available funds from the EU; under the structural funds, individual projects must provide 'match funding' to the EU's contribution, usually constituting more than half the cost, for their application to be successful. This can come from a number of sources, including Member-State funding. Member States are also encouraged, within limits, to further the aims of EU policy by independent investment of their own funds (e.g. EU/AT, 2006). The limits are imposed to ensure that such activity does not work to the detriment of cohesion policy, by allowing the richer Member States to develop faster than their poorer counterparts. These limits, known as the state aid rules, have at times seemed to constrain the development of rural telecommunications: 'the Broadband Gap', for example, makes a commitment to clarifying state aid rules and their applicability to broadband projects (European Commission, 2006).

To date, Member States have almost always engaged with the planning and funding of European rural Information-Society policy at a national or regional level. The more local or 'community' level has only been prominent through the small-scale LEADER community initiative. EU rural development policy 2007–13 has now mainstreamed the LEADER approach, and the notion of using the local level for planning rural ICT activities has come to the fore in the other policy domains (European Commission, 2005c; European Commission, 2006). The 'Broadband Gap' communication concludes that 'local/regional authorities are best placed to plan a broadband project that takes into account local needs and technological requirements' (European Commission, 2006: 8). This draws from the more detailed Commission work (European Commission, 2005c) which discusses the increasing importance of the local dimension for the development of the Information Society and advocates integrated development and endogenous growth (very much in line with LEADER principles). Quite how local-level strategies will integrate with policies at the regional, Member-State, and EU levels is not yet clear.

Explaining the rural 'broadband gap'

There is consensus that simply providing the technology is not enough to ensure that it makes a significant impact on the economy and society in disadvantaged rural areas. While the rural-specific part of European Information-Society policy might be the provision of broadband, it also includes measures to encourage take-up and effective use of ICTs which are rural relevant. The e-inclusion strand of *i2010* (European Commission, 2005b) is an example of this. Effective use in deprived rural areas would provide a self-help means of improvement, a justification for public investment in the infrastructure, and generate enough demand for the market to want to make provision in the future. Without market interest, the public sector might be locked into funding the next generations of technology in rural areas.

In attempting to explain the existing rural 'broadband gap', we clearly need to understand both the dynamics of broadband *supply*, and of differentiated uptake or *demand*, and the interrelationships between supply and demand. There is of course nothing unusual about a new network technology being deployed initially in metropolitan areas, where the costs of deployment per subscriber are lower than in rural areas, and where the demand for a new service is easier to establish. The interconnected territorial logic of supply and demand for newly deployed broadband services is explained in the Commission's 'Broadband Gap' communication:

> Despite the general increase in broadband connectivity, access in more remote and rural regions is limited because of high costs due to low density of population and remoteness. Population scarcity limits the exploitation of economies of scale, entails lower rates of demand and reduced expected returns from investment. Remoteness often implies the need of bridging longer distances from the local exchanges to the premises and to the backbone. Commercial incentives to invest in broadband deployment in these areas often turn out to be insufficient.
>
> (European Commission, 2006: 5)

As noted earlier, at the beginning of 2005, DSL broadband was available to 85 per cent of households in Europe (EU15 plus Norway and Iceland), but to only 62 per cent of rural households (European Commission, 2006). Predictably, levels of broadband uptake are also lower in rural areas (8 per cent of rural households, 18 per cent of urban households), explained both by more constrained supply and by lower levels of demand. The extent of the 'demand gap' becomes more apparent when we look at technologies that are more mature in terms of their adoption and hence less constrained by the availability of the technology in question; Figure 8.1 shows the percentage of households with a personal computer at home, an Internet connection at home and a broadband connection at home, for 'thinly populated areas', 'intermediate areas' and 'densely populated areas', for Europe as a whole (EU25) in 2004. A substantial 'rural gap' exists for both PCs and the Internet (a 14 percentage point deficit between the level of household uptake in thinly populated areas and in densely populated areas, in both cases).

How might this persistent rural technology demand gap be explained, and what implications might such explanations have for the likely future exploitation of broadband in rural areas? This section briefly explores some of the generally accepted barriers to the full exploitation of broadband, and where appropriate links them to aspects of the rural economy and society that might make the barrier even more problematic.

From a society perspective, certain groups are deemed to be more likely to ignore the opportunities afforded by broadband (just as they have ignored those

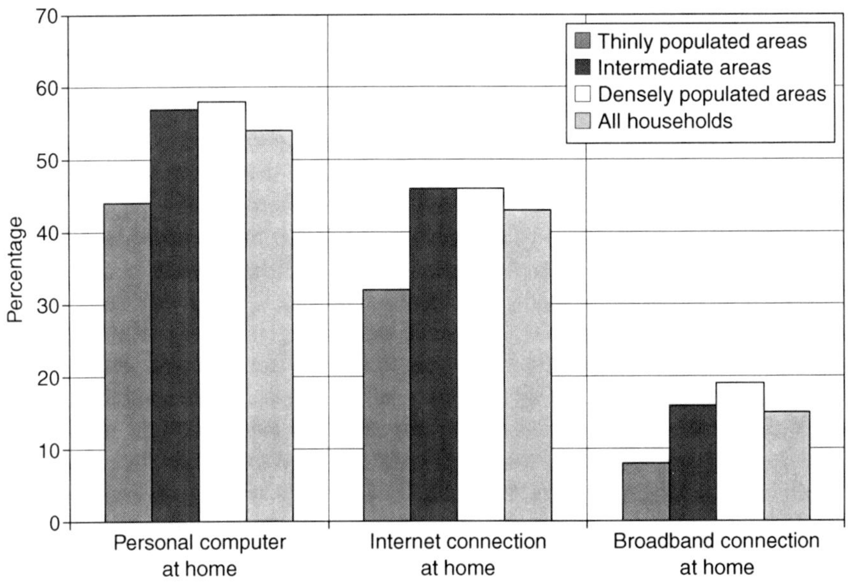

Figure 8.1 Household access to ICTs for EU25 in 2004: % of households.

previously offered by PCs and the Internet). Commentators offer slightly different lists of the 'at-risk' groups, but there is something of a consensus around the main ones as: people with low incomes and/or social status, those with disabilities, older people and those with low educational attainments. These groups will lag in terms of take-up whether they are in urban or rural settings.

In some cases, rural areas might find these at-risk groups even more problematic simply because there are proportionately more of them. Statistics from a recent EU project (Copus, 2006) highlight that 'demographic ageing is an important issue throughout large parts of the developed world, but it is especially evident in the PR [predominantly rural] regions of some Member States' (p. xii); that unemployment rates are generally significantly higher in rural areas, as is 'hidden unemployment'; and that the rural adult population's level of educational attainment is lower than in urban areas. In the agricultural sector there also appears to be a predominance of part-time working, seasonal working and multiple job-holding – typical patterns for people on low incomes. These same societal categories are also 'at-risk' groups for social exclusion more generally, which in rural areas is often exacerbated by the lack of local services. This lack is often not problematic for those who commute to more urban areas for work, but for those who are tied to their locality, services delivered locally are essential.

One means of improving local services would be to employ ICTs to *deliver* them. However, unless the local population most likely to need local services (older people and those on low incomes, for example) can be persuaded to exploit broadband in order to receive services, then such ventures will have disappointing results. Another means of improving local services would be by using ICTs to streamline the system so that local deliverers could work more efficiently.

Although we do not have statistics for the *business* uptake of broadband technologies in rural and urban areas, as with the population as a whole there are 'structural' characteristics of rural area economies that might reasonably be expected to lead to lower levels of broadband uptake and use.

Within the economy as a whole, certain trends can be discerned in different levels or speeds of take-up and exploitation of broadband. Statistics comparing the take-up of various e-business technologies make it clear that large enterprises on average are well ahead of small ones; there are also variations in the use of technologies/applications between different sectors (Reis, 2006). Even where new technologies are adopted by small businesses, there are also thought to be differences in how firms which rely on local markets might respond to broadband opportunities as compared with those remote from their markets; however, it could also be argued that the limitations of reliance on local markets should make a means of reaching more distant markets more attractive to such firms (Grimes, 2003).

These universal issues of take-up apply to rural, as well as other, areas; and might be exacerbated by rurality. The size of rural enterprises tends to be small, with self-employment being slightly more important in rural regions than urban ones (Copus, 2006). Farms, and their diversification enterprises, are typically very small and often family-run. Standard measures and notions of competitiveness might be difficult to apply to such firms, which could involve a lot of informal, part-time and seasonal employment, underemployment and an intimate relationship between work and the family.

One of the sectors reported on by Reis (2006) – manufacture of products based on: food, beverages, tobacco, textile, leather, wood, pulp and paper; publishing and printing – might serve as an agriculture proxy measure in comparative terms. This category's take-up is low for all the indicators in this study (e-commerce purchases and sales; LAN and intranet; and 'external integration of business processes'). However, although in parts of the EU – particularly the central, eastern and southern states – the agricultural sector still accounts for more than 25 per cent of the regional employment, in most rural regions the primary sector accounts for less than 10 per cent of total employment, and such regions are characterised by structures very similar to those of their urban neighbours (Copus, 2006). The service sector supplies the most employment across Europe as a whole and, although less dominant in the rural regions, it still represents on average more than half of their employment.

Rural Information-Society policy interventions focus on the more deprived areas. Agriblue data (Agriblue Working Group, 2004) show economic activity rates are lower; unemployment rates are significantly higher; and the agricultural sector is in a period of decline, with an aged workforce, increasing reliance on part-time workers and underemployment common. Some change (e.g. diversification, sectoral shifts) is already underway, but 'to retain and strengthen existing enterprise, measures will be required to increase high value-added economic activity, stimulate innovation and technology transfer, promote the development of quality systems and encourage access to foreign markets' (p. 19). The adoption of new technologies would appear to be central to such activities, but this cannot be seen as an automatic response from those firms/farms which need to make the changes: characterised by microbusinesses, an elderly workforce with below average levels of education, part-time working and multiple job-holding. The lack of aptitude for entrepreneurial change implied by such factors is exacerbated by young people and those on higher incomes commuting to more urban areas for work (Reis, 2006), and the life/work relationship of both farming families and some 'lifestyle' firms (Agriblue Working Group, 2004).

The above discussion suggests that the opportunities afforded by ICTs might benefit many firms in rural areas; however, it would seem unlikely that these same firms would inevitably make this transition. 'Dispersed delivery of education and training, including for mature students, is likely to prove an important means of increasing the rate of entrepreneurship and innovation in rural and peripheral areas' (Reis, 2006). And it cannot be automatically assumed that adopting e-business applications will make firms competitive – they will also need business advice and support if they are to be successful in new ventures or more global markets. The provision of advice, support and training in remoter areas is notoriously expensive, but is a service that could be made more efficient by the increased use of ICTs, although delivery through remote means might come up against some of the very factors it was aiming to address.

Conclusions

Information-Society policy, from European to local level, now recognises that market forces will not provide a good standard of broadband infrastructure to all geographical areas, and rural areas are clearly seen as candidates for public support in cases of market failure. There is also clearly an understanding that the provision is only advantageous if potential recipients take it up, and exploit the capabilities of the technology. Functional use is important not only to make the investment cost-effective in achieving policy goals, but also to decouple rural area telecommunications from public funding in the future: unless there is enough demand for the next upgrade of telecommunications standards to attract private investment, the public sector might be the only feasible way to fund the next generation of infrastructure in rural areas. However, policy interventions to supply broadband to certain technologically lagging regions are far more assured in securing their desired outcomes (a broadband network for local people to subscribe to if they wish) than those aimed at ensuring take-up and exploitation. This is far more dependent on the local economic and social context of the rural areas.

There are then a number of important 'positives' that can be drawn from the current situation. First, it is clear that, due to a combination of market forces and policy interventions, broadband technologies *are* being deployed in rural areas, albeit with an inevitable lag compared with urban areas, which are prioritised in the roll-out of any new network technology. Second, although there remains a significant 'rural gap' in ICT uptake and use (apparent in PC adoption and subscribing to the Internet, as well as broadband), this is at least in part explained by structural differences in the characteristics of rural (as opposed to urban) society and economy (reflected, for example, in the age structure of the population, and the industrial and enterprise mix of the economy).

It is reasonable to conclude that the rural areas of Europe, or at least many of them, *are* participating in the Information Society, and that (many) rural residents and rural businesses *are* sharing in the benefits of so doing. Far from being held back by a digital divide, many of Europe's rural areas are beginning to see the rhetoric of distance transcendence actually being realised, with benefits to rural quality of life and to rural enterprise. For the residents of many of Europe's rural areas, enhanced mobility options coupled with the widespread availability and use of ICTs have made the constraints and limitations imposed by 'rurality' fewer than they have ever been before – new vistas and opportunities are opening up for rural Europe.

There are, though, two major qualifications to this optimistic conclusion. First, it is clear that not all of Europe's rural areas are in a position to derive the benefits that participation in an Information Society could bring. For those relatively prosperous countries – including Denmark, Sweden, Norway, Germany, the Netherlands, Belgium, Luxembourg, the UK, Austria and Switzerland – that are leading the way in embracing the Information Society, the 'rural gap' (in the uptake and use of ICTs) seems relatively small, indeed in some cases is non-existent (Richardson, 2003). In southern Europe (and particularly in Greece and Portugal), and in central and eastern Europe (with the exceptions of Estonia and Slovakia), however, levels of participation in the Information Society are notably lower, and the 'rural gap' notably wider (Demunter, 2005). For such areas, policy intervention with respect both to the deployment of broadband infrastructures and stimulation of their use, within broader rural/regional development strategies, will remain necessary for many years to come.

The second qualification with respect to the above optimistic conclusion concerns those within the relatively prosperous and generally Information Society-embracing rural areas who, for various reasons – including age, infirmity, poverty, lack of education – are currently not able to participate in the Information Society. This heterogeneous group risk being doubly disadvantaged in future, in that not only will they not derive the benefits from the new network technologies reaped by the rest of society, but, also, the proliferation of *electronic* access and service delivery channels are likely to lead to changes in *physical* access and service delivery that may well have deleterious impacts upon the quality of life of the elderly, the poor and the immobile living in rural areas. For such groups, policy intervention remains necessary, both to stimulate, where appropriate, the effective uptake and use of the new technological opportunities, but also, where it is less appropriate, to ensure that the technologies are harnessed by those responsible for *delivering* services in order to provide effective and efficient service delivery to those unable to participate directly in the Information Society.

References

Agriblue Working Group. (2004) *Agriblue: Sustainable Territorial Development of the Rural Areas of Europe*, Brussels: European Commission.

Bangemann, M. (1994) *Europe and the Global Information Society – Recommendations to the European Council*, Brussels: High-Level Group on the Information Society.

Bijker, W., Hughes, T. and Pinch, T. (eds) (1987) *The Social Construction of Technological Systems*, Cambridge, MA: MIT Press.

Castells, M. (1999) 'The Informational City Is a Dual City: Can It Be Reversed?', in D. Schon, B. Sanyal and W. Mitchell (eds) *High Technology and Low Income Communities*, Cambridge, MA: MIT Press.

Castells, M. (2001) *The Internet Galaxy*, Oxford: OUP.

Copus, A. (2006) *Study on Employment in Rural Areas (SERA) Final Deliverable*: http://ec.europa.eu/agriculture/publi/reports/ruralemployment/sera_report.pdf.

Cornford, J. (2003) 'The Evolution of the Information Society and Regional Development in Europe', in C. Avgerou and R. Lebre la Rovere (eds) *Information Systems and the Economics of Innovation*, Cheltenham: Edward Elgar.

Demunter, C. (2005) *Statistics in Focus: The Digital Divide in Europe*: European Communities, http://epp.eurostat.cec.eu.int/cache/ITY_OFFPUB/KE-NP-05–038/EN/-KS-NP-05–038-EN.PDF.

EU/AT (2006) *Ministerial Declaration, 11 June 2006, Riga, Latvia*: http://europa.eu.int/information_society/events/ict_riga_2006/doc/declaration_riga.pdf.

European Commission (1994) *Europe and the Global Information Society: Recommendations to the European Council*: www.ispo.cec.be/infosoc/backg/bangeman.html.

European Commission (1997) *Cohesion and the Information Society (COM (97) 7/3)*, Brussels: European Commission.

European Commission (2002) *eEurope 2005: An Information Society for All*, Brussels: CEC.

European Commission (2003) *Competitiveness, Sustainable Development and Cohesion in Europe: From Lisbon to Gothenburg*, Luxembourg: Office for Official Publications of the European Communities.

European Commission (2004) *The Common Agricultural Policy Explained*, Brussels: European Commission Directorate-General for Agriculture.

European Commission (2005a) *Common Actions for Growth and Employment: the Community Lisbon Programme (COM (2005) 330 Final*, Brussels: European Commission.

European Commission (2005b) *i2010 – A European Information Society for Growth and Employment (COM (2005) 229 Final)*, Brussels: European Commission.

European Commission (2005c) *Commission Staff Working Document eInclusion Revisited: The Local Dimension of the Information Society (SEC (2005) 206)*: http://ec.europa.eu/employment_social/news/2005/feb/eincllocal_en.pdf.

European Commission (2006) *Bridging the Broadband Gap (SEC (2006) 354 and SEC (2006) 355)*, Brussels: European Commission.

European Commission (no date a) Europe's Regions and the Information Society: http://europa.eu.int/information_society/regwor/reg/index_en.htm.

European Commission (no date b) *The Common Agricultural Policy and the Lisbon Strategy*: http://ec.europa.eu/agriculture/lisbon/index_en.htm.

European Commission Directorate-General Regional Policy (2006) *Annual Management Plan 2007*: http://ec.europa.eu/dgs/regional_policy/document/amp2007_en.pdf.

European Council (1999) *Council Regulation (EC) No. 1257/1999 on Support for Rural Development from the European Agricultural Guidance and Guarantee Fund (EAGGF)*: http://defra.gov.uk/erd/docs/council.htm.

European Council (2005) Council Regulation (EC) No. 1698/2005 of 20 September 2005 on Support for Rural Development by the European Agricultural Fund for Rural Development (EAFRD), *Official Journal of the European Union L277*.

European Council (2006) Council Decision of 20 February 2006 on Community Strategic Guidelines for Rural Development (Programming Period 2007 to 2013) (2006/144/EC), *Official Journal of the European Union L55*.

European Parliament and European Council (2006) Regulation (EC) No. 1080/2006 of the European Parliament and of the Council of 5 July 2006 on the European Regional Development Fund and Repealing Regulation (EC) No. 1783/1999, *Official Journal of the European Union L210*. 49.

Gillespie, A. (1999) 'The Regional Dimension to the European Union's Telecommunications Policies', paper presented at *Europe Confronts the Telecommunications Revolution: The Social, Cultural and Economic Aspects* in UCLA, California, 11 February 1999.

Gillespie, A., Richardson, R. and Cornford, J. (2001) 'Regional Development and the New Economy', *Cahiers/Papers of the European Investment Bank* 6 (1): 109–32.

Grimes, S. (2002) 'The Role of Telematics in Integrating Ireland into Europe's Information Society', *European Planning Studies* 10 (8): 971–86.

Grimes, S. (2003) 'The Digital Economy Challenge Facing Peripheral Rural Areas', *Progress in Human Geography* 27 (2): 174–93.

Lowe, P. and Ward, N. (1998) *A 'Second Pillar' for the CAP? The European Rural Development Regulation and its Implications for the UK*, Newcastle: Centre for Rural Economy, University of Newcastle.

Lowe, P., Ray, C., Ward, N., Wood, D. and Woodward, R. (1998) *Participation in Rural Development: A Review of European Experience*, Newcastle: Centre for Rural Economy, University of Newcastle.

MacKenzie, D. and Wajcman, J. (1999) 'Introductory Essay: The Social Shaping of Technology', in D. MacKenzie and J. Wajcman (eds) *The Social Shaping of Technology*, Buckingham: Open University Press.

McLuhan, H. (1964) *Understanding Media: The Extensions of Man*, London: Sphere Books.

Reis, F. (2006) *Statistics in Focus: The Internet and Other Computer Networks and Their Use by European Enterprises to Do eBusiness*: http://epp.eurostat.ec.europa.eu.

Richardson, R. (2003) *ESPON 1.2.2: Telecommunication Services and Networks: Territorial Trends and Basic Supply of Infrastructure for Territorial Cohesion*, Brussels: European Commission.

Technopolis (2002) *Final Report for the Thematic Evaluation of the Information Society*: http://ec.europa.eu/regional_policy/sources/docgener/evaluation/doc/information_society.pdf.

Toffler, A. (1980) *The Third Wave*, New York: William Morrow.

Williams, R. and Edge, D. (1996) 'The Social Shaping of Technology', in W. Dutton (ed.) *Information and Communication Technologies: Visions and Realities*, Oxford: OUP.

Woodward, R. (1998) 'The Complex Nature of Social Exclusion in Rural Areas', paper presented at *What the Brochure Doesn't Say Seminar* in Kendal, organised by CHS.

Postscript

Sarah Skerratt and Grete Rusten

This book has addressed three themes, which the authors propose as being contested, and of significance, when researching ICTs within rural settings. It has then explored the relevance of these themes within Information-Society policy context – from European level through to local levels in rural areas in different European countries. The various studies featured in the chapters bring together the discussion about motivations, structures, challenges and effects of ICT use, for individuals and households through to SMEs. The authors now conclude the analyses presented above with a brief Postscript, synthesising those key comparative threads which resonate across chapters, and which give pointers towards research priorities of the future. In addition, we highlight those policy imperatives implied by the research presented above.

When examining our first theme of *understanding ICTs in rural SMEs and how they are embedded within SME practices*, Rusten, Ellingsen and Kristiansen (Chapter 2) conclude their analysis by highlighting the inherent variety of website experiences, roles and content across production categories, frequency and volume or orders and market range. Their research also illustrates different practices and challenges in the way firms and customers communicate and trade, showing that ICT is very much dependent on various other conditions such as trust and regulations (e.g. restrictions on the importing of farm products due to market protection and health risk) as well as practical arrangements such as transport. This variety must, they argue, be taken into account when seeking to understand the role (and potential) of the web for SMEs, rather than a reliance on international management literature pertaining to larger multinationals' strategies for an online presence. Bryson (Chapter 3) takes us through a stimulating historical journey, arguing how we can often over-privilege an analysis of *present* technological developments (the Internet) over those of the recent past, such as the telephone, and in so doing, omit the fact that SMEs have been adapting to technological opportunities and challenges for a number of business generations. He highlights the 'curious conflict' between the end of geography analysts and those who continue to argue for clustering and agglomeration as key elements of business success. He concludes by arguing for the importance of close proximity, co-presence and co-location as sources and stimulus to business creativity – that is, components of business practice within which ICTs become integrated in an iterative way.

Our second theme of *the persistence of place* is reviewed in two different ways and contexts by Kleppe and Hosea (Chapter 4) and Skerratt (Chapter 5). Kleppe and Hosea examine the ways in which place-based authenticity – defined through terroir products – is deliberately marketed and made available through online channels. They conclude that the marriage between spatial and technological dimensions grant rural areas the opportunity to develop new, high-value markets for local food products at potentially much lower costs than traditional marketing methods, and lead to the empowerment of local people who develop skills and know-how in marketing their locale. Place-based associations add value to products and help consumers to distinguish and choose between goods. Further, the value of local production may represent symbolic and economic elements that give local communities or regions a positive reputation. This may eventually attract customers as well as lead to tourist visits. Skerratt focuses on ways in which place persists as an 'active context', filtering the digital experiences of rural inhabitants through their use of shared ICT facilities in their rural places. She concludes her analysis by highlighting the participation environments (and even participatory environments) which remain integral to rural experiences of ICTs, and thus move our understanding beyond the notion of individualised access as the only measure of digital literacy in rural areas.

The importance of social and cultural 'fit' is the third theme we explore; that is, the ongoing importance of ICTs being built upon, and indeed leading to further developments within, language use and expression, and domestic purchasing, socialising and information-retrieval behaviours. Gannon (Chapter 6) critiques the dominance of the 'friction of distance' thesis as *the* underlying rationale explaining rural applications of ICTs, where rural is argued to be *the* motivator to ICT adoption and use by people living in rural communities. Rather, she describes the complexity of motivations, reasons and priorities expressed by individuals within rural households, and shows that, although many of these are place-relevant, few can be explained as purely *place-driven.* Gannon demonstrates how the very characteristics of rural areas can lead to observable behaviours which appear as responses to poor broadband speeds and lack of rural shops and long travelling distances to information and services. Thus, we see an interplay (rather than clear causal relationships) between ICTs and place, as technologies are appropriated by individuals within households to fit their local worlds. MacLeod (Chapter 7) examines a very specific ICT adaptation – that of the 'technologisation' of Anglo/American dominance on the Internet and how this integrates with users who speak Gaelic. She explores Crystal's (2002) thesis: that an endangered language will make progress if its speakers make use of technology. She concludes her analysis stating that, only through continued development of language technologies which enable speakers to comfortably live through Gaelic on the Internet and ICT-enabled applications, will technology be truly positioned to support, rather than diminish, minority languages in the European context. Further, language can be a way to form virtual communities of interest within cultures but across geographies.

An underpinning theme throughout our review of 'being rural in a digital age' is that of *the implications of our research findings for the feasibility and trajectory of Information-Society policies at local, regional, national and European levels.* This is explored by Talbot and Gillespie (Chapter 8), whose analysis concludes that such policies now largely recognise that market forces will not provide all geographical areas with a good standard of broadband infrastructure. They note that many rural areas *are* participating in the Information Society. However, not all of Europe's rural areas are in a position to derive the benefits that participation in an Information Society could bring. There is a need to identify and respond to heterogeneity within rural populations, since to assume ubiquity of access, skills, confidence and willingness, will lead to an under-exploitation of ICTs with long-lasting digital-divide implications. Importantly, they conclude that the proliferation of electronic access and service-delivery channels are likely to lead to changes in physical access and service delivery that may well have deleterious impacts upon the quality of life of the elderly, the poor and the immobile living in rural areas. Therefore, policy intervention remains necessary, since an inclusive digital society is not inevitable.

Thus all authors within this volume argue in different ways and in varied contexts for an ongoing recognition of complexity – reflecting the economic, social and cultural relations of rural place. The findings and analyses presented in preceding chapters give evidence that increase our understanding of the ways in which rural digital divides are comprised of diverse experiences and issues that lie 'beyond access' (Hellawell, 2001), being overlain by social relations (some near, some distant) and geographical distance. Our analyses necessarily question an acceptance of fully predictable, and often metropolitan-based, forms of ICT-related behaviours, preferences and adaptations. Our combined research, as presented in this book, complements those analyses which typically shortcut to a 'death of distance' unifying rhetoric which agglomerates individual experiences (as people or as SMEs) along a single, linear trajectory of 'progress' towards a unifying, place-less norm.

The excitement and prospects associated with such diversity have been described above. We look forward to research, policy and practice environments that enable such richness to continue to be an asset rather than a hindrance in the changing, inclusive experiences of rurality in a digital age.

References

Crystal, D. (2002) *Language Death*, Cambridge: Cambridge University Press.

Hellawell, S. (2001) *Beyond Access: ICT and Social Inclusion*, London: Fabian Society.

February 2007

Index

eBooks – at www.eBookstore.tandf.co.uk

A library at your fingertips!

eBooks are electronic versions of printed books. You can store them on your PC/laptop or browse them online.

They have advantages for anyone needing rapid access to a wide variety of published, copyright information.

eBooks can help your research by enabling you to bookmark chapters, annotate text and use instant searches to find specific words or phrases. Several eBook files would fit on even a small laptop or PDA.

NEW: Save money by eSubscribing: cheap, online access to any eBook for as long as you need it.

Annual subscription packages

We now offer special low-cost bulk subscriptions to packages of eBooks in certain subject areas. These are available to libraries or to individuals.

For more information please contact webmaster.ebooks@tandf.co.uk

We're continually developing the eBook concept, so keep up to date by visiting the website.

www.eBookstore.tandf.co.uk